Karel R Tuesday

A Gentle Introduction
to the Art of Dynamic
Object-Oriented
Programming in
Ruby

Bergin, Stehlik, Roberts, Pattis

Joseph Bergin

Mark Stehlik

Jim Roberts

Richard Pattis

Parts of this work are derived from Karel++: A Gentle Introduction to the Art of Object-Oriented Programming by Joseph Bergin, Mark Stehlik, Jim Roberts, and Richard Pattis, copyright © 1997 by John Wiley. Used with permission.

Published by Joseph Bergin, Software Tools

April, 2013

ISBN 978-0-9851543-9-4

Karel R Tuesday
A Gentle Introduction to the Art of Dynamic

Object-Oriented Programming in Ruby

Joseph Bergin, Mark Stehlik, Jim Roberts, Richard Pattis

Preface

The programming landscape has changed significantly since the initial publication of Karel the Robot in 1981. Today there are new programming languages, new programming paradigms, and new and more powerful computers. Pascal no longer enjoys the popularity it did in the 1980s. However, the concepts of Karel are still as vibrant and valid an introduction to the programming and problem-solving processes as they were when first introduced. However, the object-oriented programming paradigm has begun to dominate the world of commercial software production. And dynamic scripting languages, such as Ruby and Python have come storming onto the scene.

Karel R Tuesday updates Karel J Robot to provide a means of introducing novice programmers to dynamic object programming. This book maintains the simplicity of the original and yet provides instruction that is thoroughly object-oriented from the beginning. Where the original Karel the Robot used a syntax and methodology derived from Pascal, the present text is 100% Ruby. In object-oriented programming, a computation is carried out by a set of interacting objects. Here, the objects are robots that exist in a simple world. There can be one or several robots assigned to a task. The programming task is divided into two parts. The first part is defining the capabilities of the robots that are needed. The second is providing a description of the task for the robots to perform. The programmer uses his or her problem solving skills on both parts of this task. This version like Karel J Robot puts a lot of emphasis on polymorphism, the primary distinction between procedural programming and object-oriented programming. Additionally, languages like Ruby have many of the characteristics of Lisp/Scheme, in that functions are first-class objects and can be passed as data for later execution. There is also an introduction to simple but important design patterns, such as those that have recently revolutionized software practice.

Like its predecessors, Karel R Tuesday is a Turing complete language that can be mastered in a few weeks. While not convenient for many tasks, it is theoretically possible to solve any computer programming problem in this simple language. This gives it educational power. Instead of using many many language features to solve problems, students must apply a few simple tools in combination to solve some hard problems. This puts the focus clearly on problem solving rather than language syntax. At the same time they are learning the core of an important modern programming language and the core concepts of the object-oriented programming paradigm. Ruby also has the advantage of having relatively little syntax to learn.

We believe that most people will not actually have to program a computer as part of their everyday lives, either now or in the future. However, many people will need to be able to use a computer and will occasionally need to do something with the machine beyond the "ordinary." Simply put, they will have to solve some type of computer problem. We solve various kinds of problems every day; problem solving is part of our lives. This book will introduce you to problem-solving approaches that can be used with computers. Unfortunately, some people believe programming requires a "different" way of thinking. We don't agree with this statement. Instead of changing the way you think, this book will change how you apply your problem-solving skills to different kinds of problems.

The original Karel the Robot used procedures as the fundamental problem solving medium, as is appropriate in procedural programming. Here we apply our problem solving skills, instead, to the design of classes that describe objects (robots), since classes are the primary means of breaking a complex problem into manageable parts in object-oriented programming. The skills of procedural programming and object-oriented programming are very similar, though we look at problems from a slightly different perspective when using object-oriented programming.

For the experienced student programmer, this edition should provide insights into the problem-solving and program design processes that will make the student an even better programmer. It will also improve understanding of computer science concepts such as polymorphism, loop invariants and recursion. For individuals who want to begin a thorough sequence of training and education in programming, computer science, or both, Karel R Tuesday provides a solid foundation on which to begin your work.

For novice programmers, this book will give some insight into the programming process from two distinctly different points of view: the planner's and the implementer's. All the problems can be thought about, discussed, and planned in English. Once you have developed your plan, the actual syntax of the robot programming language has very few rules to get in your way as you become the implementer or programmer.

For individuals who do not want to program but need to have a feel for the process, Karel R Tuesday is an excellent tool for providing that insight.

Supplements

An Instructor's Manual will be available for the text, and contains numerous pedagogical suggestions for teaching the material based on many years of using Karel the Robot, Karel ++, Karel J Robot, and Object-Orientation in introductory programming courses at the college level.

Software to simulate Karel R Tuesday is available on the Web. http://csis.pace.edu/~bergin. It was built with Ruby 1.9, using Tk Graphics under Eclipse on a Macintosh.

Joseph Bergin	Pace University
Mark Stehlik	Carnegie-Mellon University
Jim Roberts	Carnegie-Mellon University
Richard Pattis	University of California, Irvine

July, 2012

Dedication. The authors would like to dedicate this work to the memory of Kristen Nygaard, who, along with his friend and colleague Ole-Johan Dahl, invented object-oriented programming in the 1960s and who worked since then to refine and extend it. Kristen was an interesting and lively person who worked his entire life to make things better for others, both in technology and otherwise. We, who came to know him, miss him and his continuing inspiration greatly. He died suddenly in August 2002 at the age of 75.

Contents

Personal Notes

1 The Robot World

This chapter introduces a class of robots and sketches the world they inhabit. In later chapters, where a greater depth of understanding is necessary, we will amplify this preliminary discussion.

1.1 The Robot World

Robots live in a world that is unexciting by today's standards (there are no volcanoes, Chinese restaurants, or even ipods), but it does include enough variety to allow robots to perform simply stated, yet interesting, tasks. Informally, the world is a grid of streets that robots can traverse. It also contains special things that a robot can sense and manipulate.

Figure 1-1 is a map illustrating the structure of the robot world, whose shape is a great flat plane with the standard north, south, east, and west compass points. The world is bounded on its west side by an infinitely long vertical wall extending northward. To the south, the world is bounded by an infinitely long horizontal wall extending eastward. These boundary walls are made of solid neutronium, an impenetrable metal that restrains robots from falling over the edges of the world.

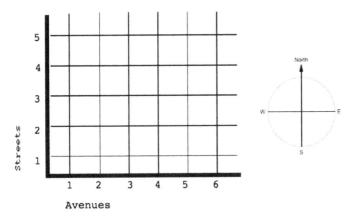

Figure1-1 The Robot World

Crisscrossing the world are horizontal streets (running east-west) and vertical avenues (running north-south) at regular, one-block intervals. To help you distinguish between streets and avenues, remember that the A in "Avenue" points north and the V points south. A corner, sometimes called a street corner or intersection, is located wherever a street and an avenue intersect.

One or more robots can occupy any corner, facing any of the four major compass directions. Any number of robots may occupy the same corner, because the streets and avenues are quite wide. We will often work with only one robot at a time, however. Robots are referenced by names so that we can send them messages individually. When we work with a single robot we will often call it karel[1], though you are free to name the robots that you create with any names you like.

Both streets and avenues have numbers; consequently, each corner is identified uniquely by its street and avenue numbers. The corner where 1st Street and 1st Avenue intersect is named the origin. The positions of robots and other things in this world can be described using both absolute and relative locations. The absolute location of the origin, for example, is the intersection of 1st Street and 1st Avenue. An example of a relative location would be to say that a robot is two blocks east and three blocks north of some thing in the world. The origin also has a relative location; it is the most southwesterly corner in the robot world. Sometimes we will describe a robot task using language that gives a different interpretation to the robot world, with north as up, south down, and west and east being left and right, respectively. This is how we (in the Northern Hemisphere) normally look at maps, of course.

Besides robots, two other kinds of things can occupy this world. The first of these kinds of things is a *wall section*. Wall sections are also fabricated from the impenetrable metal neutronium, and they can be manufactured in any desired length and pattern. They are positioned half way between adjacent street corners, effectively blocking a robot's direct path from one corner to the next. Wall sections are used to represent obstacles, such as hurdles and mountains, around which robots must navigate. Enclosed rooms, mazes, and other barriers can also be constructed from wall sections. Figure 1-2 shows some typical wall arrangements a robot might find in the world. Robots are objects since, as we shall see, they have behavior. Walls are simpler stuff, however.

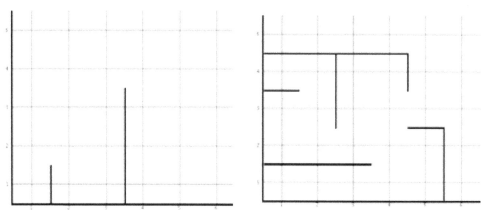

Fig 1-2-A North-South Wall Segments   Fig 1-2-C. A Maze of Wall Segments

---

[1]The name Karel is used in recognition of the Czech dramatist Karel Čapek, who popularized the word robot in his play R.U.R. (Rossum's Universal Robots). The word robot is derived from the Czech word robota, meaning "forced labor."

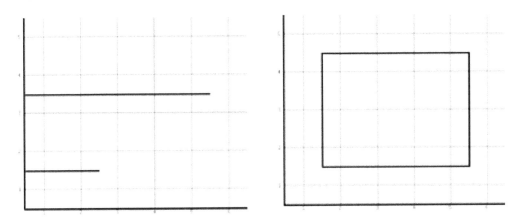

Fig 1-2-B East-West Wall Segment   Fig1-2-D A Room With No Doors or Windows

Figure 1-2 Different Wall Segment Arrangements in the Robot World

The second kind of thing in the world is a *beeper*. Beepers are small plastic cones that emit a quiet beeping noise. They are situated on street corners and can be picked up, carried, and put down by robots. Some tasks require one or more robots to pick up or put down patterns made from beepers or to find and transport beepers. Figure 1-3 shows one possible pattern of beepers. Beepers are small so there can be several on a corner, and they don't interfere with robot movement. There can even be an infinite number on a corner. Like walls, beepers have no behavior, so are not objects. They can be manipulated by objects, however.

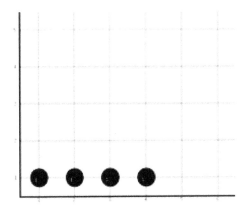

Figure 1-3 One Pattern of Beepers in the Robot World

1.2 Robot Capabilities

Let's now shift our attention away from the robot world and concentrate on the robots themselves. Robots are mobile; a robot can move forward (in the direction it is facing), and it can turn in place. Robots can also perceive their immediate surroundings using rudimentary senses of sight, sound, direction, and touch. They have behavior.

A robot sees by using its TV camera, which points straight ahead. This camera is focused to detect a wall exactly one-half block away from the robot. A robot also has the ability to hear a beeper, but only if the robot and the beeper are on the same corner; the beepers beep very quietly. By consulting its internal compass, a robot can determine which direction it is facing. Finally, each robot is equipped with a mechanical arm that it can use to pick up and put down beepers. To carry these beepers, each robot wears a soundproof beeper-bag around its waist. A robot can also determine whether it is carrying any beepers in this bag by probing the bag with its arm. A robot can also use its arm to determine whether there are other robots on the same corner that it occupies. Finally, a robot can turn itself off when its task is complete.

As you might expect, robots are made in factories. All robots come from the main factory, Karel-Werke, which can actually supply several different models of robots. When we need a robot for a task, we can use the standard model, or we can write a specification for a new model. Karel-Werke is able to build specialized robots that are modifications or extensions of the existing models.

Whenever we want a collection of robots to accomplish a task in the robot world, we must supply a detailed set of instructions that describe any special features of the robots that are needed and also explain how to perform the task. For most tasks one robot is all that is needed. When a robot is ordered from the factory, it is delivered to the robot world by helicopter. The helicopter pilot sets up the robots according to our specifications and sends each new robot a sequence of messages to detail its task, which it is then able to carry out. This sequence of instructions is sometimes called its script, or its main task.

What language do we use to program (here we use *program* to mean "write instructions for") robots? Instead of programming these robots in English, a natural language for us, we program them in a special programming language. This language was specially designed to be useful for writing robot programs. The robot programming language, like any natural language, has a vocabulary, punctuation marks, and rules of grammar, but this language, unlike English, for example, is simple enough for robots to understand. However, it is a powerful and concise language that allows us to write brief and unambiguous programs for them. This language is built from and based on the Ruby Programming Language.

1.3 Tasks and Situations

A *task* is something that we want a robot to do. The following examples are tasks for robots:

- Move to the corner of 15th St. & 10th Ave.
- Run a hurdle race (with wall sections representing hurdles).
- Escape from an enclosed room that has a door.
- Find a beeper and deposit it on the origin.
- Escape from a maze.

A *situation* is an exact description of what the world looks like. Besides the basic structure of the world, which is always present, wall sections and beepers can be added. To specify a situation completely, we must provide answers for the following questions.

- What is each robot's current position? We must specify both the robot's location (which corner it is on) and what direction it is facing.
- What is the location and length of each wall section in the world?
- What is the location of each beeper in the world? This information includes specifying the number of beepers in each robot's beeper-bag.

Situations are specified in this book by a small map or brief written description. If we know the number of beepers that each robot has in its beeper-bag, then the maps in Figure 1-4 completely specify different situations. The initial situation for any task is defined to be the situation in which all of the robots are placed at the start of the task. The final situation is the situation that each robot is in when it turns itself off. Figure 1-4 shows six initial situations that are typical for tasks that a single robot will accomplish in the coming chapters.

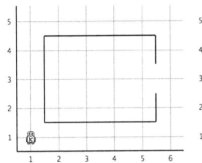

Fig A. A room has one door. Robot is at the origin, facing North and must enter the room

Fig B. A diagonal line of beepers Robot is facing East and must pick all beepers.

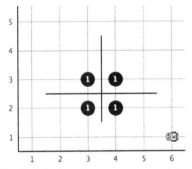

Fig C. A "+" wall arrangement with beepers. From a starting position robot must pick the beepers

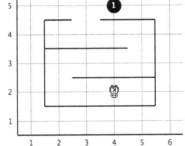

Fig D. Robot must escape the maze and pick the beeper.

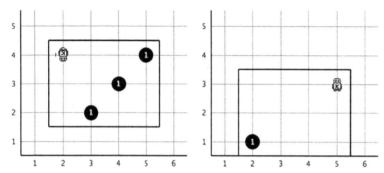

Fig E. Beepers are scattered in a box. Robot is facing South in the North-West corner. Robot must pick all the beepers in the box.

Fig F. A box with one beeper. Robot is facing North in the North-East corner. Robot must find the Beeper.

Figure 1-4 Six Sample Tasks for a Robot to Perform

1.4 Robots and Objects

Robots are examples of things called Objects. An *object* is an electronic thing, though it is useful to think of objects as if they were real, just as robots can be real. Objects can **do** things and they can **remember** things. We can ask robots (and objects in general) to do the things they know how to do, and we can ask them about the things they remember. We will explore this idea throughout this book. Ruby is a computer language in which it is easy to create objects, and in particular, robots. The Robot Programming Language was created using ideas like the ones presented in this book. In Chapter 4 we shall see other, somewhat more abstract, kinds of objects. Objects can be used to represent things like robots or ideas like a game strategy. The key idea, however, is that objects have behavior and can be asked to exhibit that behavior, either by carrying out some action or by giving us some information that it has remembered.

1.5 Important Ideas From This Chapter

robot
task
situation
program
object
do, remember

1.6 Problem Set

The purpose of this problem set is to make sure that you have a good understanding of the robot world and the capabilities of robots before moving on to robot programming.

1. Which of the following directions can a robot face?

- northeast
- east
- south-southwest

- north
- 164 degrees
- vertical
- down

2. What things other than robots can be found in the robot world?

3. Which of the things listed in Problem 2 can a robot manipulate or change?

4. What reference points can be used in the robot world to describe a robot's exact location?

5. How many robots can we have in a given robot world?

6. Give the absolute location of each robot in each of the worlds shown in Figure 1-5. Give a relative location of each robot in the worlds.

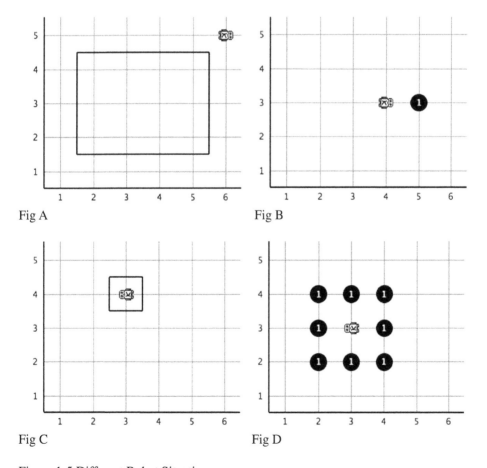

Fig A   Fig B

Fig C   Fig D

Figure 1-5 Different Robot Situations

2 Primitive Instructions and Simple Programs

This chapter begins our study of the Robot Programming Language. We will start with a detailed explanation of the primitive instructions that are built into every robot's vocabulary. Using these instructions, we can instruct any robot to move through the world and handle beepers. Section 2.6 shows a complete robot program and discusses the elementary punctuation and grammar rules of the robot programming language. By the end of this chapter we will be able to write programs that instruct robots to perform simple obstacle avoidance and beeper transportation tasks.

Before explaining the primitive instructions of the robot programming language, we must first define the technical term *execute*: A robot executes an instruction by performing the instruction's associated action or actions. The robot executes a program by executing a sequence of instructions (script) that are given to it by the helicopter pilot. Each instruction in such a sequence is delivered to the robot in a message, which directs one robot to perform one instruction in the program.

2.1 Changing Position

Every robot understands two primitive instructions that change its position. The first of these instructions is **move**, which changes a robot's location.

move

> When a robot is sent a **move** message it executes a **move** instruction and moves forward one block; it continues to face the same direction. To avoid damage, a robot will not move forward if it sees a wall section or boundary wall between its current location and the corner to which it would move. Instead, it turns itself off. This action, called an error shutoff, will be explained further in Section 2.7.

From this definition we see that a robot executes a **move** instruction by moving forward to the next corner. However, the robot performs an error shutoff when its front is blocked.

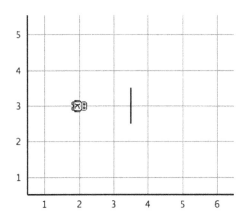

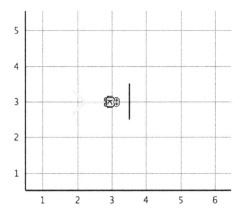

Figure 2-1 A: A Robot in the Initial
Situation before
a move Instruction

Figure 2-1 B: A Robot in the Final
Situation after Executing
a move Instruction

Figure 2-1 shows the successful execution of a **move** instruction. The wall section is more than one half-block away and cannot block this robot's move.

In contrast, Figure 2-2 shows an incorrect attempt to move. When this robot tries to execute a **move** instruction in this situation, it sees a wall section. Relying on its self-preservation instinct, it performs an error shutoff.

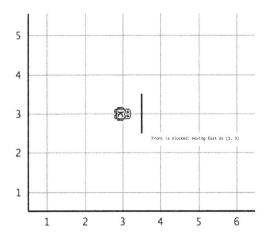

Figure 2-2 The Result of a robot Attempting to move When Its Front Is Blocked Is an Error Shutoff.

2.2 Turning in Place

The second primitive instruction that changes a robot's position is **turn_left**. This instruction changes the direction in which the robot is facing but does not alter its location.

turn_left

> When a robot is sent a **turn_left** message it executes a **turn_left** instruction by pivoting 90 degrees to the left. The robot remains on the same street corner while executing a **turn_left** instruction. Because it is impossible for a wall section to block a robot's turn, **turn_left** cannot cause an error shutoff.

A robot always starts a task on some corner, facing either north, south, east, or west. A robot cannot travel fractions of a block or turn at other than 90 degree angles. Although **move** and **turn_left** change the robot's position, after executing either of these instructions, the robot still is on some corner and still is facing one of the four compass directions.

Karel-Werke's designer purposely did not provide a built-in **turn_right** instruction. Would adding a **turn_right** to the primitive instructions allow the robot to perform any task it cannot accomplish without one? A moment's thought-and the right flash of insight-shows that the **turn_right** instruction is unnecessary; it does not permit robots to accomplish any new tasks. The key observation for verifying this conclusion is that a robot can manage the equivalent of a **turn_right** instruction by executing three **turn_left** instructions.

2.3 Finishing a Task

We need a way to tell a robot that its task is finished. The **turn_off** instruction fulfills this requirement.

turn_off

> When a robot is sent a **turn_off** message, it executes a **turn_off** instruction. It turns off and is incapable of executing any more instructions until restarted on another task. The last instruction executed by every robot in a program is usually a **turn_off** instruction. This is not strictly necessary, however. The robot will generate an error (*exception*, in techno-speak) for any messages it receives after it executes **turn_off**.

2.4 Handling Beepers

Every robot understands two instructions that permit it to handle beepers. These two instructions perform opposite actions.

pick_beeper

> When a robot is sent a **pick_beeper** message, it executes a **pick_beeper** instruction. It picks up a beeper from the corner on which it is standing and then deposits the beeper in its beeper-bag. If a **pick_beeper** instruction is attempted on a beeperless corner, the robot performs an error shutoff. On a corner with more than one beeper the robot picks up one, and only one, of the beepers and then places it in the beeper-bag.

put_beeper

> When a robot is sent a **put_beeper** message, it executes a **put_beeper** instruction by extracting a beeper from its beeper-bag and placing the beeper on the current street corner. If a robot tries to execute a **put_beeper** instruction with an empty beeper-bag, the robot performs an error shutoff. If

the robot has more than one beeper in its beeper-bag, it extracts one, and only one, beeper and places it on the current corner.

Beepers are so small that robots can move right by them; only wall sections and boundary walls can block a robot's movement. Robots are also very adept at avoiding each other if two or more show up on the same corner simultaneously.

2.5 Robot Descriptions

All robots produced by Karel-Werke have at least the capabilities just described. As we will see, such robots are very primitive, and we might like robots with additional abilities. Therefore, we must have some way to describe those extra abilities so that the factory can build a robot to our specifications. Karel-Werke employs a simple robot programming language to describe both robot abilities and the lists of robot instructions, called programs. The formal name for the description of a robot instruction is **method**. The factory begins each robot creation by first building a definition of **Robota** that has no actual capabilities, but has interfaces for the above methods. The simple model of robot described above is called the **UrRobot** class[2] and it is built by actually implementing the methods. A class is a description of robots of the same kind. A class is like a production line in the factory that makes robots. The specification, or interface, of the **Robota** class in the robot programming language follows.

```
=begin
 A general framework in which robots of various kinds may be
 defined. It does not, however, define any instantiable robots.
 The actions of robots are declared, but not defined here.
=end
class Robota

  # Move one block in the current direction (provided the front is
  # clear)
  def move()
    raise "Implemented in sub-class."
  end

  # Turn 90 degrees to the left from the current direction
  def turn_left()
    raise "Implemented in sub-class."
  end

  # Pick a beeper from the current corner (provided there is one to
  # pick)
  def pick_beeper()
    raise "Implemented in sub-class."
  end

  # Put a beeper on the current corner (provided the robot has one in
  #the beeper bag)
```

---

[2]Ur is a German prefix meaning "original" or "primitive." The pronunciation of ur is similar to the sound of "oor" in "poor."

```
def put_beeper()
  raise "Implemented in sub-class."
end

# Turn off, making further actions impossible
def turn_off()
  raise "Implemented in sub-class."
end

end
```

The matching parentheses in each method def are not required in Ruby, but we shall usually write them to emphasize that we are referencing a method, rather than something else (such as a value).

Preceding the model class name is a comment to explain the purpose of the class. These comments are used by tools to provide documentation for our work. The class header is then followed by a list of instructions (methods) for this kind of robot. The list is always written indented for each level. The defs themselves are one level and the instructions defining each def are the next level. The statements starting with # are just comments that explain the purpose of the class and each method. A quoted string should have matching quotes. The raise statements are how a robot signals an error has occurred. In general, quoted strings can use single quotes (apostrophes) as well, but they must be matched. In truth, there is a bit more defined in Robota that we are not showing here, including the names of the directions that robots can face.

Method *defs* are the descriptions of how a **Robota** would carry out each of these instructions. Namely, it would just signal that it could not do anything since the instruction isn't implemented here. It is in UrRobot that we see the first actual implementation of the methods. In fact, the robot factory won't actually release one of these skeletons. Their only purpose is in preproduction for an **UrRobot**. An **UrRobot** has all of these methods and a few more that we shall see along the way, but the factory has completed the construction and is willing to put them into the world. Think of a member of Robota as if it is a partially completed robot as it rolls off the first segment of the production line at the Karel-Werke. Or, think of it as a user manual with which a robot might be operated. The assembly line metaphor we use here is actually quite close to what really happens in Ruby.

While these instructions don't really do anything, they have the correct form for the Ruby language. The word *class* is eventually matched by *end* in the file in which it appears (robota.rb). Each method *def* is indented between two and four spaces, and the body of each of the definitions is indented an additional two to four spaces. This indenting is very important in the Robot Programming Language as it helps you to understand the structure of our instructions for the robots. You should decide on how many spaces to indent and stick to it.

The class **UrRobot** is built from the skeleton class. We sometimes say that the skeleton here defines the *interface* of the **UrRobot** class and that **UrRobot** is a sub-class of **Robota**. UrRobot just makes these incipient capabilities real. In the Robot Programming Language, we say that UrRobot *inherits* the capabilities of the skeleton class, but we shall wait a bit before we show the details of inheritance. So while a skeleton robot might "look" like a real robot, it's "legs" won't move, nor it's arm, etc. But the UrRobot is fully functional and ready to do your bidding. The mechanism to derive UrRobot from Robota is the class definition, which we discuss in detail in the next chapter, but in this case, it has a form like:

```
class UrRobot < Robota
  . . . # implementations of the inherited methods
end
```

The five methods, **move** through **turn_off**, name actions that **UrRobots** can perform. We defined each of these actions in the foregoing sections, and we will see many examples of their use throughout this book. These methods are all executed for their effect (they **do** something), but return no feedback to the robot program when executed. Later we will see additional methods that do produce feedback when executed, rather than changing the state of the robot. Said differently, the instructions here do something as opposed to telling us something that the robot remembers: robots **do** things and they **remember** things.

Note that a class is not a robot. It is just a description (blueprint, specification) of robots of the same kind. The class of a robot tells us its capabilities (methods). If we know the class of a robot we know what the robot can do and what it can remember. We haven't created any robots yet, but are about to do so.

A sample task for an **UrRobot** might be to start at the origin, facing east, and then walk three blocks east to a corner known to have a beeper, pick up the beeper, and **turn_off** on that corner. A complete program to accomplish this task is shown next. In this program we name the robot **karel**, but we could use any convenient name. Note that we don't capitalize the names of robots. They aren't people, after all. In Ruby, the name used to refer to an object (including a robot) is called a *reference variable* and the convention is not to capitalize these in our Ruby programs. The names of classes like UrRobot, on the other hand, are usually capitalized. Constants like EAST are written in all capital letters.

```
#!/opt/local/bin/ruby
require "ur_robot"

def task()
    karel = UrRobot.new(1, 1, EAST, 0)
          # Deliver the robot to the origin (1,1),
          # facing east, with no beepers.
    karel.move()
    karel.move()
    karel.move()
    karel.pick_beeper()
    karel.turn_off()
end

task()
```

Complete programs will be discussed in the next section. And note that we haven't discussed how the beeper to be picked got on the corner. This will be explained below and in the appendices. But note that there are three things here. First is the prerequisites needed in this file (require…). Then there is a definition of a *top-level* method named task. Finally there is an invocation of that method, requesting that the helicopter pilot actually read out the instructions of the task. The first line (shebang) will be discussed later.

2.6 A Complete Program

In this section we describe a task for a robot named karel and a complete program that instructs it to perform the task. The task, illustrated in Figure 2-3, is to transport the beeper from 1st Street and 4th Avenue to 3rd Street and 5th Avenue. After karel has put down the beeper, it must move one block farther north before turning off.

The following program instructs karel to perform this task. The program uses all of the methods available to robots in the **UrRobot** class, a few new words from the robot programming vocabulary, and punctuation symbols such as the period and comma. We will first discuss karel's execution of this program, and then analyze the general structure of all robot programs.

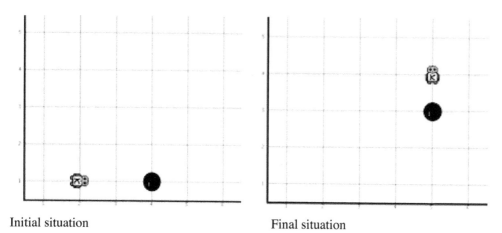

Initial situation   Final situation

Figure 2-3 The Initial and Final Situations of Karel's task

```
#!/opt/local/bin/ruby
require "ur_robot"

def task()
    karel = UrRobot.new(1, 2, EAST, 0)
    karel.move()
    karel.move()
    karel.pick_beeper()
    karel.move()
    karel.turn_left()
    karel.move()
    karel.move()
    karel.put_beeper()
    karel.move()
    karel.turn_off()
end

task()
```

See the Appendix for more on the details of the above including the *require* statement.

We must note that this is not the only sequence of messages that will correctly perform the stated task. Although it is obvious and direct, this is just one of many sequences that will accomplish the task.

The first line points to the location of the Ruby processor (on my computer – yours may be different). It is called a shebang (sharp-bang). The next line here make the name UrRobot available here, and refers to the file ur_robot.rb which contains the complete definition of UrRobot. The third line (omitting the blank line) introduces the main task block and we will use this form in every program. It introduces the name of a method called task. Any name will do for this, but it will be helpful for us to think of the *main task* of a robot this way. This def is eventually matched with an end that completes the definition. The fourth line creates a robot we will refer to as karel, and the remaining indented lines following that are the task for karel. The creation of a robot (called here a delivery specification) is actually a message to the class UrRobot, which is itself an object.

Note that Ruby is *case-sensitive*, meaning that capitalization of words matters. EAST is not the same as east. These two names might refer to different things, or to nothing at all. After the end of the def we come to the last line which is an invocation of the task method. We give its name, any optional parameters (discussed later) and optional parentheses. All of the parentheses above are optional in Ruby, actually, but if you write them, you cannot have any space between the method name and the parentheses. The task method is just a way for us to collect the statements together and give them a name collectively, a kind of abstraction.

A set of messages to one or more robots is called a *task*. A task, if correctly written, can be executed by the Ruby system. The first instruction in the main task block constructs the robot, associates the name **karel** with it, and delivers it, ready to run, from the factory to 1st Street and 2nd Avenue, facing East with no beepers in its beeper-bag. This statement can be thought of as a delivery specification or a message to the factory itself. It instructs the helicopter pilot how to set up the robot when it is delivered. The delivery specification also names the specific type or class of robot that we want delivered. Here we want an **UrRobot**.

The remaining lines of the main task block instruct karel how to carry out the task. These messages are sent to karel by the helicopter pilot, as described next.

2.6.1 Executing a Program

Before a program can be executed in a world, the program is read at the factory to make sure it has no errors. We will discuss errors later; for now, we will assume that our program is correct. But the check at the factory is very cursory. It will check that the def is matched by an end, for example, but not for names misspelled.

How is a program executed? A program execution is begun after the helicopter pilot delivers the robot to the required corner and sets it up according to the delivery specification. Here we require that the **UrRobot karel** be set up on 1st Street and 2nd Avenue, facing East, and with zero beepers in its beeper-bag. Then, for each additional command in the main task block, the pilot sends a corresponding electronic message to the robot named in that command. The message gives the instruction that the named robot is supposed to perform. These messages are relayed by the pilot to the robot through a special robot control satellite that hovers over the world. Since a robot can execute only one instruction at a time and since the satellite has a very limited communication capacity, only one message can be sent at a time. The pilot must wait for instruction completion before sending the next message. When the robot completes the current instruction, it sends a reply back to the pilot through the satellite indicating that the next message can be sent. Messages from the main task block are sent sequentially without omitting any messages in a strict top-to-bottom order. The pilot continues sending messages until either all messages in the main task block have been sent or the pilot attempts to send a message to a robot that has executed a **turn_off** or has performed an error shutoff.

It is also possible for robots to send messages to each other. When this occurs, the robot sending the message waits for the reply before continuing. This is to guarantee that the satellite communication channel is never overloaded. There is a subtle point here, however. The helicopter pilot only reads out the messages in the main task block. These messages contain the names of the robot's methods. The robot itself knows how to carry out the details of that method. We shall see how important this distinction is in the next chapter. A robot will only react to message sent specifically to it. This is important to remember when we have several robots.

To determine what a program does, we simulate, or *trace*, its execution. Simulating or tracing a robot program means that we must systematically execute the program exactly as the pilot and robots would, recording every action that takes place. We can simulate a robot program by using markers on a sheet of paper (representing robots and the world) or walking around on a rectangular grid. We simulate a robot program by following the sequence of messages in the order the pilot reads them to the robot. We will discuss tracing later, but in order to become proficient robot programmers, we must understand exactly how the pilot reads the program and the robot executes it. The ability to simulate a robot's behavior quickly and accurately is an important skill that we must acquire.

Let's follow a simulation of our program. In the following simulation (2, 4) means 2nd Street and 4th Avenue. In the following annotation we explain exactly what state the robot is left in after the execution of the instruction. Note that the symbol # (the hash symbol) is used in the simulation to introduce comments into our robot programs. Each comment begins with the # mark and continues to the end of the line. These comments are ignored by the pilot and by the robots; they are included only to aid our own understanding of the program. Here we use them to explain in detail each instruction as it will be executed. We note, however, that if the program is changed in any way, the comments are likely to become invalid.

```
def task()
    karel = UrRobot.new(1, 2, EAST, 0)
                    # A new robot named karel is
                    # constructed and delivered to
                    # (1,2), facing east. karel has
                    # no beepers in its beeper-bag.
    karel.move()         # karel moves east to (1, 3)
    karel.move()         # karel moves east to (1, 4)
    karel.pick_beeper()  # karel picks 1 beeper
                         # 1 beeper in bag
    karel.move()         # karel moves east to (1, 5)
    karel.turn_left()    # karel remains on (1, 5), faces north
    karel.move()         # karel moves north to (2, 5)
    karel.move()         # karel moves north to (3, 5)
    karel.put_beeper()   # karel puts 1 beeper
                         # down, now 0 beepers in bag
    karel.move()         # karel moves north to (4, 5)
    karel.turn_off()     # karel remains on (4, 5) facing north
                         # and shuts off
end

task()
```

Karel is done and we have verified that our program is correct through simulation by tracing the execution of the program.

2.6.2 The Form of Robot Programs

Now that we have seen how a robot executes a program, let's explore the grammar rules of the robot programming language. The factory and pilots pay strict attention to grammar and punctuation rules, so our time is well spent carefully studying these rules. We start by dividing the symbols in a robot program into three groups. The first group consists of special symbols. It has members such as the punctuation marks like the parentheses (and), and the period. The next group of symbols consists of names such as robot and class names, **karel** and **UrRobot**. We also use names to refer to instructions, like **put_beeper** and **turn_left**. The third and last group of symbols consists of reserved words. We have already seen a few of these like `class` and `def`.

Reserved words are used to structure and organize the primitive instructions in the robot programming language. They are called reserved words because their use is reserved for their built-in purpose. These reserved words may not be reused for other purposes in a robot program, such as robot names. To make the reading of programs easier, we may write robot programs using both upper- and lowercase letters as well as the underscore character, but we must be consistent. The robot programming language is case-sensitive, meaning that the use of upper- and lowercase letters in a word must be consistent each time the word is used. For example, `require` is always spelled with all lowercase letters. If we use the word **Require** in a robot program it would refer to something else, perhaps the name of a robot.

Since robot programs need to be read by humans as well as robots, it is helpful to be able to put explanatory material into the program itself. The language therefore permits comments to be inserted into the text of the program. As we have seen in the foregoing program, a comment begins anywhere on a line with the special symbol # (the hash mark). The comment terminates only when the line does. Anything may follow the comment symbol on the same line. A multi-line comment begins with =begin in the left margin of a line and terminates with =end, also in the left margin. Anything in between these is a comment, ignored by Ruby.

Every robot program consists of a task to be completed by one or more robots. We will put the main task block into a task method, though it isn't essential:

```
def task()
   .  .  .
end
```

The main task block always ends with the reserved word end. We then *invoke* the method by giving its name. In our metaphor, these are the instructions read by the helicopter pilot. In practice, however, these would be executed if you give your computer the command:

ruby tester.rb

where all of the above program (including the require) is in the file named tester.rb. See Section 1 of the Appendix for hints on executing robot programs.

If we needed specialized robots to perform various parts of the task, the class declarations of those robots could precede the task list, including the definitions of any new instructions defined in the class declarations. Classes can also be in separate files. We will go into this in detail in Chapter 3.

The main task block itself normally starts with a list of definitions, called declarations. In the above program we have one declaration, which declares that the name **karel** will be used as the name of a robot in class **UrRobot**. Declarations introduce new names and indicate how they will be used in the rest of the program. We could also declare names for several different robots, even robots of different classes. The declarations of robots can best be thought of as delivery specifications to the factory. They always contain information about how and where the robot should be placed in the world. They don't need to be at the beginning of a task, though we often put them there. They do need to appear before we try to ask them to do anything. After all, we have to deliver a robot before we can ask it to do something. In Ruby the declaration of a name is just its first use to the left of the assignment (=) operator. Its existence is declared and the name is associated with an initial value. The *assignment operator* is pronounced something like "let it be", as in let karel be a reference to a new UrRobot…

Every program has one main task block, even when the entire program is spread over separate files. Most of the statements in the main task block are messages to the robots declared in the declaration list. The main exception here is the delivery instruction, which causes the factory to construct and deliver a new **UrRobot** named karel to 1st Street and 2nd Avenue (we always list streets first), facing east, with no beepers in its beeper-bag. When delivered, the robot is set up and ready to receive messages sent to it. Since robots are delivered by the factory in helicopters, we don't need to be concerned about walls in the world that might impede delivery to any corner. The helicopter will be able to fly over them.

We can send messages to several different robots from the same main task block, so we need to specify which robot is to carry out each instruction. Thus, if we have a robot named karel and want it to move, we send the message **karel.move()**. This seems redundant here when there is only one robot, but it is required nevertheless. An instruction that causes a robot to perform one of its own instructions, such as move, is known as a message statement. The instruction named in a message statement (**move**) is called the message, and the robot (**karel**) is the receiver of the message. Messages are the means of getting a robot to execute an instruction.

Execution always begins with the first instruction of the main task block. Robots are not automatically shut down at the end of a program; the **turn_off** instruction should be used for that purpose. The indenting of the main task block indicates the instructions that will be executed. If we reach the end of the instructions in the main task block and any robot is still on because it hasn't yet executed a **turn_off** instruction, it means that at least one **turn_off** instruction has been omitted from the program. This is not an error, but turning off your robots when you are done with them is useful as their appearance will change to show you that they are done.

Observe that the program is nicely indented as well as commented. It is well organized and easy to read. This style of indenting is not necessary for the Ruby system to correctly interpret your program. It is the means by which you, the Robot Programmer, can easily see what statements belong with what parts.

The importance of adopting a programming style that is easy to read by humans cannot be overemphasized.

We note, for completeness, that instruction statements in a def block (such as our main task block) can be terminated by semicolons. These will be ignored if present. On the other hand, a pair of matching parentheses at the end of each message, while not required, will be included for the present, even though experienced Ruby programmers usually omit them. Ruby has a flexible format (syntax) that sometimes is easier to write than to read; especially for beginners.

2.7 Error Shutoffs

When a robot is prevented from successfully completing the action associated with a message, it turns itself off. This action is known as an *error shutoff*, and the effect is equivalent to receiving a **turn_off** message. However, turning off is not the only way such a problem could be addressed. An alternative strategy could have the robot just ignore any message that cannot be executed successfully. Using this strategy the robot could continue executing the program as if it had never been required to execute the unsuccessful instruction.

To justify the choice of executing an error shutoff, rather than just ignoring messages in such situations, consider the following: Once an unexpected situation arises-one that prevents successful execution of an instruction-a robot probably will be unable to make further progress toward accomplishing the task. Continuing to execute a program under these circumstances will lead to an even greater discrepancy between what the programmer had intended for the robot to do and what it is actually doing. Consequently, the best strategy is to have the robot turn off as soon as the first inconsistency appears.

So far, we have seen three instructions that can cause error shutoffs: **move**, **pick_beeper**, and **put_beeper**. We must construct our programs carefully and ensure that the following conditions are always satisfied.

- A robot executes a **move** instruction only when the path is clear to the next corner immediately in front of it.
- A robot executes a **pick_beeper** instruction only when it is on the same corner as at least one beeper.
- A robot executes a **put_beeper** instruction only when the beeper-bag is not empty.

We can guarantee that these conditions are met if, before writing our program, we know the exact initial situation in which the robot will be placed.

2.8 Programming Errors

In this section we classify all programming errors into four broad categories. These categories are discussed using the analogy of a motorist with a task in the real world. It should help clarify the nature of each error type. You might ask, "Why spend so much time talking about errors when they should never occur?" The answer to this question is that programming requires an uncommon amount of precision, and although errors should not occur in principle, they occur excessively in practice. Therefore we must become adept at quickly finding and fixing errors by simulating our programs.

A *lexical* error occurs whenever the robot program contains a word that is not in its vocabulary. As an analogy, suppose that we are standing on a street in San Francisco and we are asked by a lost motorist, "How can I get to Portland, Oregon?" If we tell the motorist, "fsdt jkhpy hqngrpz fgssj sgr ghhgh grmplhms," we commit a lexical error. The motorist is unable to follow our instructions because it is impossible to decipher the words of which the instructions are composed. Similarly, the robot executing a program must understand each word in a program that it is asked to execute.

Here is a robot program with some lexical errors:

```
deg task()                  # misspelled word
   karel = UrRobot(1, 2, EAST, 0) # missing '.new'
   karel.move()
   karel.mvoe()             # misspelled instruction
   karel.pick()             # unknown word
   karel.move()             # ok
   karel.turn_right()       # unknown word
   karel.turnLeft           # unknown word
   karel.move               # ok
   karel.put_beeper();      # ok
   Karel.move()             # unknown word
   karel.turn_Left()        # unknown word
end

task()
```

The last two errors occur because the robot programming language is case-sensitive. The word turn_left is not the same as turn_Left, nor is karel the same as Karel.

Even if the pilot recognizes every word in a program, the program still might harbor a *syntax* error. This type of error occurs whenever we use incorrect grammar or incorrect punctuation. Going back to our lost motorist, we might reply, "for, Keep hundred. just miles going eight." Although the motorist recognizes each of these words individually, we have combined them in a senseless, convoluted manner. According to the rules of English grammar, the parts of speech are not in their correct positions. We discussed the grammar rules for basic robot programs in Section 2.6.2.

The following program contains no lexical errors, but it does have syntax errors.

```
def = task()                    # misplaced = sign
   karel = UrRobot.new(1, 2, EAST 0) # missing comma
   karel.move(                   # missing parenthesis
   karel..move()                 # extra period
   karel.pick_beeper()           # ok
   karel.move ()                 # space before the parentheses
   karel.move(),                 # misplaced comma
                                 # missing 'end'
```

If our program contains syntax errors, the factory will discover them when our program is checked there. It will also discover some, but not all, lexical errors. In both cases, the factory has no conception of what we meant to say; therefore, it does not try to correct our errors. Instead, the factory informs us of the detected errors and doesn't build the robot. This action is not an error shutoff, for in this case the robot never has a chance to begin to execute the program. While discussing the next two categories of errors, we will assume that the factory finds no lexical or syntax errors in our program, so it builds the robot and the pilot delivers it and begins to execute the program.

The third error category is called an *execution* error. Unlike (some) lexical and (all) syntax errors, which are detected at the factory, the pilot can only detect these errors while the program is running or during a simulation of its execution. Execution errors occur whenever a robot in the world is unable to execute an instruction successfully and is forced to perform an error shutoff. Returning to our motorist, who is trying to drive from San Francisco to Portland, we might say, "Just keep going for eight hundred miles." But if the motorist happens to be facing west at the time, and takes our directions literally, the motorist would reach the Pacific Ocean after traveling only a few miles. At this point, the motorist would halt, realizing that he or she cannot follow our instructions to completion.

Likewise, a robot turns off if asked to execute an instruction that it cannot execute successfully. Instructing a robot to **move** when the front is blocked, to **pick_beeper** on a corner that has no beeper, and to **put_beeper** when the beeper-bag is empty are examples of execution errors, and each one results in an error shutoff.

If a lexical error is detected during execution, such as mistyping the name used to refer to a robot (Karel instead of karel), the program will also be halted and you will need to correct the error and execute it again. The computer system will *raise* an exception, perhaps a name error that will be printed on your computer screen in a console window.

The final error class is the most insidious, because pilots, the factory, and robots cannot detect this type of error when it occurs. We label this category of error an *intent* error. An intent error occurs whenever the program successfully terminates but does not successfully complete the task. Suppose our motorist is facing south when we say, "Just keep going for eight hundred miles." Even though these instructions can be successfully followed to completion, the motorist will end up somewhere in Mexico, rather than Oregon.

Here is an example of an intent error in a robot program: Beginning in the situation shown in Figure 2-4, karel is to pick up the beeper, move it one block to the north, put the beeper down, move one more block to the north, and **turn_off**.

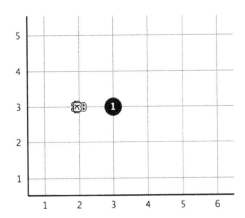

Figure 2-4 Karel's Initial Situation

```
def task()
    karel = UrRobot.new(3, 2, EAST, 0)
    karel.move()
    karel.pick_beeper()
    karel.move()
    karel.turn_left()
    karel.move()
    karel.put_beeper()
    karel.move()
    karel.turn_off()
end
```

There are no lexical, syntax, or execution errors in this program. As far as karel and the helicopter pilot are concerned, when the **turn_off** is executed, everything is perfect. However, look at the task and look at the program. What is the error? The task is to move the beeper one block to the north, yet karel also moved the beeper one block to the east. The intent was a northerly move, but the final result was an easterly move. The program does not satisfy the requirements of the stated task and thus contains an error of intent.

Remember that a robot does not understand the task for which we have programmed it. All that the robot can do is execute the instructions corresponding to messages we have sent it in our program. Thus, there is no way for a robot to know that the program did not accomplish what we intended. Similarly, the pilot has no way to know what we intended. He or she only knows what is actually written in the program itself.

2.8.1 Bugs and Debugging

In programming jargon, all types of errors are known as *bugs*. There are many apocryphal stories about the origin of this term. In one story the term bug is said to have been originated by telephone company engineers to refer to the source of random noises transmitted by their electronic communications circuits. Another story originated with the Harvard Mark I Computer and Grace Murray Hopper, later Admiral. The computer was producing incorrect answers, and when engineers took it apart trying to locate the problem, they found a dead moth caught between the contacts of a relay, causing the malfunction: the first computer bug. Other stories abound, so perhaps we shall never know the true entomology of this word.

Perhaps the term bug became popular in programming because it saved the egos of programmers. Instead of admitting that their programs were full of errors, they could say that their programs had bugs in them. Actually, the metaphor is apt; bugs are hard to find, and although a located bug is frequently easy to fix, it is difficult to ensure that all bugs have been found and removed from a program. Debugging is the name that programmers give to the activity of removing errors from a program.

2.8.2 A Note About Indentation

We have stressed the importance of indentation. In reality the Ruby language processor is very tolerant about how we write our programs. But our brain isn't so forgiving. The previous task, could have been written as follows:

```
    def task()
  karel = UrRobot.new(3, 2, EAST, 0)
    karel.move()
        karel.pick_beeper()
    karel.move()
    karel.turn_left(); karel.move()
        karel.turn_off()
  end
  end
```

which is much harder for our brain to process. Note that since we put two statements on one line Ruby requires that we separate them with a semicolon, but that doesn't make it much easier for us. As our programs get more complex this becomes even more important. The visual structure can be as important as the logical structure of our programs for us to work easily with them.

2.9 A Task for Two Robots

We are not restricted to using only a single robot to perform a task. We can have as many as we like. We shall see in later chapters that robots can communicate in sophisticated ways. For now, here is a simple task for two robots.

Karel is at 3rd Street and 1st Avenue on a corner with a beeper, facing East. Carl is at the origin facing East. Karel should carry the beeper to carl and put it down. Carl should then pick it up and carry it to 1st Street and 3rd Avenue. The beeper should be placed on this corner. Both robots should face East at the end.

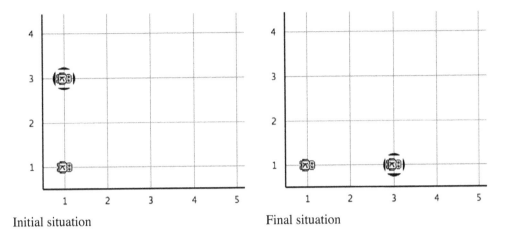

Initial situation   Final situation

Figure 2-5. Initial and Final Situations for the Two Robot Task

```
def task()
    karel = UrRobot.new (3, 1, EAST, 0)
    carl = UrRobot.new (1, 1, EAST, 0)
    karel.pick_beeper()
    karel.turn_left()
    karel.turn_left()
    karel.turn_left()
    karel.move()
    karel.move()
    karel.put_beeper()
    carl.pick_beeper()
    carl.move()
    carl.move()
    carl.put_beeper()
    karel.turn_off()
    carl.turn_off()
end

task()
```

Did you find the intent error here? How can you fix it? Is there more than one way to fix it?

2.10 Separating Out the Task

In the above examples, we have shown the instructions for our robot(s) in the main task block. It is useful to separate them out. This makes it slightly more flexible to actually execute the code in our programs. However, it isn't essential to do this in Ruby and the following will actually work, though the style is not preferred.

Here is the program of Section 2.6 written in the alternate style.

```
#!/opt/local/bin/ruby
require "ur_robot"

karel = UrRobot.new(2, 2, EAST, 0)
karel.move()
karel.move()
karel.pick_beeper()
karel.move()
karel.turn_left()
karel.move()
karel.move()
karel.put_beeper()
karel.move()
karel.turn_off()
```

Here we don't write a task block (method) at all. Using our metaphor of the helicopter pilot, she begins reading these instructions, perhaps written on a sheet of paper. This doesn't seem very important in this simple example, but will become so very soon. We will prefer to capture the task in a method. Since the statements aren't enclosed in a def, they are just executed. We can say they are at *top level*. In our preferred format, the invocation of task is the only statement at top level.

2.11 An INFINITY of Beepers

We note for completeness, though we can't use the information yet, that a robot can be delivered with infinitely many beepers in its beeper-bag. If such a robot puts down a beeper or picks a beeper, the number of beepers in the beeper-bag does not change. It is still INFINITY.

```
karel = UrRobot.new(3, 2, EAST, INFINITY)
```

We will use this information in later chapters. It is also possible, though rare, for a corner to contain an infinite number of beepers. Since programs are finite, however, there is no way to put down or pick up an infinite number of beepers.

2.12 Some Terminology

Robots are examples of programming constructs called **objects**. Objects have two capabilities: they do things and they **remember** things. The things that robots do are move, pick_beeper, etc. We will learn some things about remembering in Chapter 4 and later. We ask an object to do something by sending it a message. We can also ask an object something about what it has remembered with a message. Beepers and walls in the robot world are not objects, however. You can't send them messages. As a person, you are something like an object. You can receive messages. You can do things. You can remember things. You respond to the messages you receive.

We refer to Robots using names. These names are called **variables**. This is because they can vary. A name can refer to different robots at different times, just as in your world, the name karel can refer to different people at different times. Sometimes a robot (and in general, an object) needs to refer to itself. When you refer to yourself you probably use a special *name*, like *me*. Likewise any robot can refer to itself with the special name self.

A file containing Ruby code usually ends in .rb. File names are usually written in all lower case, but that isn't essential. A require statement at the beginning of a file refers to another file whose definitions are required. A require caused the contents of the file to be loaded and made available. Any top-level commands in the file (i.e. not part of any definition) will be executed when the file is loaded.

2.13 Important Ideas From This Chapter

object
variable (reference)
bug
method
message
lexical error
syntax error
execution error
intent error
class
self

2.14 Problem Set

The purpose of this problem set is to test your knowledge of the form and content of simple robot programs. The programs you are required to write are long but not complicated. Concentrate on writing grammatically correct, pleasingly styled programs. Refer back to the program and discussion in Section 2.6 for rules and examples of correct grammar and punctuation. Each of these problems requires a single robot of the **UrRobot** class. In each case we assume it will be named karel. This is not required, however, and you are, in general, free to name your robots with other names. Verify that each program is correct by simulating karel's actions in the appropriate initial situation.

1. Start a robot in the initial situation illustrated in Figure 2-6 and simulate the execution of the following program. Karel's task is to find the beeper, pick it up, and then turn itself off. Draw a map of the final situation, stating whether an error occurs. If an execution or intent error does occur, explain how you would correct the program. This program has no lexical or syntactic errors.

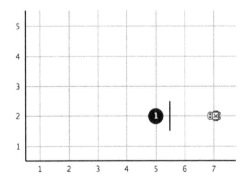

Figure 2-6: Initial Situation for Problem 1

```
def task()
    karel = UrRobot.new(2, 7, WEST, 0)
    karel.move()
    karel.turn_left()
    karel.turn_left()
    karel.move()
    karel.turn_left()
    karel.move()
    karel.turn_left()
    karel.move()
    karel.pick_beeper()
    karel.turn_off()
end

task()
```

2. Carefully inspect the following program and correct all lexical and syntactic errors. Hint: There are nine errors. Three are syntactical, and four lexical. (Yes, there are other errors too, and some are a bit hard to classify with what you know now.) Confirm that each word is in an appropriate place and that it is a correctly spelled instruction name or reserved word. You may use the program in Problem 1 as a model for a lexically and syntactically correct program.

```
def job()
    karel = UrRobot(2, 7, West, 0)
    karel.move()
    karel.move()
    karel.pick_beeper()
    karel.move; ()
    karel.turn_left()
    move ()
    karol.move()
    karel.turn_right
      karel.put_beeper()
    karel.put_beeper()
    karel.turn_off
```

3. What is the smallest lexically and syntactically correct robot program? You will need to do a bit of research outside this book in the Ruby literature to discover the answer to this one. Alternatively, you can experiment with a Ruby system to discover the answer.

4. In most cities and towns we can walk around the block by repeating the following actions four times:

walk to the nearest intersection

turn either right or left (the same one each time)

If done correctly we will return to our original starting place. Program karel to walk around the block. Will your program succeed for the initial situation in Figure 2-7?

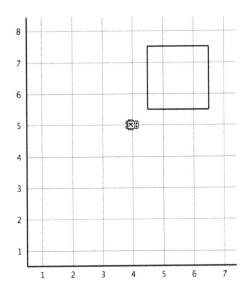

Figure 2-7 Initial Situation for the Walk Around the Block Task

5. Every morning karel is awakened in bed when the newspaper, represented by a beeper, is thrown on the front porch of the house. Program karel to retrieve the paper and bring it back to bed. The initial situation is given in Figure 2-8, and the final situation must have karel back in bed (same corner, same direction) with the newspaper.

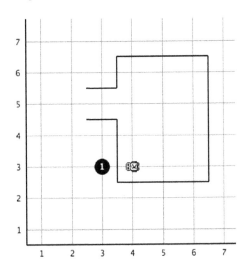

Figure 2-8: Initial Situation for the Newspaper Retrieval Task

6. The wall section s in Figure 2-9 represent a mountain (north is up). Program karel to climb the mountain and then plant a flag, represented by a beeper, on the summit; karel then must descend the other side of the mountain. Assume that karel starts with the flag-beeper in the beeper-bag. Remember that karel is not a super-robot who can leap to the top of the mountain, plant the flag, and then jump down in a single bound. As illustrated, karel must closely follow the mountain's face on the way up and down.

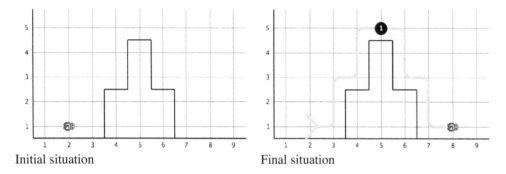

Initial situation   Final situation

Figure 2-9: The Mountain Climbing Task

7. On the way home from the supermarket, karel's shopping bag ripped slightly at the bottom, leaking a few expensive items. These groceries are represented by -you guessed it- beepers. The initial situation, when karel discovered the leak, is represented in Figure 2-10. Program karel to pick up all the dropped items and then return to the starting position.

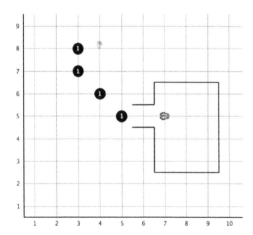

Figure 2-10 Initial Situation for the Grocery Pickup Task

8. Write a program that instructs karel to rearrange the beeper pattern as shown in Figure 2-11.

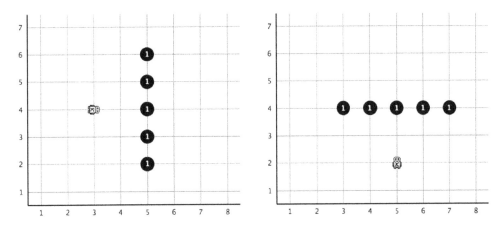

Figure 2-11 The Rearrange the Beepers Task

9. Karel is practicing for the Robot Olympics. One of karel's events is the shuttle race. The shuttle race requires karel to move around two beepers in a figure 8 pattern. Write a program that instructs karel to walk a figure 8 pattern as fast as possible (fast implies as few instructions as possible). Karel must stop in the same place it starts and must be facing the same direction.

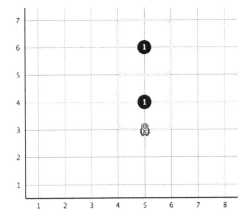

Figure 2-12 The Shuttle Race and karel's Figure 8 Path

10. Suppose we want a robot named karel to move from the origin to the intersection of 100'th street and 100'th avenue. How many different programs can we write to do this? What is the minimum number of instructions the robot will need to execute in order to carry this out? What is the minimum number of instructions you need to write (using just the knowledge gained from this chapter) in order to do it?

11. A robot named karel is at the origin facing North with one beeper in its beeper bag. Three blocks east of it is another robot named carl, facing East with no beepers. There are no wall section s or beepers in the world. Have karel walk to carl and give carl the beeper. Carl should then carry the beeper two blocks north and put it down. Both robots should then return to their original locations, facing the original directions.

12. How long would it take for a robot to put down an INFINITY of beepers?

13. If a robot named karel is on a corner with an infinite number of beepers and it picks one up, how many are left on the corner? How many are in the beeper-bag?

3 Extending the Robot Programming Language

This chapter explains the mechanics of specifying new classes of robots and adding new instructions to the robot vocabulary. It also discusses methods for planning, implementing, and testing our programs. The ability to extend the robot vocabulary combined with these techniques can simplify our work in writing robot programs.

3.1 Creating a More Natural Programming Language

In Chapter Two, we saw a robot perform a complex task. We also saw that it takes many messages to perform such a task. Writing so many messages is verbose and error prone.

Let's look at a particularly clumsy aspect of robot programming. Suppose that we need to program a robot to travel over vast distances. For example, assume that, starting at 3rd Avenue and 2nd Street, the robot must move east along 2nd Street for ten miles (a mile is eight blocks long), pick up a beeper, and then move another five miles north. Because a robot understands about moving *blocks* but not *miles*, we must translate our solution into instructions that move the robot one block at a time. This restriction forces us to write a program that contains 120 move messages. Although the conversion from miles to blocks is straightforward, it results in a very long and cumbersome program.

The crux of the problem is that we think in one language, but must program robots in another. Rather than make programmers the slaves of the machine, continually forced to translate their powerful ideas into the robot's primitive methods, Karel-Werke turned the tables and endowed robots with a simple mechanism to learn the definitions of new methods.

The robot programming language permits the robot programmer to specify new classes of robots. These class descriptions provide specifications of new robot instructions. Karel-Werke will then use the class descriptions to create robots able to interpret the new messages.

A robot's learning ability is quite limited. Karel-Werke builds each robot with a *dictionary* of useful method names and their definitions, but each definition must be built from simpler instructions that robots already understand. By providing robots with a dictionary of instructions that perform complex actions, we can build a robot vocabulary that corresponds more closely to our own. Given this mechanism, we can solve our programming problems using whatever instructions are natural to our way of thinking, and then we can provide robots with the definitions of these instructions.

We can define a **move_mile** instruction as eight **move** messages. Then, when a robot is told to move_mile in a program, it looks up the method definition associated with this message name and executes it. Now our unwieldy beeper-moving program can be written with a **move_mile** definition, containing eight move messages, and another 15 move_mile messages. This program, containing these 23 messages, would be quite an improvement over the original program, which needed more than 120 messages to accomplish the task.

Although both programs move the robot exactly the same distance, the smaller program is much easier to read and understand. In complicated problems, the ability to extend a robot's vocabulary makes the difference between understandable programs and unintelligible ones. We will explore in detail this extremely important definition mechanism in the next two sections.

3.2 A Mechanism that Defines New Classes of Robots

Back in Chapter 2 we saw the declaration of the primitive UrRobot class. Users of the robot language can also declare new classes of robots and the factory will be able to deliver them, just as it does the standard robots. To specify a new class of robots, we include a class specification in the declaration section at the beginning of our robot program or in a separate file. Isolated from a program, the typical form of the specification is shown in the following template.

```
class <new-class-name> [ < <old-class-name> ]³
      <list-of-new-methods>
end
```

The class specification uses the reserved word **class**, and the special symbols like < to separate the various parts of the declaration. This general form includes elements delimited by angle brackets, < and >, which must be replaced with appropriate substitutions when we include a class specification in a robot program. Angle brackets are not part of the robot programming language, just a way we can set off locations in a program structure where actual language elements may appear. In this case, <new-class-name> must be replaced by a new name. This name can be built from letters, digits, and the underscore character, but must not match the spelling of any reserved word. As we shall see a few other characters such as the question mark are also legal. Names must also begin with a letter or underscore. Class names always begin with an upper-case letter. The replacement for < old-class-name > is the name of some existing class, often UrRobot. New methods that apply to this class of robot will replace <list-of-new-methods>, and we will soon see how to define these new methods.

In the specification above, the square brackets indicate that what is enclosed is optional. And note that if it is used, that it begins with a literal less than symbol, <. Distinguish between angle brackets used to denote place holders, from the less than used to introduce the old-class-name if it exists. Suppose that we would like to solve the mile mover problem discussed in the introduction to this chapter. Suppose also that, in addition to the new capabilities, we want the robots of the new class to have all of the functionality of the standard UrRobot class. We can do so with a new class specification as follows.

```
require "ur_robot"

# Defines robots that can move a mile at a time
class MileWalker < UrRobot

    # Move 8 blocks = 1 robot world mile
    def move_mile
        # instructions omitted for now
    end # of move_mile

end # of class MileWalker
```

The name of the new class of robots is **MileWalker**, which also names its main new capability. We also indicate, by giving the name of the **UrRobot** class after the <, that mile walkers are to have all of the capabilities of members of the UrRobot class. We needed the *require* to make the name UrRobot visible in

---

³There are a few other things we can include in a robot class declaration. These will be introduced in future chapters. It is possible also, that < old-class-name> is missing, in which case the < is not written.

this new class. We shall put this code in the file mile_walker.rb. As a shorthand we say that UrRobot is the *parent* class of MileWalker or that MileWalker is a *subclass* of UrRobot. We also say that robots of the new class *inherit* all the capabilities of the parent class. Therefore, mile walkers know how to move and turn_left, just like members of the UrRobot class. They can also pick and put beepers and turn themselves off. In keeping with a common Ruby convention, the name of the class begins with a capital letter, and since it is a catenation of words, each internal word also begins with a capital letter: MileWalker.

Here we have a list of only a single new method. Each method in the list is written with its definition indented, and the detail of these will be shown just below. This specification says that when a robot in this class is first turned on it will be able to execute **move_mile** methods as well as all methods inherited from the **UrRobot** class. Think of a mile walker as having been created in the factory by passing down the UrRobot production line and then being passed to an additional production line to install the additional capabilities. We shall see in the future, that this additional processing can also modify the basic instructions as well as install new ones. Again, this metaphor of the production line is quite close to what really happens.

Thus, we will see later that the names of instructions can be either new names or the names of methods already existing in the parent class. In this latter case we can give new meaning to methods as we shall see in section 3.6. Again, keeping with the Ruby convention, method names are all lower-case letters, but multiple words are separated with underscores: move_mile. You would do well to follow these conventions in your own programming as they make communication easier. Some authors prefer to use bumpyWords for methods and connect run-on words with upper case letters: moveMile. We won't use this alternate convention, but you may read programs that do use it. Note that class names are, by convention, singular nouns, written with bumpy words but the files they reside in are all lower case. It is best if they end with the file extension rb: mile_walker.rb.

The methods of a class define what capabilities an object in that class has. They also define what messages you can send to such an object. Don't confuse the two, however. The message is how you *talk* to an object. The method is what it does when it gets a message. Different objects can have different methods associated with a given message as we shall see. The names of methods that cause objects to do something are normally verbs or verb phrases that describe the action, such as move, or pick_beeper.

The class declaration introduces the names of new robot methods, but we have not yet explained how they are to be carried out. In the next section we will see how to define the new capabilities.

3.3 Defining the New Methods

As we declare a new robot class we need to define all of the new instructions introduced in it. These definitions are part of the class declaration in the declaration part of the robot program. The form of a simple instruction definition is as follows.

```
def <method_name> [(<more>)]
    <list_of_instructions>
end
```

As we see, we begin with the reserved word **def** and the definition ends with the word **end**. We have to give the name of the method we are defining, of course. It is possible that there are additional parameters, optionally within parentheses. If so, they are separated by commas. We shall see some of this in Chapter 4. Starting on the second line, we give a list of instructions, similar to a main task block, indented an additional few spaces, that tells a robot of this class how to carry out the new method. This list of instructions is sometimes called a *block* in the robot programming vocabulary, though Ruby uses that term in a specific way to be discussed later. For example, our move_mile method in the MileWalker class would be written within that class as shown below. Most of the instructions in the list of instructions will be messages. Note that it is acceptable to put blank lines between the various instructions and definitions if you think that helps you read the code. It is also acceptable to terminate your instructions with semicolons. We will largely avoid this practice, however.

```
require "ur_robot"
class MileWalker < UrRobot
    def move_mile()
        move()
        move()
        move()
        move()
        move()
        move()
        move()
        move()
    end
end
```

This block is like a main task block, but it is also different, since the messages in it are not prefaced here with the name of any robot. The reason for the difference is that in the main task block, we need to tell some particular robot to carry out an instruction, so we say something like karel.move( ) to get a robot named karel to move. Here, however, a robot of the **MileWalker** class will eventually carry out this instruction when it is sent a **move_mile** message. The robot will carry out this instruction list itself. Since it is moving itself and not another robot, it sends the message to *self*. Every message is directed to a particular object, even if it is the same object executing the code in question. In fact, each of the move instructions in the block could have been written as self.move() instead, to emphasize this. We shall do this occasionally, but it is optional.

If we have a MileWalker named lisa, we can get it to walk a mile with either

```
lisa.move_mile()
```

or

```
lisa.move()
lisa.move()
lisa.move()
lisa.move()
lisa.move()
lisa.move()
lisa.move()
lisa.move()
```

In the former case, lisa will move itself eight times upon receiving the single move_mile message.

The complete robot program for the above is:

```
require "ur_robot"

class MileWalker < UrRobot
    def move_mile()
        move()
        move()
        move()
        move()
        move()
        move()
        move()
        move()
    end
end

def task()
   lisa = MileWalker.new(3, 2, EAST, 0)
   # Declare a new MileWalker lisa.
   lisa.move_mile()
   lisa.move_mile()
   lisa.move_mile()
   lisa.move_mile()
   lisa.move_mile()
   lisa.move_mile()
   lisa.move_mile()
   lisa.move_mile()
   lisa.move_mile()
   lisa.move_mile()
   lisa.pick_beeper()
   lisa.turn_left()
   lisa.move_mile()
   lisa.move_mile()
   lisa.move_mile()
   lisa.move_mile()
   lisa.move_mile()
   lisa.turn_off()
end

task()
```

Here the main task block is within this same file. Actually it can be in any file in your program. Often, when we write a class (in a file) we also put a main block in it as well, just to test it. If you want to put the main task in a different file, that file will need to import the MileWalker class with a statement such as:

```
require "mile_walker"
```

One thing we have not talked about yet is how the beepers (and walls) get into the world in the first place. The world is also an object and it accepts messages like any object does. One of the messages is place_beepers. The usage of this is discussed in the Appendix. As a result, a program to be run with the software provided with this book looks a bit different, since we also need to make the world visible in a window and place beepers and walls into it.

We can now give a better definition of the word *program*. A program is a description of the objects that will be used (the classes), creation of objects from the classes, and a description of what we want those objects to actually do. Prior to the example above, the programs have been a bit incomplete since much is hidden in the definition of UrRobot, for example. Here, however, we see both the description of a new class of robots (objects) and the task we want them to perform.

Notice that having a move_five_miles instruction here would be useful. Contemplate writing the program without defining any new instructions. It requires 122 messages to be sent to the robot. This is not hard to write with a good text editor, but once it is written, it is tedious to verify that it has exactly the right number of move commands.

3.4 The Meaning and Correctness of New Methods

A robot is a machine, a device completely devoid of intelligence. This is something that robot programmers must never forget. The robot does not "understand" what we "mean" when we write a program. It does exactly what we "say". There is no room for interpretation. A robot class declaration is a description to the robot factory that tells it how to construct robots of this class. At the robot factory the entire declaration part of any robot program is read and examined for errors. As part of the manufacturing and delivery process the robots are given the definitions of each of the new methods of their class. Each robot stores the definitions of the methods in its own dictionary of methods. Thus, when we tell a robot of the MileWalker class to move_mile, it receives the message, consults its dictionary to see how it must respond, and then carries out the required actions. The helicopter pilot does not have to read this part of the program when setting up robots for delivery since the robot already knows how to move_mile. It is the robot, itself, that will execute the method when it receives the move_mile message. Objects are autonomous in this regard. They know their own methods and execute the methods themselves when sent appropriate messages.

In a robot's world, just because we define a new method named move_mile, it doesn't necessarily mean that the instruction really moves the robot one mile. For example, there is nothing that prevents using the following method definition

```
def move_mile()
   move()
   move()
   move()
   move()
   move()
   move()
end
```

According to robot programming rules of grammar, this is a perfectly legal definition for it contains neither lexical nor syntax errors. However, by defining move_mile this way, we tell a robot that executing a move_mile instruction is equivalent to executing six move instructions. The robot does not understand what a move_mile method is supposed to accomplish; its only conception of a move_mile instruction is the definition we provide. Consequently, any new method we define may contain an intent error, as this example shows.

Besides intent errors, a new method can cause execution errors if it is defined by using primitive instructions that can cause error shutoffs. Can this incorrect definition of move_mile ever cause an error shutoff? The answer is yes, because we might encounter a wall before we completed six moves. However, it is possible to write a set of instructions for a robot to execute in which it would seem that nothing is wrong with this version of move_mile. Thus we might gain false confidence in this incorrect method and be very surprised when it fails us later. This example is somewhat trivial because the error is obvious. With a more complex defined method we must take care to write a definition that really accomplishes what its name implies. The name specifies what the method is intended to do, and the definition specifies how the method does what the name implies. The two must match exactly, if we are to understand what our programs mean. If not, one or both must be changed.

When simulating a robot's execution of a defined method, we must adhere to the rules that the robot uses to execute these instructions. Robots execute a defined method by performing the actions associated with its definition. Do not try to shortcut this process by doing what the method name means because the robot does not know what a defined method means; the robot knows only how it is defined. We must recognize the significance of this distinction and learn to interpret robot programs as literally as the robot does. The meaning of names is supposed to help a human reader understand a program. If the actual instructions defining the meaning of a name are at variance with the meaning of the name, it is easy to be misled.

3.5 Defining New Methods in a Program

In this section we display a complete robot program that uses the method definition mechanism. We will first trace the execution of the program (recall that tracing is just simulating the execution of the methods in the order that a robot does). We will then discuss the general form of programs that use the new method definition mechanism. The task is shown below in Figure 3-1: it must pick up each beeper in the world while climbing the stairs. Following these figures is a program that correctly instructs a robot to accomplish the task.

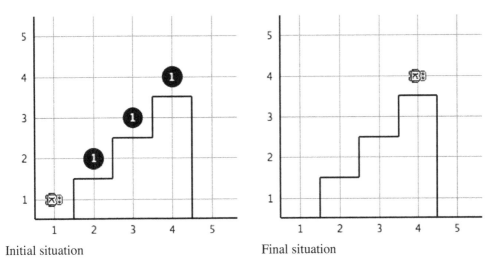

Initial situation   Final situation

Figure 3-1 A Stair Cleaning Task for karel to Perform

```
require "ur_robot"

class StairSweeper < UrRobot
   #Robot turns right by executing three turn_left instructions
   def turn_right()
      self.turn_left()
      self.turn_left()
      self.turn_left()
   end

   #Robot climbs one stair
   def climb_stair()
      self.turn_left()
      self.move()
      self.turn_right()
      self.move()
   end
end

def task()
   alex = StairSweeper.new(1, 1, EAST, 0)
   alex.climb_stair()
   alex.pick_beeper()
   alex.climb_stair()
   alex.pick_beeper()
   alex.climb_stair()
   alex.pick_beeper()
   alex.turn_off()
end

task()
```

Next, we provide an annotated version of the same program that numbers each instruction and message in the order in which it is executed, starting with the delivery specification instruction #0.

```
class StairSweeper < UrRobot
   #Robot turns right by executing three turn_left instructions
   def turn_right()
      # to here from  #4,    #13 or  #22
      self.turn_left()#5,    #14 or  #23
      self.turn_left()#6,    #15 or  #24
      self.turn_left()#7,    #16 or  #25
      # return to      #4,    #13 or  #22
   end
```

```
    #Robot climbs one stair
    def climb_stair()
        # to here from    #1,    #10 or   #19
        self.turn_left()  #2,    #11 or   #20
        self.move()       #3,    #12 or   #21
        self.turn_right() #4,    #13 or   #22
        self.move()       #8,    #17 or   #26
        # return to       #1,    #10 or   #19
    end

def task()
    alex = StairSweeper.new(1, 1, EAST, 0) #0
    alex.climb_stair() #1
    alex.pick_beeper() #9
    alex.climb_stair() #10
    alex.pick_beeper() #18
    alex.climb_stair() #19
    alex.pick_beeper() #27
    alex.turn_off()    #28
end

task()
```

To verify that this program is correct, we trace the execution of it, carefully simulating the execution of the instructions. Only one instruction can be executed at a time in the robot world. When a program is executing, we call the current instruction the *focus of execution*. When the helicopter pilot starts to execute a program, the focus is initially on the first instruction within the main task block.

In this sample program the initial focus is the climb_stair message, which is annotated as #1. The climb_stair message is sent through the satellite to the robot alex. When alex receives this message, the focus of execution passes from the pilot to alex. The pilot, who must wait until the instruction has been completed, is very careful to remember where he or she was in the program when the climb_stair message was sent. Alex, upon receiving this message, consults its list of dictionary entries and goes to the definition of climb_stair. In the sample program the new execution point is annotated as "to here from #1".

Alex focuses on the list of instructions defining the new method, climb_stair, and encounters a turn_left message (marked as #2). Alex trains the focus of execution on the turn_left message, executes it, and then focuses on #3, move. Alex executes this move and focuses on #4, turn_right. Since this is not a primitive instruction, alex must retrieve its definition from its dictionary. It then focuses on the instruction list from the definition of turn_right and executes the three turn_left instructions, #5, #6, and #7. Having completed the execution of the turn_right method, alex now returns its focus to the place in which the turn_right message occurred within climb_stair. Alex shifts focus to #8 and executes the move. After alex performs this move it is finished executing the method climb_stair so it yields execution back to the pilot since it has completely carried out the task required by the message climb_stair. The focus of execution returns to the place in the program marked #1, and the pilot sends alex the pick_beeper message that is marked #9. With this message, the focus of execution is again passed from pilot to robot. Alex also interprets and carries out this pick_beeper instruction and yields focus back to the pilot at #10. The pilot then sends alex another climb_stair message. Alex repeats this same sequence of steps a second time for this climb-stair message marked #10 and the pick_beeper that follows. It is then repeated yet again for the third climb_stair and pick_beeper messages. Alex is finally instructed to execute the turn_off instruction, after which the program's execution is complete.

Notice that a method definition can become alex's focus from any place in the program that sends alex that message. The pilot and the robot must always remember the place in the program where they were when the focus changes. This allows the execution to return to its correct place and continue executing the program. It is important for us to understand that no complex rules are needed to execute a program containing new methods. Tracing the execution of this program was a bit tedious because each step is small and simple, but alex is not equipped to understand anything more complicated. Alex can follow a very simple set of rules that tell it how to execute a program. Yet we can use these simple rules, coupled with every robot's willingness to follow them, to command the robot to perform complicated tasks.

We should now understand how the helicopter pilot and the robots work together to execute a program that includes the method definition mechanism. It is best to think about the execution of the program as if a robot (or any object) that receives a message) itself executes whatever method that object has corresponding to the message. So it is alex that executes climb_stair and turn_right, not the pilot. The helicopter pilot only executes the main program block.

We next turn our attention toward program form, and we make the following observations about the stair-cleaning program.

* The names defined within a robot class, including the names of the parent class and the parent of the parent, etc. (collectively called *ancestors*), are called the *dictionary* of the class.

* The full declaration of UrRobot does not need to be included in your robot programs, since it is *factory standard*, though we need to *require* it. Any other class that you need to define must be completely written in the declaration part, along with the definitions of all of its methods.

* Names used within a file, but not defined there, need to be imported (i.e. required) unless they are built in to Ruby.

* The class definitions of your robot classes are normally placed in separate files where the name of the file is the closely related to the name of the class, with .rb appended to the end. So the StairSweeper class would naturally appear in a file named stair_sweeper.rb. The main method can be in this file or not as long as you import any needed classes into it. In fact, main task block can be in a file of its own that is not a robot class at all. We shall see this later. The Appendix shows how you can execute your robot programs.

The class dictionary entries are not permanent and the world does not remember any definitions from program to program. Each time we write a robot program, we must include a complete set of all dictionary entries required in that program. They can be spread over several files, however.

3.6 Modifying Inherited Methods

Earlier in this chapter we built the class MileWalker that gave robots the ability to walk a mile at a time. Notice that they retained their ability to walk a block at a time as well. Sometimes we want to build a class in which some previously defined instruction is redefined to have a new meaning. For example, suppose we had a problem in which a robot always needed to move by miles, but never by blocks. In this case it would be an advantage to create a class with a new definition of the move instruction so that when a robot in this class was told to move, it would move a mile. This is easily done, though the code is a bit messier.

```
require "ur_robot"

class MileMover < UrRobot
    #Move 8 blocks = 1 robot world mile
    def move()
        super()
        super()
        super()
        super()
        super()
        super()
        super()
        super()
    end
end
```

We say that the new definition of move in this class *overrides* the original definition inherited from the class UrRobot since it has the same name (and no parameters). We now have a problem, since to move a mile we need to be able to move eight blocks, but we are defining move to mean move a mile here. Therefore, we can't just say move eight times because that is **this** instruction. (See Problem 11.) Instead, we need to indicate that we want to use the original, or overridden, instruction, move, from class UrRobot. We can do this since UrRobot is the parent class. We just need to use the message super(), which is a way to name the method of the same name in the super class. There is more on this in Chapter 4

Now if we complete the above program with

```
def task()
    karel = MileMover.new(5, 2, NORTH, 0)
    karel.move()
    karel.pick_beeper()
    karel.move()
    karel.put_beeper()
    karel.turn_off()
end

task()
```

Karel will find the beeper at $(13, 2)$ and will leave it at $(21, 2)$.

> **Messages**: Now we can begin to explore a very important idea. A large program may have several different methods with the same name; move, for example. If so, they will be in different classes. When you send a message to an object, it will, if it understands the message at all, use the method from its own class to carry out the message. It won't matter what name you use to refer to the object, it knows itself and what class it belongs to and will *choose* the right version of the method, because it knows only its own version. But it is also possible to send a message to the robot in a different way as when we said super(). We will discuss this again under the heading *polymorphism*.

Notice now that if we had several different robots in the same program and we sent each of them the same messages, they might each respond differently to those messages. In particular, a MileWalker only moves a block when told to move, while a MileMover, moves a mile.

3.7 An Ungrammatical Program

Before reading this section, quickly look at the small program in the example below, and see if you can find a syntax error.

```
require ur_robot

class BigStepper < UrRobot
   def long_move()
      move()
      move()
      move()
   end

def task()
   BigStepper tony.new(5, 2, north, 0)
   tony.long_move()
   tony.turn_left()
   tony.turn_off()
end
```

While there are a lot of errors in this fragment, the only grammatical error is the missing end for the class. It is the only one the factory will catch on its check. This example illustrates the common programming mistake of omitting quote marks around a string ("ur_robot"). The program is also wrongly indented in task block, but that isn't an error, just ugly. The definition of long_move appears to define the instruction correctly. Did you spot the quoting mistake? And did you find the other errors in this example?

The factory reads the declaration part of a program and the main task block of the program to check for lexical and syntax errors. A reader (human or otherwise) discovers syntax errors by checking *meaningful* components of the program and checking for proper grammar and punctuation. Examples of meaningful components are class declarations, method definitions, and the main task block. In effect we verify the meaningful components separately. Let us illustrate how the factory finds the mistake in the program above using this examination. Remember that the factory only reads the program's words and is not influenced by our meaning or intention.

The factory examines the new robot class declaration. It has a name, a parent class, and a list of features. The punctuation all checks out as well. Then it sees the class name and method name in the instruction definition. It then looks for a block to include with the definition. Each def and class must end with an end and so it will find the missing end error. At some point in the analysis, perhaps first, and perhaps later, it will check to see that the require is correct. It will find what looks like a name and a name could refer to anything including the string that is needed here, representing a Ruby file. While in fact this name has not been defined, the factory won't discover that, since it looks at structure and not content. In summary, little things make a big difference in programming. There is one more lexical error. Did you get it? The factory won't.

Note that the program processor won't catch all of your errors. It cannot catch intent errors, of course, but in Ruby it will also miss some of your lexical errors, such as misspelled words. These will only be caught when you execute the program. For example, the fact that north isn't effectively defined in the above example will only be found when the program executes. Here it isn't a misspelling, but the fact that the name north doesn't refer to anything that is the problem. And yes, it should be NORTH, of course, not north.

We are rapidly becoming experts at analyzing programs. Given a robot program, we should now be able to detect grammar and punctuation errors quickly. We should also be able to simulate programs efficiently. Nevertheless, the other side of the programming coin, constructing programs, may still seem a little bit magical. The next few sections take a first step toward demystifying this process.

Oh yes, the above program never actually invokes the task method, so nothing can be executed in any case. This is an intent error.

3.8 Tools for Designing and Writing Robot Programs

Designing solutions for problems and writing robot programs involve problem solving. One model[4] describes problem solving as a process that has four activities: definition of the problem, planning the solution, implementing the plan, and analyzing the solution.

The initial definition of the problem is presented when we are provided figures of the initial and final situations. Once we examine these situations and understand what task a robot must perform, we begin to plan, implement and analyze a solution. This section examines techniques for planning, implementing and analyzing robot programs. By combining these techniques with the new class and instruction mechanism, we can develop solutions that are easy to read and understand.

As we develop and write programs that solve robot problems, these three guidelines must be followed:

* our programs must be easy to read and understand,

* our programs must be easy to debug, and

* our programs must be easy to modify to solve variations of the original task.

3.8.1 Stepwise Refinement - a Technique for Planning, Implementing, and Analyzing Robot Programs

In this section, we will discuss *stepwise refinement*, a method we can use to construct robot programs. This method addresses the problem of how we can naturally write concise programs that are correct, simple to read, and easy to understand.

It may appear natural to define all the new classes and methods that we will need for a task first, and then write the program using these instructions. But how can we know what robots and which new instructions are needed before we write the program? Stepwise refinement tells us first to write the program using any robots and instruction names we desire, and then define these robots and their instructions. That is, we write the sequence of messages in the main task block first, and then we write the definitions of the new instruction names used within this block. Finally, we assemble these separate pieces into a complete program.

---

[4]G. Polya, How to Solve It, Princeton University Press, 1945, 1973.G. Polya, How to Solve It, Princeton University Press, 1945, 1973.

There are possibly many kinds of stepwise refinement, actually, especially in object-oriented programs. Here we explore only one kind, called *procedural decomposition*. It lets us defer hard detail work while we get an overall view of our problem and its possible solution. Let's give it a try.

We will explore this process more concretely by writing a program for the task shown in Figure 3-2. These situations represent a harvesting task that requires a robot to pick up a rectangular field of beepers.

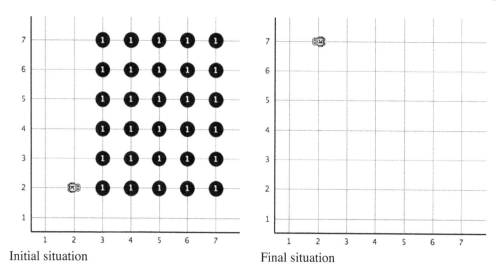

Initial situation   Final situation

Figure 3-2 The Harvest Task

Our first step is to develop an overall plan to guide us in writing a robot program that allows karel to perform the task. Planning is probably best done as a group activity. Sharing ideas in a group allows members to present different plans that can be thoughtfully examined for strengths and weaknesses. Even if we are working alone, we can think in a question and answer pattern such as the following.

Question: How many robots do we need to perform this task?

Answer: We could do it with one robot that walks back and forth over all of the rows to be harvested, or we could do it with a team of robots.

Question: How many shall we use?

Answer: Let's try it with just one robot named mark, for now.

Question: How can mark pick a row?

Answer: Mark could move west to east across the southern most unpicked row of beepers, picking each beeper as it moves.

Question: How can mark pick the entire field?

Answer: Mark could turn around and move back to the western side of the field, move north one block, face east, and repeat the actions listed above. Mark could do this for each row of beepers in the field. Since mark is not standing on a beeper we will move it to the first beeper before starting to harvest the first row.

If this idea seems like it might work, our next step is to write out the main task block of the program using English-like new message names. We briefly move from planning to implementing our plan. Even though this is done on paper, we should still concentrate on correct syntax and proper indenting to reduce errors when we copy our program into the computer. Suppose we call the class of the new robot by the name Harvester.

```
def task()
   mark =  Harvester.new(2, 2, EAST, 0)
   mark.move()
   mark.harvest_one_row()
   mark.return_to_start()
   mark.move_north_one_block()
   mark.harvest_one_row()
   mark.return_to_start()
   mark.move_north_one_block()
   mark.harvest_one_row()
   mark.return_to_start
   mark.move_north_one_block()
   mark.harvest_one_row()
   mark.return_to_start()
   mark.move_north_one_block()
   mark.harvest_one_row()
   mark.return_to_start()
   mark.move_north_one_block()
   mark.harvest_one_row()
   mark.return_to_start()
   mark.turn_off()
end
```

Notice that what we have really done here is to design a new class of robot that can respond to three new messages. We can think of a robot class as a mechanism for creating *service* providers; the robots. These robots, a kind of object in object-oriented programming, provide specific services when sent messages requesting the service. Here we seem to require three different services, harvest_one_row, return_to_start, and move_north_one_block, beyond the basic services that all UrRobots can provide.

Before we continue with this plan and begin to work on the new instructions, harvest_one_row, return_to_start and move_north_one_block, we should analyze our original plan looking at its strengths and weaknesses. We are asking if we are requesting the right services. Our analysis might proceed as follows.

Question: What are the strengths of this plan?

Answer: The plan takes advantage of the new instruction mechanism and it allows mark to harvest the beepers.

Question: What are the weaknesses of the plan?

Answer: Mark makes some *empty* trips.

Question: What are these empty trips?

Answer: Mark returns to the starting point on the row that was just harvested.

Question: Why are these bad?

Answer: Because robots (and computers) are valuable resources that should generally be used efficiently. Some tasks must be done "on time" if solving them is to confer any benefit. Moreover, programmer time is very valuable.

Question: Can mark pick more beepers on the way back?

Answer: Instead of harvesting only one row and then turning around and returning to the start, mark can harvest one row, move north one street and come back to the west harvesting a second row. Mark can then move one street north to begin the entire process over for the next two rows. If mark repeats these steps two more times the entire field of beepers will be harvested.

Again we analyze this new plan for its strengths and weaknesses.

Question: What advantage does this offer over the first plan?

Answer: Mark makes only six trips across the field instead of twelve. There are no empty trips.

Question: What are the weaknesses of this new plan?

Answer: None that we can see as long as there are an even number of rows.

When we are planning solutions, we should be very critical and not just accept the first plan as the best. We now have two different plans and you can probably think of several more. Let's avoid the empty trips and implement the second plan.

```
def task()
   mark =  Harvester.new(2, 2, EAST, 0)
   mark.move()
   mark.harvest_two_rows()
   mark.position_for_next_harvest()
   mark.harvest_two_rows()
   mark.position_for_next_harvest()
   mark.harvest_two_rows()
   mark.move()
   mark.turn_off()
end
```

Let us commit to this plan. We must now begin to think about planning the new instructions harvest_two_rows and position_for_next_harvest.

3.8.2 The Second Step-Planning harvest_two_rows and position_for_next_harvest

Our plan contains two subtasks: one harvests two rows and the other positions mark to harvest two more rows. The planning of these two subtasks must be just as thorough as the planning was for the overall task. Let's begin with harvest_two_rows.

Question: What does harvest_two_rows do?

Answer: harvest_two_rows must harvest two rows of beepers. One will be harvested as mark travels east and the second will be harvested as mark returns to the west.

Question: What does mark have to do?

Answer: Mark must pick beepers and move as it travels east. At the end of the row of beepers, mark must move north one block, face west, and return to the western edge of the field picking beepers as it travels west.

Continuing to use English-like message names, we can now implement this part of the plan.

```
class Harvester < UrRobot
  def harvest_two_rows()
      harvest_one_row_moving_east()
      go_north_to_next_row()
      harvest_one_row_moving_west()
  end
  ...
end
```

We analyze this plan as before looking for strengths and weaknesses.

Question: What are the strengths of this plan?

Answer: It seems to solve the problem.

Question: What are the weaknesses of this plan?

Answer: Possibly one-we have two different instructions that harvest a single row of beepers.

Question: Do we really need two different harvesting instructions?

Answer: We need one for going east and one for going west.

Question: Do we really need a separate instruction for each direction?

Answer: Harvesting is just a series of pick_beepers and moves. The direction mark is moving does not matter. If we plan go_to_next_row carefully, we can use one instruction to harvest a row of beepers when mark is going east and the same instruction for going west.

Our analysis shows us that we can reuse a single dictionary entry (harvest_one_row) instead of defining two similar instructions, making our program smaller. Here is the new implementation.

```
# Before executing this, the robot should be facing East,
# on the first beeper of the current row.
def harvest_two_rows()
   harvest_one_row()
   go_to_next_row()
   harvest_one_row()
end
```

The comment written in this method is called a *precondition*. In order to guarantee that the method does what it is supposed to do, any message naming this method must first guarantee that the precondition is true. Otherwise the method may not carry us toward our goal. It is very important to notice when preconditions are needed and to include them in your methods. Note that we could also deduce a postcondition here. When the precondition is true beforehand, the method will leave the robot facing West, but one block North of where it started. It is often useful to state these in your methods as well.

Let's now plan position_for_next_harvest.

Question: What does the position_for_next_harvest instruction do?

Answer: This instruction is used when mark is on the western side of the beeper field. It moves the robot north one block and faces mark east in position to harvest two more rows of beepers.

Question: What does mark have to do?

Answer: Mark must turn right to face north, move one block and turn right to face east. We implement this instruction as follows.

```
class Harvester < UrRobot

   . . .
   # Before executing this, the robot should be facing West,
   # on the last corner of the current row.
   def position_for_next_harvest()
      turn_right()
      move()
      turn_right()
   end

   def turn_right()
      turn_left()
      turn_left()
      turn_left()
   end
   . . .
```

We should analyze this instruction to see if it works properly. Since it seems to work correctly, we are ready to continue our planning and in the process define more new instructions.

3.8.3 The Third Step-Planning harvest_one_row and go_to_next_row

We now focus our efforts on harvest_one_row and finally go_to_next_row.

Question: What does harvest_one_row do?

Answer: Starting on the first beeper and facing the correct direction, mark must harvest each of the corners that it encounters, stopping on the location of the last beeper in the row.

Question: What does mark have to do?

Answer: Mark must execute a sequence of harvest_corner and move instructions to pick all five beepers in the row.

Question: How does mark harvest a single corner?

Answer: Mark must execute a pick_beeper instruction.

Question: Will this method appear in a message in the main task block?

Answer: Probably not. It is just a helper.

We can implement harvest_one_row and harvest_corner as follows.

```
class Harvester < UrRobot

    ...
  def harvest_one_row()
      harvest_corner()
      move()
      harvest_corner()
      move()
      harvest_corner()
      move()
      harvest_corner()
      move()
      harvest_corner()
  end

  def harvest_corner()
      pick_beeper()
  end
  ...
```

We again simulate the instruction and it seems to work. We now address the instruction, go_to_next_row.

Question: What does go_to_next_row do?

Answer: This instruction moves mark northward one block to the next row.

Question: Didn't we do that already? Why can't we use position_for_next_harvest? [5]

Answer: It will not work properly. When we use position_for_next_harvest, mark must be facing West. Mark is now facing East so position_for_next_harvest will not work.

Question: What does mark have to do?

Answer: Mark must turn left to face North, move one block, and turn left to face West.

The following is the implementation of this new instruction.

```
class Harvester < UrRobot
    ...
    # Before executing this, the robot should be facing East,
    # on the last corner of the current row.
    def go_to_next_row()
        turn_left()
        move()
        turn_left()
    end
    ...
```

We can use simulation to analyze this instruction and show that it is correct and our program is done.

Notice that some of our methods have preconditions. This means that the user (whoever sends the message) must guarantee that the precondition is true. If not, the program will not behave correctly. However, the wise programmer can limit the possible damage here, by making such methods harder to use by the unwary programmer (including herself). Note that harvest_one_row and go_to_next_row are not intended to be used in the main task block at all, but are really just here to help us decompose the solution sensibly. Ruby will let us hide the names of methods so that users can be warned to use the methods only within this class, rather than throughout the program. Ruby actually has several forms of *visibility*, Here go_to_next_row might better be changed to be a hidden method. Then we only need to worry about the precondition while we write this class, since it is less likely to be used (or abused) elsewhere in a larger program. While less important, perhaps, other helper methods should also normally be made private. This makes the class simpler for others to use, since there are fewer options and the intent of the class is usually clearer. The mechanism in Ruby to hide a name is to create a protected section of the class definition. A method defined in the protected section can be referenced in subclasses, but not otherwise. If it is in a private section it is visible only within the class itself. The public section, which is the normal thing, has methods visible everywhere.

---

[5]At this point you should simulate the instruction position_for_next_harvest on paper. Start with mark facing west and see where the robot is when you finish simulating the instruction.

3.8.4 The Final Step-Verifying That the Complete Program is Correct

Since we have spread this program out over several pages, we print it here so you will find it easier to read and study.

```ruby
require "ur_robot"

class Harvester < UrRobot
    # Before executing this, the robot should be facing East,
    # on the first beeper of the current row.
    def harvest_two_rows()
       harvest_one_row()
       go_to_next_row()
       harvest_one_row()
    end

    # Before executing this, the robot should be facing West,
    # on the last corner of the current row.
    def position_for_next_harvest()
       turn_right()
       move()
       turn_right()
    end

  private # the rest of the methods are invisible

    def turn_right()
       turn_left()
       turn_left()
       turn_left()
    end

    def harvest_one_row()
        harvest_corner()
        move()
        harvest_corner()
        move()
        harvest_corner()
        move()
        harvest_corner()
        move()
        harvest_corner()
    end

    def harvest_corner()
        pick_beeper()
    end
```

```
    # Before executing this, the robot should be facing East,
    # on the last corner of the current row.
    def go_to_next_row()
        turn_left()
        move()
        turn_left()
    end
  end

  def task()
  world = RobotWorld.instance()

    world.read_world("../worlds/fig3-2.kwld")
    mark =  Harvester.new(2, 2, EAST, 0)
    mark.move()
    mark.harvest_two_rows()
    mark.position_for_next_harvest()
    mark.harvest_two_rows()
    mark.position_for_next_harvest()
    mark.harvest_two_rows()
    mark.move()
    mark.turn_off()
  end

  if __FILE__ == $0
    screen = window(10, 80) # (size, speed)
    screen.run do
        task()
    end
  end
```

We are not done. We have used simulation to analyze the individual instructions in the program to see if they work correctly. We have not examined how they work in concert as one large robot program. We must now simulate mark's execution of the entire program to demonstrate that all the parts work correctly to be sure the program is correct. We may have relied on some invalid assumptions when writing the instructions that move mark between rows, or we may discover another error in our planning or implementing; maybe our analysis was wrong. A skeptical attitude toward the correctness of our programs will put us in the correct frame of mind for trying to verify them.

Stepwise refinement blends the problem solving activities of planning, implementing and analyzing into the programming process. It is a powerful programming technique and can shorten the time required to write correct robot programs.

Note: The above program also shows a bit more about how to run the graphical simulation that comes with this book. Instead of just invoking the task, we create both a screen and a world. The world keeps track of what is in the robot world, such as beepers and walls. In the above, we read the contents from a text file. We also create the screen, which is the visual representation of the world and shows the robots in action. But to use it we need to tell the screen to run the task. Note do ... end construct. It is called a block in Ruby terminology. It encapsulates some code without naming it as a def does. This will be discussed later, but for now you can utilize it to see the robots in action. RobotWorld is another class and the window method knows how to create a KarelWindow. Just like the new method, the window method requires parameters, in this case the size of the window to show (in streets and avenues) and the speed with which to run the simulation between 0 (very very slow) and 100 (very very fast).

Also note: The above does something else that we will start to use now. For the first time, we have created a class that you might consider using in the future for other programs. This means you might want to require it in some other Ruby file. But we have also put the simulation run into the same file but wouldn't want the simulation to run just because we have required it. Therefore we enclose the creation of the screen and the run command in a special if statement. This statement is discussed in general in Chapter 5 but for now, all we need to know is that an if is always matched with an end, just as a def. An if encloses a set of statements that are executed conditionally. Here the condition is pretty esoteric, but it means that the enclosed statements will only be executed if the program is run directly, rather than just loaded with require. Literally, if the current program ($0) is the same one as the one defined in this file (__FILE__). When you *require* something a different program loads the file.

3.9 Advantages of Using New Instructions

It is useful to divide a program into a small set of instructions, even if these instructions are executed only once. New instructions nicely structure programs, and English words and phrases make programs more understandable; they help convey the intent of the program. Read back through the programs we have just written and see if you can find any place where they are confusing or difficult to understand.

We could, of course, use a different plan to solve the above (or any) problem. It is useful to think in terms of services required. For example, in the harvester example above, it might be useful to think of harvest_field as a service. Fulfillment of this service would result in harvesting of an entire field, as the name suggests. We could easily add this feature to the Harvester class. Its implementation could be all of the statements of the main task block above except the first and last. It would also be possible to create a new class, say FieldHarvester, that adds just this new instruction, and that is derived from the Harvester class above.

```
require "harvester"

class FieldHarvester < Harvester

   def harvest_field()
      move()
      harvest_two_rows()
      position_for_next_harvest()
      harvest_two_rows()
      position_for_next_harvest()
      harvest_two_rows()
      move()
   end
end

def task()
   world = RobotWorld.instance()
   world.read_world("../worlds/fig3-2.kwld")
   jim = FieldHarvester.new(2, 2, EAST, 0)
   jim.harvest_field()
   jim.turn_off()
```

```
      end

   if __FILE__ == $0
      screen = window(10, 80)
      screen.run do
         task()
      end
   end
```

To use this new class we could include its definition as well as the definition of the Harvester class in a single file. We prefer to put them into separate files, but then we need to require the file that contains the Harvester class in the file that contains the FieldHarvester: require "harvester".

You can also spread a Ruby (hence robot) program over several files. Suppose that we put the above definition in a file named "field_harvester.rb" and put the definitions of the Harvester class in another different file "harvester.rb." Either or both or neither could contain a main task block. We could actually specify a task within a different file, say "harvest_task.rb" that contains only the following lines. Separating our robot definitions into separate files makes it easier to reuse them in other programs.

```
   require "field_harvester"

   def task()
      world = RobotWorld.instance()
      world.read_world("../worlds/fig3-2.kwld")
      tony = FieldHarvester(2, 2, EAST, 0)
      tony.harvest_field()
      tony.turn_off()
   end

   if __FILE__ == $0
      screen = window(10, 80)
      screen.run do
         task()
      end
   end
```

The require statements tell the factory to include things that we use, but don't define here. See the Appendix for more on the mechanics of executing programs. We have also shown a few of the world commands. Read_world sets up a world for our problem. Here it defines where the beepers go that comprise our field. We don't need to require things that are themselves required in the files we name. So, once we require "field_harvester" or, equivalently "field_harvester.rb" we automatically get "harvester.rb" and "ur_robot.rb", etc.

3.9.1 Avoiding Errors

Many novices think that all of this planning, analyzing, tracing, and simulating of programs as shown in the previous sections takes too much time. What really takes time is correcting mistakes. These mistakes fall into two broad categories:

- Planning mistakes (execution and intent errors) happen when we write a program without a well-thought-out plan and can waste a lot of programming time. They are usually difficult to fix because large segments of the program may have to be modified or discarded. Careful planning and thorough analysis of the plan can help us avoid planning mistakes.

- Programming mistakes (lexical and syntax errors) happen when we actually write the program. They can be spelling, punctuation, or other similar errors. If we write the entire program without testing it, we will undoubtedly have many errors to correct, some of which may be multiple instances of the same mistake. Writing the program in slices will both reduce the overall number of errors introduced at any one time and may prevent multiple occurrences of the same mistake (e.g., we discover a misspelling of a new instruction name). Practice helps of course. It also helps NOT to abbreviate the names we give things but to spell them out completely. Typing is not what makes programming hard, but understanding. Using real and informative names helps a lot with this. Often when you abbreviate you forget just how you spelled something and spend more time looking up your spellings than the time you spend typing them out completely. Unfortunately Ruby doesn't help you find spelling errors until you actually execute the program statement that contains the error. So in addition to careful programming, we need careful testing.

Stepwise refinement is a tool that allows us to plan, analyze and implement our plans in a way that should lead to a robot program containing a minimum of errors.

3.9.2 Future Modifications

Earlier in this chapter we said we must write programs that are easy to read and understand, easy to debug, and easy to modify. The robot's world can be readily changed and we must be able to modify existing programs to keep the robot out of trouble. It can be much simpler and takes less time to modify an existing program to perform a slightly different task than to write a completely new one. Below are two situations that differ somewhat from the Harvester task.

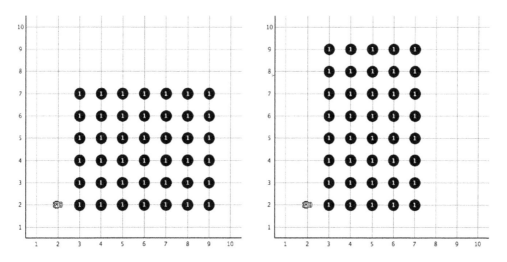

Figure 3.3 a. Longer rows   Figure 3.3 b. More rows

How difficult would it be to modify our Harvester class and the program containing it to accomplish the new beeper harvesting tasks? The second problem is easy to solve; we just add two new lines to the original main task block to solve the new task! We don't need any changes to the Harvester class itself.

What about the first problem? The change here is very different from the change in the first one since we have to pick up two additional beepers in each row. The use of new instructions allows us to quickly find where we need to make the change. There is only one instruction that actually picks up any beepers. We make a simple change to harvest_one_row as follows,

```
def harvest_one_row()
    harvest_corner()
    move()
    harvest_corner()
    move()
    harvest_corner()
    move()
    harvest_corner()
    move()
    harvest_corner()
    move()              # add these
    harvest_corner()    #
    move()              #
    harvest_corner()    # four lines
end
```

This change to the Harvester class is fine provided that we will not need to solve the original problem in the future. It is truly advantageous here to leave the Harvester class unchanged and create a new class, LongHarvester that contains this modified harvest_one_row instruction.

```
require "harvester"

class LongHarvester < Harvester
    def harvest_one_row()
        super()                     # Execute the inherited instruction
        self.move()                 # Add these
        self.harvest_corner()       #
        self.move()                 #
        self.harvest_corner()       # four lines
    end
end
```

The use of new instructions also simplifies finding and fixing intent errors. This is especially true if the instructions are short and can be easily understood. Suppose our robot makes a wrong turn and tries to pick up a beeper from the wrong place. Where is the error? If we use new instructions to write our program, and each new instruction performs one specific task (e.g., position_for_next_harvest) or controls a set of related tasks (e.g., harvest_two_rows), then we can usually determine the probable location of the error.

3.9.3 A Program Without New instructions

Below is a program that attempts to solve the original beeper planting problem with only primitive instructions. Examine the program and ask the same questions we have just explored.

- Where would we change the program to solve the first modified situation?

- Where would we change the program to solve the second modified situation?

- Suppose mark makes a wrong turn while planting the beepers. Where would we first look to correct the error?

As an example, find the single error that we included in this program.

```
if __FILE__ == $0
    world = RobotWorld.instance()
    world.read_world("../worlds/fig3-2.kwld")
    mark = UrRobot.new(2, 2, EAST, 0)
    mark.move()
    mark.pick_beeper()
    mark.move()
    mark.pick_beeper()
    mark.move()
    mark.pick_beeper()
    mark.move()
    mark.pick_beeper()
    mark.move()
    mark.pick_beeper()
    mark.turn_left()
    mark.move()
    mark.turn_left()
    mark.pick_beeper()
    mark.move()
    mark.pick_beeper()
    mark.move()
    mark.pick_beeper()
    mark.move()
    mark.pick_beeper()
    mark.move()
    mark.pick_beeper()
    mark.turn_left()
    mark.turn_left()
    mark.turn_left()
    mark.move()
    mark.turn_left()
    mark.turn_left()
    mark.turn_left()
    mark.pick_beeper()
    mark.move()
    mark.pick_beeper()
    mark.move()
    mark.pick_beeper()
    mark.move()
    mark.pick_beeper()
    mark.move()
```

```
      mark.pick_beeper()
      mark.turn_left()
      mark.turn_left()
      mark.turn_left()
      mark.move()
      mark.turn_left()
      mark.pick_beeper()
      mark.move()
      mark.pick_beeper()
      mark.move()
      mark.pick_beeper()
      mark.move()
      mark.pick_beeper()
      mark.move()
      mark.pick_beeper()
      mark.turn_left()
      mark.move()
      mark.turn_left()
      mark.pick_beeper()
      mark.move()
      mark.pick_beeper()
      mark.move()
      mark.pick_beeper()
      mark.move()
      mark.pick_beeper()
      mark.move()
      mark.pick_beeper()
      mark.move()
      mark.turn_off()
   end
```

Long lists of messages such as this may correctly solve a problem but they are very difficult to read and understand. They are also very difficult to debug and modify.

3.10 Mixins with Modules

We have noted that the processing system for our Robot Programming Language is Ruby, a modern dynamic object-oriented language. Here we will explore one aspect of the *dynamic* nature of the language. As we have said, the processor doesn't check things like the spellings of our names. This can be a bad thing as we may find our own errors much later than we would like, or not at all. But the language was designed that way for a reason. It was not an oversight. Here we shall learn why.

We have seen two cases above in which we wanted a robot class that had a turn_right instruction. This turns out to be pretty common as you might expect. Many programs also might want a turn_around instruction, or one named back_up. In fact, the Karel-Werke has seen a lot of such requests and treated it as an opportunity. They could, of course, have included these things in the standard UrRobot model, but decided on a different plan, since not all robots need these capabilities. Just as when you purchase an automobile, you can now get a robot delivered with special *value packs*. The customer specifying a class can have additional value packs installed in the robots they have delivered. Here is one such pack. We shall call it Turner and put it into a Ruby module called turner.rb.

```
module Turner
   def turn_right()
      turn_left()
      turn_left()
      turn_left()
   end

   def turn_around()
      turn_left()
      turn_left()
   end

   def back_up()
      turn_around()
      move()
      turn_around()
   end
end
```

A Ruby module is just like a class except that you can't create new objects of this type. There are two important things to note about this module. First is that it does not inherit from UrRobot, or any other robot class. Even more important is that it uses message names that are not defined here. So the turn_right method sends turn_left messages to itself, but turn_left is not defined if we aren't in a subclass of UrRobot. This seems very strange.

In fact if you try to instantiate a Turner (joe = Turner.new()) you will get an error. Such a module is called a *mixin*. This module is intended only for use within robot classes as follows. Let's go back to our StairSweeper class from earlier in this Chapter. There we wanted turn_right. An alternate way to define the StairSweeper is like this.

```
require "ur_robot"
require "turner"

class StairSweeper < UrRobot
   include Turner

   # Robot climbs one stair
   def climb_stair()
      turn_left()
      move()
      turn_right()
      move()
   end
```

```
    #Robot climbs one stair and picks a beeper from the new location
    def climb_and_pick_one()
        climb_stair()
        pick_beeper()
    end
end
```

Here we have not included the turn_right instruction, but have instead simply included Turner. We say we have mixed in the functionality of the Turner class, like mixing chocolate bits into cookies – yum.

Note that the mixin is incomplete. Note that it defines things that use the features of the other class, but not the other way about, and note that the mixin class is simple enough not to require its own constructor (more about that in Chapter 4). This makes the use free of negative consequences. We will use mixins occasionally to get common behaviors into our classes.

You can build your own mixins, of course. As you build classes in this book, and elsewhere, you can take common methods that seem generally useful and either put them into Turner, extend Turner with your own submodule, or write independent mixins. A class like StairSweeper can include any number of mixins, but we have one fundamental class like UrRobot and mixin other relatively independent, simple, other modules.

Mixins have a special advantage in that once the code is tested for such a class it is relatively safe to reuse. One of the ways to write better programs is to assure we don't have errors. One of the best ways to have fewer errors is to write less code. One way to do that is to reuse code we know works and have confidence in.

Ruby, and so the Robot Programming Language, is called *dynamic* partly because it permits this kind of programming, delaying the checking of the validity of names until the processor sees them used in action. Note that a Turner has no turn_left instruction, but if we mix it in with UrRobot, the result will have one. Here the StairSweeper object isn't (just) a Turner, or even (just) an UrRobot, but the combination. Hence it can make use of the methods of both. This is, as young people would say in about 1940, "swell."

3.11 Writing Understandable Programs

Writing understandable programs is as important as writing correct ones; some say that it is even more important. They argue that most programs initially have a few errors, and understandable programs are easier to debug. Good programmers are distinguished from bad ones by their ability to write clear and concise programs that someone else can read and quickly understand. What makes a program easy to understand? We present two criteria.

* A good program is the simple composition of easily understandable parts. Each part of the programs we just wrote can be understood by itself. Even without a detailed understanding of the parts, the plans that the programs use to accomplish their respective tasks are easy to understand.

* Dividing a program (or a large method definition) into small, easy to understand pieces is not enough. We must also make sure to name our new methods properly. These names provide a description, possibly the only description, of what the method does. Imagine what the previous programs would look like if for each meaningful method name we had used a name like first_instruction or do_it_now. The robot programming language allows us to choose any method names we want, but with this freedom comes the responsibility to select accurate and descriptive names.

It is much easier to verify or debug a program that contains new methods. The following two facts support this claim.

* New methods can be independently tested. When writing a program, we should hand simulate each method immediately after it is written, until we are convinced that it is correct. Then we can forget how the method works and just remember what the method does. Remembering should be easy, if we name the method accurately. This is easiest if the method does only one thing.

* New methods impose a structure on our programs, and we can use this structure to help us find bugs. When debugging a program, we should first find which of the new methods is malfunctioning. Then we can concentrate on debugging that method, ignoring the other parts of our program that are irrelevant to the bug.

Thus we see that there is an interesting psychological phenomenon related to the robot method definition mechanism. Because the human brain can focus on only a limited amount of information at any one time, the ability to ignore details that are no longer relevant is a great aid to program writing and debugging.

To help make our new method definitions understandable, we should also keep their lengths within a reasonable range. A good rule of thumb is that definitions should rarely exceed five to ten instructions. This limit leaves us enough room to write a meaningful method, but restrains us from cramming too much detail into any one definition. If a method's size exceeds this limit, we should try to divide it naturally into a set of smaller instructions.

This rule applies to the number of messages written within the main task block too. Most novice programmers tend to write method definitions that are too large. It is better to write many small, well-named methods, instead of a few oversized definitions.

If a new method that we write can only be executed correctly in a certain situation, then we should include comments in the definition explaining what those conditions are. For example, a method that always picks up a beeper should indicate in a comment where that beeper must appear. For example:

```
# Requires a beeper on the next corner in front.
def move_and_pick # from class Walker
    move()
    pick_beeper()
end
```

Writing understandable programs with new methods and using the technique of stepwise refinement can reduce the number of errors we make and the amount of time we spend writing robot programs. The real goal, however, is to write *beautiful* programs; programs that other programmers read with enjoyment and we read with satisfaction.

3.12 Important Ideas From This Chapter

subclass
override
dynamic language
extends (superclass, subclass)
stepwise refinement
precondition
postcondition

mixin inheritance
visibility (public, protected, private)
requires
module
include

3.13 Problem Set

The problems in this section require defining new methods for a robot named karel, or writing complete programs that include such new methods. Concentrate on writing well-structured programs, built from naturally descriptive new methods. Practice using stepwise refinement and freely define any new methods that you need. If you find yourself continually writing the same sequence of messages, it is a sure sign that you need to define that sequence as a new method. Carefully check for syntax errors in your program, and simulate karel's execution of each program to verify that it is correct.

Paradoxically, the programs in this problem set will be among the largest you will write. The instructions covered in the next chapters are so powerful that we will find that complex tasks can be solved with programs comprising a small number of these potent instructions.

1. Write appropriate definitions for the following new methods: (1) move_mile, remembering that miles are 8 blocks long; (2) slide_left, which moves karel one block to its left, but leaves it facing the same direction, and (3) move_kilo_mile, which moves karel 1000 miles forward. This last problem is difficult but a fairly short solution does exist. You may use the move_mile message in this problem without redefining it. Can any of these methods cause an error shutoff when it is executed?

2. Karel sometimes works as a pin-setter in a bowling alley. Write a program that instructs karel to transform the initial situation in Figure 3-4 into the final situation. Karel starts this task with ten beepers in its beeper-bag.

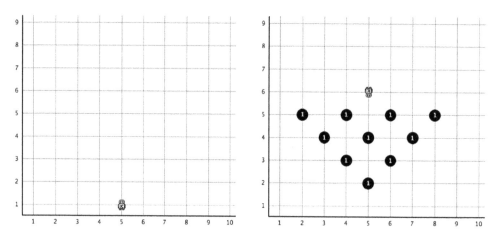

Figure 3-4 A Pin-Setting Task

3.   Rewrite the harvesting program using a different stepwise refinement.

4. Figure 3-5 illustrates a field of beepers that karel planted one night after a baseball game. Write a program that harvests all these beepers. Hint: this task is not too different from the harvesting example. If you see the correspondence between these two harvesting tasks, you should be able to develop a program for this task that is similar to the original harvesting program.

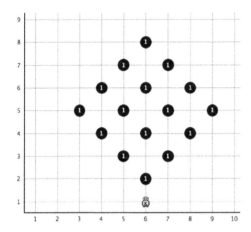

Figure 3-5 Another Harvesting Task

5. Karel wants to send greetings to the other inhabitants of the universe, so the robot needs to plant a field of beepers that broadcasts the message to alien astronomers. Program karel to plant the message of beepers shown in Figure 3-6. You may choose karel's starting position.

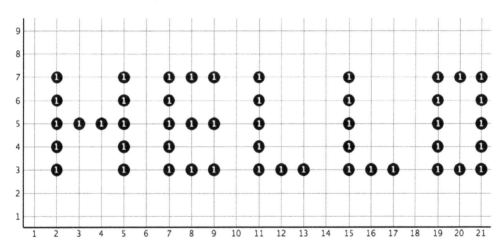

Figure 3-6 A Message for Alien Astronomers

6. Karel has received a contract from NASA (the National Aeronautics and Space Administration of the United States) to display the correct time for astronauts to read as they orbit above karel's world. The time must be displayed digitally and must fit in the situation shown in Figure 3.7. You may choose the size and shape of the digits. The program must allow you to change the time quickly so karel can rapidly update the display. For practice, display the time 10 : 52.

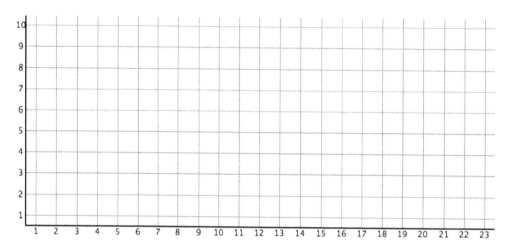

Figure 3-7 A Digital Clock

7. Karel has taken a part time job as a gardener. Karel's specialty is planting beepers. Karel's current task is to plant one and only one beeper on each corner around the "+" shaped wall arrangement as shown in the situation in Figure 3-8.

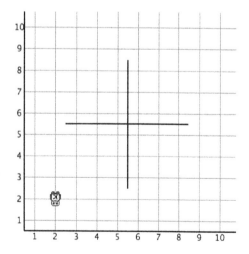

Figure 3-8 A Gardening Task

8. Karel got bored with gardening, so the robot decided to try a different part time job. The robot now installs carpets (made from beepers) in buildings in its world. Write a program that instructs karel to install a carpet in the building shown in Figure 3-9. There must be no "lumps" in the carpet so be sure that karel places one and only one beeper on each intersection in the room.

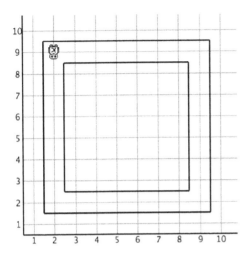

Figure 3-9 A Carpet Task

9. Program karel to arrange beepers as shown in the final situation given in Figure 3-10. Karel has exactly twelve beepers in its beeper bag. You may start karel on any convenient corner.

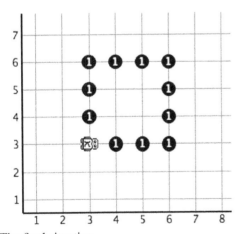

The final situation

Figure 3-10 A Box of Beepers

10. Give a specification for a class where a) the new robots have all of the capabilities of robots in class UrRobot, and b) they can also execute method pick_a_pair, which will cause such a robot to pick up two beepers (if available) from the current corner. Call this new class PickAPairRobot. Give the specification for this new class in the robot programming language.

11. Suppose we define a method in some robot class like this.

```
def move()
    super()
    move()
end
```

What will happen if we send our robot such a message? If you want to test this, start your robot facing West or South. What is the meaning of the move instruction within this method?

12. Read Problem 2.13-10 of Chapter 2 again. How short a program can you write now to carry out this task, using knowledge from this chapter?

13. Why is it important that programs be easily readable by people?

14. How can we achieve the goal of writing readable programs?

4 Polymorphism

This chapter explains the consequences of specifying new classes of robots and also introduces some objects that are not robots. Objects in different classes can behave differently when sent the same messages. This is called polymorphism. Each robot or other object behaves according to the definition of its own class.

When you build a new robot class you really want to keep it simple. Each class should define objects that do one task and do it well. As we have seen, it may be necessary to define several methods in that class to carry out the task, but we should be able to name the overall task or service that the robot class is supposed to provide. Suppose that we have two tasks to do, however. How do we handle that? One way is to have two classes, one for each task and then use a robot from each class to perform each task. This implies more than one robot in a program, of course.

4.1 Robot Teams

In this section we will introduce a very different problem-solving method. Instead of solving a problem with a single robot, suppose we have a team of robots cooperate in the task.

4.1.1 Team Basics

For example, the beeper harvesting task could be quite easily done by three robots each sent the message harvest_two_rows, if we position them appropriately two blocks apart. The first robot would harvest two rows, then the next robot would harvest the next two rows, etc. The main task block would look like the following.

```
def task()
    karel = Harvester.new(2, 2, EAST, 0)
    kristin = Harvester.new(4, 2, EAST, 0)
    matt = Harvester.new(6, 2, EAST, 0)

    karel.move()
    karel.harvest_two_rows()
    karel.turn_off()
    kristin.move()
    kristin.harvest_two_rows()
    kristin.turn_off()
    matt.move()
    matt.harvest_two_rows()
    matt.turn_off()
end
```

The problem could also be solved by six robots, of course.

We could also intersperse the operations of the three robots if we wished, rather than have one complete its task before the other makes any move:

```
def task()
    karel = Harvester.new(2, 2, EAST, 0)
    kristin = Harvester.new(4, 2, EAST, 0)
    matt = Harvester.new(6, 2, EAST, 0)

    karel.move()
    kristin.move()
    matt.move()
    karel.harvest_two_rows()
    kristin.harvest_two_rows()
    matt.harvest_two_rows()
    karel.turn_off()
    kristin.turn_off()
    matt.turn_off()
end
```

However, if we are happy to have one robot complete its task before the next begins, we can solve this in a more interesting way. We don't actually need to use three different names to refer to the three robots. We can let an existing name refer to another robot. The names of robots are called *references* for this reason. They are also called *variables* since their values can vary, or change, as the program proceeds as we see now.

```
def task()
    karel = Harvester.new(2, 2, EAST, 0)
    karel.move()
    karel.harvest_two_rows()
    karel.turn_off()

    karel = Harvester.new(4, 2, EAST, 0)
    karel.move()
    karel.harvest_two_rows()
    karel.turn_off()

    karel = Harvester.new(6, 2, EAST, 0)
    karel.move()
    karel.harvest_two_rows()
    karel.turn_off()
end
```

There is one subtle difference here. We only use one name, karel, to refer to three different robots.

In this first line we *initialize* this reference to a new robot at corner (2, 2). Then later we give this same reference a new value (*initialize* its value) by creating a new robot at (4, 2), etc. The old robot to which the name karel referred is, in a sense, discarded. We still have a team of robots, but we only need one name. We do the same in the world of people, by the way. There are several people named Karel in the real world, and who the name refers to depends on context. It is the same in the robot world.

Note, however, that once we point the name karel to the second robot (the one that starts at (4,2)), we can't refer to the original robot in this program anymore. There is no way to recover a reference once we lose it.

We can have a given reference refer to different robots at different times, and, conversely, we can have different names refer to the same robot at the same time. It is, therefore, good to separate two concepts in your mind: that of the name of a robot (a reference to a robot) and that of the robot itself (a robot, of course). These ideas will be explored later.

When we change the object to which a reference points we call it **assignment**. We use assignment to have the program remember things using reference variables like the name karel above. We use the = operator to indicate assignment. An assignment is really just an association between a name and some value, perhaps a robot. Human names are an association between words (the names) and people. When you were born, your parents assigned you a name to set up this association. But there is nothing intrinsic about this association. The same name refers to different people and, often enough, different names refer to the same person.

Finally, we emphasize that if you reach a situation in which there is no reference at all to some object, then there is no way to reconstruct a reference. The object, perhaps a robot, passes out of your program's control. A system component called the *garbage collector* will return the resources that the object uses to the factory.

In the above we had several robots, but they were all of the same class. We can have teams in which there are several different kinds of robots as well.

4.1.2 Organizers

Now that we see how a team can be put together, let's see if we can improve the structure. We have a lot of code in the main task block here and would like to delegate that control to some object to make the program both more flexible and easier to understand. We will put a new layer, actually an object, between the main task block and the three Harvester robots we use above. We shall call the new class Organizer. Unlike everything we have done up to now, organizers won't be robots, since they don't need to move, etc. They can just sit in their "office" and direct workers to jobs. In fact, an Organizer takes a role just like that of the helicopter pilot of our main metaphor and frees the pilot (main task block) from some detail.

An organizer will need to know what robots it uses for workers in some way. In this section we will choose the simplest way of all, the organizer will simply know the names of the workers and we intend that it will *know* this when it is created. Thus, our class will need a constructor, which is a special method that will be executed whenever we create such an object. UrRobots also have constructors, defined in the infrastructure of this system and they are automatically executed whenever you say something like:

```
karel = UrRobot.new(1, 1, EAST, 0)
```

The constructor for UrRobot requires that you give the four *arguments* that define the delivery specification: street, avenue, direction, and initial number of beepers.

A constructor in Ruby is a method with the special name *initialize*. Otherwise it is like any method. Also, unlike people, robots are just objects, so they can be owned (by other objects) and so we shall define our Organizer class so that an object of this class will own three robots that it will use for the harvesting task. To indicate this, within the class, a robot named karel will be referred to as @karel. This is similar to the idea that an object owns its own methods and can send messages to itself such as self.move(). An object can own other objects and refers to them similarly. Thus, our class starts out like this:

```
require "harvester"

class Organizer
    # note: there is no superclass listed here - Object by default
    def initialize()
        @karel = Harvester.new(2, 2, EAST, 0)
        @kristen = Harvester.new(4, 2, EAST, 0)
        @matt = Harvester.new(6, 2, EAST, 0)
    end
```

The organizer doesn't need any arguments for creation itself, since it isn't a robot. Actually, it does have a superclass, the built in class Object, but that one isn't named as a superclass in Ruby. It is automatically used if no superclass is specified. We create an Organizer with just:

```
charlie = Organzier.new()
```

When we execute this, the constructor (initialize) from Organizer will be invoked and so the three Harvester robots will themselves be created (invoking their constructor...). Thus the creation of one object may involve the automatic creation of others. Now we can ask the organizer to harvest_field by giving it a method:

```
def harvest_field()
    @karel.move()
    @karel.harvest_two_rows()
    @kristen.move()
    @kristen.harvest_two_rows()
    @matt.move()
    @matt.harvest_two_rows()
end
```

We neglected to turn_off the three robots. You can add that if you like. Now the main task block becomes much simpler:

```
def task()
    world = RobotWorld.instance
    world.read_world("../worlds/fig3-2.kwld")

    charlie = Organizer.new()
    charlie.harvest_field()
end
```

Within a Ruby class, a name that begins with @ is known as an *instance variable*. An alternate name is *field*. Each object of the class will have its own reference and they are distinct in different objects of the same class.

So if we were to create two different Organizer objects, each would own its own robot named @karel and there would be no conflict.

It is worth noting that the Organizer could also have the name karel (reference), if we like, rather than charlie. There will be no conflict. But you might find it easier to keep everything straight in your mind if you don't do that until you have quite a lot of practice with programming.

The objects owned by another, and normally created in the constructor, are called fields, or instance variables. The two terms arose at different times in the history of computing, with field originally referring to a simpler concept. The term instance variable (or even instance field) indicates that the *owned* object is part of the specific instance (instantiation) of the *owner*. An instance of Organizer own three instances of Harvester, referred to by three instance variables. Instance variables in Ruby are automatically private. Therefore it isn't possible to write:

```
charlie.@kristen.move()
```

The reason this sort of thing isn't allowable in Ruby is that if it @kristin were public we would be saying to other programmers who might want to use this class that it is ok to do so. But if we were to then change the *main* here to the following, it will be a disaster since kristen won't be in the correct position to harvest its two rows.

```
def task()
    ...
    charlie = Organizer.new()
    charlie.@kristen.move()
    charlie.harvest_field()
end
```

The big idea is that each object should be in control of its own internal *state*. Then the programmer that writes the class has the possibility of avoiding programming errors. This brings up an extremely important topic: *object invariants*, sometimes called *class invariants*. An invariant in this context is something that is always maintained in the true state. It is an invariant of the Organizer class that upon creation the helper robots are correctly positioned with respect to the field and not moved except via harvest_field. This is necessary for the correct operation of harvest_field, of course, as the correct positioning is a precondition of harvest_field. It is the purpose of constructors in object oriented languages to set the objects up so that any needed invariants are true. Then the public methods can expect that the invariant is true when they begin, but must also be sure to re-establish it before they finish. Non-public methods are helper methods for the public methods and they may avoid maintaining invariants if they are only invoked by public methods which do keep invariants true. But this also means that fields of an object must be hidden if they participate in any way in the statement of an invariant. So the three helper names should be hidden. And starting a name with an @ symbol is the Ruby way of defining and hiding a field.

Note that given the above description, we don't yet have a complete description of the invariant for the Organizer class, since harvest_field doesn't restore the invariant we have stated. We must also add to it the statement that an Organizer will only harvest one field. It is a *single use* object, unless we modify it somewhat. In Chapter 5 we will learn some techniques by which we could make the organizer simply do nothing if asked to harvest_field a second time.

4.2 Similar Tasks

Sometimes we want to do several tasks, but the tasks are very similar. How can we build the classes to take advantage of the common parts of the task and yet distinguish the specific differences?

Often we use inheritance to solve this problem. After all, we have seen several kinds of robots already and all have a move method. We didn't need to write that method in all the classes, only in those in which move should do something different than the version inherited from UrRobot. We can do more, however.

Here is a task for a team of robots. Suppose we want to lay down beepers in a field that has five rows and four columns. Suppose that we want the odd numbered rows (first, third, and fifth) to have two beepers on each corner and we want the other rows to have three beepers on each corner.

One good way to solve this is to have two different kinds of robots: TwoRowLayers and ThreeRowLayers. A two-row layer will put down two beepers on each corner that it visits while laying beepers and a three-row layer will put three instead.

However, it is good to recognize that these two kinds of robots are very similar in their overall behavior, only differing in one aspect of their behavior. In particular, we will have a method called lay_beepers that implements the way a robot lays down a full row of beepers. This will be identical in both our new classes, since each will lay a row of the same length. This method will call another method called put_beepers, that will be different in each of our classes. It will put down two beepers when received by a TwoRowLayer, and three when received by a ThreeRowLayer. However, if we write lay_beepers twice, once in each class, we will be wasting effort. Worse, if the problem changes to one that requires rows of length five instead of four, we have two places to change the program. If we change only one of them the program will be broken, but it may not be immediately obvious why, especially if we have left the problem alone for a few days before modifying it.

We can capture the commonality of their behavior in a special class called an *abstract* class. An abstract class is one that the robot factory never actually manufactures, but uses as a kind of template for the construction of more specialized robots.

```
# Abstract class to lay a row of beepers
class BeeperLayer < UrRobot
    # Puts beepers on four corners as defined by a subclass
    def lay_beepers()
        move()
        put_beepers()
        move()
        put_beepers()
        move()
        put_beepers()
        move()
        put_beepers()
        move()
        turn_off()
    end
end
```

Here we define BeeperLayer as such a class. We give it a new lay_beepers method in which we describe laying down a row of length four. For each corner we visit (other than the starting corner) we execute put_beepers(). This is a new method is not defined in this class. It is simply missing. This is similar to the situation we saw at the end of Chapter 3 with Mixins, except here it is a robot class that references an undefined method, not a mixin. If we try to create a BeeperLayer and send it the lay_beepers message we will get an error. Note, of course, that Ruby has no way to advertise that this class is abstract. It looks fine until you recognize that put_beepers is missing. The class and method comments are all we have to indicate this to the reader.

In effect an abstract class is a template with a hole (put_beepers) that can be filled for a specific use. One of the advantages of object-oriented programming is that it permits something called *reuse*. Note that an abstract class provides a general framework via its non-abstract methods for something to occur, and lets you fill (reuse) the holes in the template in different ways for different purposes. This idea of reusing the holes in a basic structure is very important and powerful. Here is an analogy that might be helpful in understanding abstract classes. Suppose you want to build a home music system from various components. Suppose you have decided on all the elements except the amplifier. You can purchase and even assemble the other components, though they won't be very useful yet. However, the standards adopted by manufacturers assure you that whichever amplifier you later buy will plug properly into the rest of your system. Your skeleton system is something like an abstract class, not usable in itself, but very usable when extended.

Since we didn't give a definition to put_beepers, a robot of this type wouldn't know what to do when given this message, so the factory doesn't make any of these robots for delivery. It is useful, however, as a partial specification of other classes that extend this one. These extensions are not abstract and they will give a definition for put_beepers, while also inheriting lay_beepers. Thus, any new subclasses automatically have the same version of lay_beepers, even if we need to modify it in the future. Next we see two such subclasses.

```
#Puts two beepers on each corner when asked to lay_beepers
class TwoRowLayer < BeeperLayer
   def put_beepers()
      put_beeper()
      put_beeper()
   end
end

#Puts three beepers on each corner when asked to lay_beepers
class ThreeRowLayer < BeeperLayer
   def put_beepers()
      put_beeper()
      put_beeper()
      put_beeper()
   end
end
```

Each of these two classes extends BeeperLayer and so has the same lay_beepers method. The lay_beepers method calls put_beepers. We will use a robot reference named lisa to refer alternately to a succession of two- and three-row layers. A class that is not abstract is sometimes called *concrete*, but that is not a special Robot programming (or Ruby) word.

```
def task()
    lisa = TwoRowLayer.new(1, 3, EAST, INFINITY)
    lisa.lay_beepers()
    lisa = ThreeRowLayer.new(2, 3, EAST, INFINITY)
    lisa.lay_beepers()
    lisa = TwoRowLayer.new(3, 3, EAST, INFINITY)
    lisa.lay_beepers()
    lisa = ThreeRowLayer.new(4, 3, EAST, INFINITY)
    lisa.lay_beepers()
    lisa = TwoRowLayer.new(5, 3, EAST, INFINITY)
    lisa.lay_beepers()
end
```

Each time the name lisa refers to a two-row layer it puts two beepers at each corner on which it is asked (within lay_beepers) to put_beepers, and each time it refers to a three-row layer it puts three beepers on each corner. Again, this is just like the situation with people. If I know two people named Bill and I say to each "Bill, move." and one of the Bills always moves slowly and the other always moves quickly, then I can expect them to act in their usual way. Even if I refer to them with a generic name, they will likely behave as they always do: "Friend, move." And note that it isn't the name that moves, but, rather, the person (object) to which the name refers.

Notice that starting with the second assignment here, each time we make an assignment we let the name lisa refer to a different robot. This means that no name at all refers to the previous robot. We can no longer send instructions to a robot if we have no reference to it. The robot factory will know that this is the case and collect the unusable robot back using its garbage collector. The resources it uses will be recycled.

The fact that each robot always interprets each message it gets, directly or indirectly, in terms of the methods defined by its own class, is called *polymorphism*. It is impossible to make a robot behave differently than the definition of its class, no matter what reference is used to refer to it. While it is not important to minimize the number of names used in a program, understanding polymorphism is fundamental. You will see later, perhaps only after leaving the robot world for true Ruby programming, that we often use a name to refer to different variables at different times and that we just as often refer to a given robot by different names at different parts of a large program. The key to understanding is to simply remember that it is the robot itself, not the name by which we refer to it, that determines what is done when a message is received. (Truth in advertising: actually, since Ruby is a dynamic language it is possible to change a robot's behavior and we will explore a bit of that later in book. Still, the class of an object never changes.)

Finally in this section we should look at what it is that makes programs easy to understand and to modify. Often we have the choice, when designing a program, to have a single robot perform a complex task or to have a team of robots each performing some part of that task. Which is to be preferred? In the extreme, it is possible to build a single robot class that will solve all of the problems in this book--a super-super-super-duper-robot. Should we do that, or should we build a lot of simpler classes each of which solves a single task?

The answer to the above is clear to those who have had to live with large programs. Large programs are usually written to solve significant problems. Such programs take a significant amount of time and money to develop and the problems that they solve are usually ever changing. This is due to the fact that the organizations that want the programs are continually evolving. Yesterday's problems are usually similar to tomorrow's problems but they are seldom identical. This means that programs must change and adapt to the problems they intend to solve.

Because of the way people think, it is difficult to understand and modify large programs. This is largely because of the amount of detail in them. It is therefore useful if they are built out of small and easy to understand parts. The implication of this for robot programming is that you will be building better skills if you build small robot classes with a single, simple to understand purpose, rather than a large, complicated, do everything class that can solve all problems. With the small classes you can choose a set of robots to perform much of a complex task and write other simple classes to perform the rest, rather than to have to understand all of the interconnections in a complex class. This is similar to what we learned in the previous chapter. Small methods are better than big ones. The same is true for classes. We will see this again in Section 4.4.

Polymorphism also helps us here, since it means that when we design a robot to perform a certain simple task we can be assured that it will always perform that task when sent a message, independent of how that message reaches it. If we design our classes well, our robots will be trustworthy. We can also use polymorphism as we did above to factor out the common behavior of a set of classes into a superclass, like BeeperLayer, that may be abstract or not. Mixins can also help us to reuse code that we have written and tested.

4.3 Object Oriented Design -- Clients and Servers

In section 3.8 we learned a useful technique for designing a single class. We learned to ask what services (methods) are needed from that class and designing complex tasks as a decomposition into simpler tasks. Now we are going to look at design from a broader perspective. Here we will learn to recognize that we may need several classes of robots to carry out some task, and these robots may need to cooperate in some way. We will discuss only the design issues, leaving implementation until we have seen some more powerful ideas.

Suppose that we want to build a robot house as shown in Figure 4-1. Houses will be built of beepers, of course. In the real world, house building is a moderately complex task that is usually done by a team of builders, each with his or her own specialty. Perhaps it should be the same in the robot world.

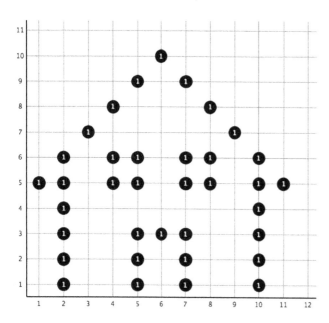

Figure 4-1 A House Building Task.

If you look back at some of our earlier examples, you will find that there are really two kinds of instructions. The first kind of instruction, such as **harvest_two_rows** in the Harvester class is meant to be used in the main task block. The other kind, like **go_to_next_row**, is meant primarily to be used internally, as part of problem decomposition. For example, the instruction **go_to_next_row** is unlikely to be used except from within other instructions, and so we might want to make it private. The first kind of instruction is meant to be public and defines in some way what the robot is intended to do. If we think of a robot as a server, then its client (the main task block, or perhaps another robot) will send it a message with one of its public instructions. The client is one who requests a service from a server. A Harvester robot provides a harvesting service. Its client requests that service. The place to begin design is with the public services and the servers that provide them. The server robot itself will then, perhaps, execute other instructions to provide the service. We can use successive refinement to help design the other instructions that help the server carry out its service.

The easiest way to get a house built is to call on the services of a **Contractor**, who will assemble some appropriate team to build our house. We tell the contractor robot **build_house** and somehow the job gets done. The client doesn't especially care how the contractor carries out the task as long as the result (including the price) are acceptable. (Here the costs are low, since robots don't need to send their children to college.) Notice that we have just given the preliminary design for a class, the Contractor class, with one public method: **build_house**. We may discover the need for more methods and for more classes as well. We also know that we will probably need only a single robot of the Contractor class. Let's name it kristin, to have a working name. Similar to the Organizer from earlier in this Chapter, a Contractor doesn't need to be a robot, since it doesn't need to carry out robot actions. It will direct the actions of other objects that are robots.

Now we examine the task from kristin's standpoint. What does it need to do to build a house? One possibility is to place all of the beepers itself (but then it would need to be a robot). But another way is to use specialist robots to handle well-defined parts of the house: for example, walls, the roof, and the doors and windows. Kristin will *delegate* the work to other robots. Well, since we want the walls to be made of bricks (beeper-bricks, that is), we should call on the services of one or more **Mason** robots. The doors and windows could be built by a **Carpenter** robot, and the roof built by a **Roofer** robot.

The **Contractor**, kristin, needs to be able to gather this team, so we need another method for this. While it could be called by the client, it probably should be called internally by the contractor itself when it is ready to begin construction. Kristin also needs to be able to get the team to the construction site. We will want a new Contractor method **gather_team**. We shall make the task of gathering the team more flexible here than we did with Organizers.

Focusing, then, on the smaller jobs, the **Mason** robot should be able to respond to a **build_wall** message. The contractor can show the mason where the walls are to be built. Similarly, the **Roofer** should be able to respond to **make_roof**, and the **Carpenter** robots should know the messages **make_door** and **make_window**. We might go a step farther with the roofer and decide that it would be helpful to make the two gables of the roof separately. So we would also want a **Roofer** to be able to **make_left_gable** and **make_right_gable**.

However, we can also make the following assumption. Each specialized worker robot knows how to do its own task and also knows the names of the tasks and subtasks that it must do. If the contractor simply tells it to **get_to_work**, then it already knows what it should do. Therefore, we can factor out this common behavior into a ruby abstract class named **Worker**. This is an example of a general concept called an *interface*. Just as with Robota giving the interface for robot actions, Worker gives the general protocol for workers: they know how to **get_to_work**.

```
class Worker < UrRobot
   def get_to_work()
      raise NotImplementedError.new('get_to_work error')
   end
end
```

It is useful to note that this class has the desired method, but if you try to invoke it directly, it generates an error. The purpose of this is to help us, the robot programmers, avoid errors. The intention is that we will inherit this class in and then override the get_to_work method to do the right thing. The above also emphasizes that even the exceptions that define errors are objects in Ruby. NotImplementedError is built in to Ruby and we need to create a new object to signal such an error. It will be raised if you create a Worker when this method has not yet been overridden. While it is possible for a running program to handle such errors being raised, we don't discuss that in this book.

```
class Roofer < Worker
   def get_to_work()
      make_roof()
   end
...
```

It extends Worker which itself inherits from UrRobot, so it inherits all of the methods of both of its superclasses, but it immediately overrides get_to_work to invoke make_roof (which we don't show here). The purpose of the interface was only to help assure that we don't forget the get_to_work method. The Carpenter and Mason classes also start out similarly, but their get_to_work methods send messages (to self) appropriate for each of them. The rest of the Roofer class has the following structure, but we have not shown the details of most of the methods.

```
    private

    def make_roof()
       make_left_gable()
       make_right_gable()
    end

    def make_left_gable()
       # TODO
    end

    def make_right_gable()
       # TODO
    end
```

The other classes also extend this interface and provide an implementation of the get_to_work method. Here we show outlines of the new methods. Each class implements get_to_work in a different way. We also mark each method telling whether it is public or private. We mark remaining work with # TODO (i.e. "to do").

```
class Mason < Worker
   def get_to_work()
      build_wall()
      move_to_second_wall_base()
      build_wall()
   end

private

   def build_wall()
      # TODO
   end

   def move_to_second_wall_base()
      # TODO
   end
end

class Carpenter < Worker
   def get_to_work()
      # TODO
   end

private

   def make_window()
      # TODO
   end
```

```
    def make_door()
        # TODO
    end

  end
```

The above code gives us an outline for the helper classes. Let's look more deeply at the Contractor class. We are about to introduce a large number of important concepts in a small space, so you may want to make a list of important ideas as we go.

Since the team of builders is assembled by the contractor it needs to have some way to learn who they are and it must have some reference to each of them so that it can send them messages. No object can send a message to another unless it has a reference. To do this, we introduce a new feature of Ruby that we haven't seen before: the *array*. An array is just a linear collection of references, similar to a shopping list. It has a first item, and a variable number of entries. It may seem odd at first but the ordering of the items starts at 0, not 1, but we won't really need to use that knowledge yet. Ruby also has the nice feature that it can process all of the elements of an array (or certain other similar structures) very simply. First, however, we need to create an empty array when we create a Contractor. An empty array in Ruby is represented by just a matching pair of square brackets: [ ]. An array is an object, like any other and it has methods, including **push**, which adds an item to the end of the list. We will want each Contractor object to carry a list: a list of its workers.

We also need to associate a name with this array so that we can refer to it from various places. In Ruby, an assignment is used to make such associations, just as when we create a new robot. The name we will use for this list is @workers, declaring it to be a field or instance variable, since it begins with @. This implies that each contractor object has its own list as well as the fact that the list is private to that contractor. We will, in a moment, create the empty list and assign it a name with just

```
@workers = []
```

We do that in its constructor. A constructor in Ruby, as we said earlier, is just a method with the special name initialize. It is invoked when you send the new message to a class. So, putting all of this together, the Contractor class starts out like this:

```
# Manage a team of worker robots, each of which knows their job
class Contractor
    def initialize()
        @workers = []
    end
```

It is the constructor that is actually invoked to initialize the reference. We write an initialize method, but normally we don't invoke it directly.

Note that @workers = [] is really just a Ruby shorthand for @workers = Array.new(). Ruby has many such shorthands as we shall see. But this is an especially helpful shorthand for a new (empty) array, since Ruby also can say something like [2, 3, 5, 7, 11] for a certain array of prime numbers. Other languages use the name *list* for the same concept as what Ruby calls an array: a sequential but extendable collection of values. We shall sometimes use the word list as well.

Interfaces, Abstract Classes, Modules, Mixins: Only classes and modules are actually explicit Ruby concepts. A class defines objects. A module defines functionality that can't be instantiated (with new). The other terms are just ideas that help us organize our thoughts, which is extremely important, since it is the thinking that is the hard part about programming.

An interface of an object is is nothing more or less than the set of messages that the object can respond to. It is defined by the public methods of its class and those of all of its ancestors. A Ruby class can extend one other class and can mix in other methods from modules. It can also define new methods. All of the public methods become part of the interface.

Actually, in Ruby, everything is an object. Even a class is an object and so has an interface. We have seen the *new* message being sent to classes already. Even numbers like 42 are objects and can respond to messages. We shall see this in Chapter 5, especially. But note that the UrRobot class, while it is an object, is NOT a robot object. It is a class object. You can extend the interfaces of class objects just as you can other objects. For example you could (but we have not) define a how_many method of UrRobot that would tell you how many UrRobots have been created in a program.

An abstract class has some holes and usually some additional structure. It is just a trick we use to organize our thinking. A hole in an abstract class is created by either forcing a method to cause the program to fail by raising some exception, or it contains a method that calls another that doesn't exist. In the latter case it expects that the user will either create a concrete (i.e. ordinary) subclass to supply these methods, or it will use a mixin to do so. But a class is abstract only because we build it precisely to contain these holes.

By way of analogy, a class is like a blueprint for an object (robot, for example), containing information about how to build it. An interface is like a user's manual, showing how it can be used, but not built. An abstract class is a partially built structure that requires some completion.

Also, Mixin is just a concept. Some languages, such as Ruby have a mechanism by which we can create complex things from simpler parts. Actually most languages do this, but a mixin is a coherent set of functionality that might be needed by other things, such as objects. In Ruby, we use Modules to define mixins and include them as needed.

The names interface, mixin, and abstract class are just high level conceptual aids to help us, the programmer, think about the fundamental purpose of our classes. An interface makes a requirement that some method needs to be implemented. A mixin, while closely related, actually defines the behavior that will be mixed in, not the requirement that it must be built in the future. An abstract class provides a hole that needs to be filled, either in a sub class or with a mixin.

Now that we have the constructor we see how to put the team together. We assume a (private) method gather_team to do this. And it will send the push message to the array three times to add a Mason, a Roofer, and a Carpenter. But instead of writing @workers.push(something) we can just say @workers << something. The << operator is a shorthand for push for arrays.

```
def gather_team()
   worker = Mason.new(1, 2, EAST, INFINITY)
   @workers << worker
   worker = Roofer.new(5, 1, EAST, INFINITY)
   @workers << worker
   worker = Carpenter.new(1, 5, EAST, INFINITY)
   @workers << worker
end
```

As we said, *push* adds an item to the end of the list. You can think of the "end" of the list as the front or the back, the top or the bottom, just so that you are consistent in how you think of it. Actually, we can simplify the **gather_team** method. Up until now we have given robots specific names when we created them. And in the above we do so. But we just create the three robots (by invoking their constructors) as an argument to push. These objects are anonymous (no names), but the list into which we put them maintains a reference to each of them separately.

```
def gather_team()
   @workers << Mason.new(1, 2, EAST, INFINITY)
   @workers << Roofer.new(5, 1, EAST, INFINITY)
   @workers << Carpenter.new(1, 5, EAST, INFINITY)
end
```

The method is shorter, but there is more going on in each statement. We create a robot, and we also append it to the list of workers. The third robot pushed in to the array has no individual name, but we can refer to it using an expression instead. It is @workers[2] if you need to reference it individually. The important thing is the reference and not the name. Here we store the references in an array.

Note that the objects (Workers) we put into the array all have the same interface. This is an extremely good practice, as is naming the array so that it signals what the interface of its contents is. Ruby doesn't insist on this, however, but programming can get very messy if you break this rule.

Finally, build_house is the method the Contractor uses to (a) gather its team, and (b) tell each of the workers to get to work.

```
# Put the entire team to work
def build_house()
   gather_team()
   @workers.each do |worker|
      worker.get_to_work()
   end
end
```

We recognize the message gather_team, of course. But the structure of the *each* method is something new for us. If we have a collection like an array then we can use such a structure to process all of it. The word each is followed by some code in a block (i.e. do...end). Such code is called a *block*. A block contains statements, such as the message to an object "worker", but it can also contain one or more *parameters*. The parameters if present are written, separated by commas, between vertical stroke symbols, as in I worker I. The statements in the block are executed several times, once for each element of the array (hence the method name each). For each execution of the block an item is taken from the array (in the order they appear there) and the parameter name is made to be a reference to that value. Only then are the statements of the block executed. One of the very few odd rules in Ruby is that the symbol do must appear on the same line as the each to which it applies.

The idea is that the block statements will be executed once for each element of the collection (once for each worker, in this problem) and that the worker variable will be made a reference to each of them in turn, once each. Since we have put three worker objects into the list, the statement worker.get_to_work() will be executed three times and each time, worker will refer to a different object. We shall look at this again in Chapter 6. A method like each in class Array is an example of a general concept called *Iterator*. Method *each* iterates (repeats) over the elements of its object (an Array) to execute some defined behavior (the block). We shall see more of this in Chapter 6. We promise you will like it.

Since we know here (but not in general) how many elements the list contains this statement:

```
@workers.each do |worker|
    worker.get_to_work()
end
```

is exactly the same as these six statements

```
worker = @workers[0]
worker.get_to_work()
worker = @workers[1]
worker.get_to_work()
worker = @workers[2]
worker.get_to_work()
```

or even these three statements

```
@workers[0].get_to_work()
@workers[1].get_to_work()
@workers[2].get_to_work()
```

since the elements of a list can be indexed to retrieve a reference to an individual element. We won't use this indexing here, and simply present it to show how the *each* method *unrolls*. We prefer to use the *each* method, of course, since it guarantees that all of the elements of the list will be processed even if there are more (or less) than three. It even works when there are none at all, then doing nothing.

With all of this built, all we need to do to build the house is create a Contractor and tell it to build_house:

```
def task()
    kristen = Contractor.new()
    kristen.build_house()
```

```
end
```

Note that the Contractor kristin is a server. Its client is the main task block, which delivers messages to it. But note also that kristin is a client of the three helpers since they provide services (wall services...) to kristin. In fact, it is relatively common in the real world for clients and servers to be mutually bound. For example, doctors provide medical services to grocers who provide food marketing services to doctors.

In object-oriented programming, this idea of one object *delegating* part of its task to other objects is very important. When one bit of code asks an object to perform some action or retrieve some information, the receiver of the message will often delegate the work to another object. In this world, that object could be another robot, or something else entirely as we shall see. Delegation in this way helps us break up a large program into small, understandable, parts. And, of course, delegation models what happens in the real world. It is nearly the same in the object-oriented world. Delegation is a big idea. One object carries out part of its task by asking another to do something for it.

> **References**: A reference variable in Ruby is a name or expression that points to some object value (here a robot type or an array). For example, we have often used the name karel as a reference to a robot. There are some rules that you need to know about references that will also help you understand polymorphism. The first rule is that a reference in Ruby can point to anything. So a name karel could refer to a robot, or an array, or .... The object that is referred to is always and ever determined by the class named when it was created. So karel = MileWalker.new(...), creates a mile walker that always remains a mile walker independent of which reference points to it. Thus objects in Ruby have permanent types, defined by their classes, but references have no types at all.
>
> Objects never change their type, and their type is what determines what messages they will respond to successfully. See Duck Typing in Section 4.9.

Before we move on, let us step back a few paces and try to get some perspective. Here we have used something we call an abstract class (Worker) to define the structure of a protocol, but without adding any real functionality. The actual operations are added in the classes that extend the interface. However, there is no requirement in Ruby that we do anything like that. We could, instead have just not written the Worker class at all, and then, of course, not extended it in Roofer, Mason, and Carpenter. They would extend UrRobot instead. Had we done that everything would have worked exactly the same (except for the error messages if we goof). If we correctly added get_to_work to each of the worker classes, then the contractor would correctly invoke it. Had we forgotten then it would have been an error, but an *unknown method* error, rather than a *not implemented* error. So in retrospect, it seems like there was very little benefit for the three lines we wrote and the inclusion of the extra superclasses in Roofer, Mason, and Carpenter. The real benefit, however, is in advertising to ourselves and to other programmers what our intent is in our program, nothing more. We declare, by writing this way that we intend to give each worker this functionality and that we will depend on it in the Contractor class. Without this declaration of intent, we would, perhaps, have to spend more time reading code to discover the intent. When we make mistakes, and we will, we want it to be as obvious as possible what those mistakes are. The structure we have built here helps in that, even if, in the strict rules of programming, it wasn't necessary.

Some other programming languages have stricter rules than Ruby and they might require something like what we have done here. Such languages generally find more errors since they enforce more rules.

4.4 Choreographers

There is an even more interesting way to carry out some complex tasks if we let one robot directly coordinate the actions of some others. One robot can serve as a Choreographer to the others, which themselves do whatever the Choreographer does.

Before we show the details it will be helpful to cover some background

4.4.1 The Devil is in the Details

Here we want to discuss some ideas of Ruby and the larger object-oriented world. We have focused so far in the book on methods. Methods define what happens when a message is sent to an object. A method is an *encapsulation* of any sort of behavior of an object. An encapsulation is just a packaging of something, like peas in a pod. An *abstraction* is a named encapsulation. So a method is actually an abstraction. Encapsulated means that its details are hidden. But it also has a name. Abstraction and encapsulation are very important ideas in computing. A method may also have *parameters* that help it carry out the behavior. Our methods so far have all implicitly had the *self* parameter, though it isn't obvious. The initialize method of robot classes also has street, avenue, direction, and initial number of beepers as parameters. The **read_world** method of the world has a String object as a parameter. The string names the file containing a description of the world. When we create a method we give names to the parameters. When we invoke a method, usually by sending a message to an object, such as a robot, we provide values, called *arguments*, to match the parameters. In the body of the method, the parameter acts like an initialized variable.

However, we can, perhaps at the top level of a file, also define a simple method that does not appear to be part of any class. We have already done this with the task method. Here is another example:

```
def do_many_moves(robot)
    robot.move()
    robot.move()
    robot.move()
end
```

This is not a method of any of our robot classes and it can't be sent as a message to any robot. Instead we invoke the method by simply giving its name and some argument, perhaps a robot of some kind, but actually, any object that understands the move message will do, since within the method we do send messages to an object. The name robot used here is intended as a hint to other programmers about the intent, but Ruby won't demand that it be a robot, only that it have a move method. A call of this will look like the following:

```
do_many_moves(charlie)
```

and when it is called, it will send the move message three times to the object referred to by the name charlie.

A simple top-level method like this is actually a method of the class called *Object*, which is built in to Ruby. Invoking the method as we have done is implicitly sending a message to an instance of this Object class. Ruby is very uniform in this way. Everything is an object. Objects have behavior. Methods encapsulate this behavior and every method is part of some class.

Actually, there are two different kinds of simple methods. Some are invoked simply for the effect they have, such as moving a robot. Others, however, are used to compute something like a mathematical function, such as the square-root. The new method of Class objects does this, returning a fresh object. We could, for example, give the Contractor class a method that would tell us how many workers it was managing. Such a method has a return value as well as possible parameters. We shall see quite a lot of this sort of method starting in Chapter 5.

An interesting feature of Ruby is that methods themselves are objects (of class *Method*). This is not true of all computer languages. It means that we can do things with them, such as pass them as parameters to other methods.

But there is a fundamental idea about methods that needs to be understood thoroughly and this is the essence of Polymorphism. A message is always interpreted by the object that receives the message. We discussed this before when we introduced the MileMover robots. Each class could have a different version of some method, even a built-in robot method like move. The robot that receives a move message was created in some class and it knows what move method it has. In fact that object knows no other move method (except that it has a way to access the methods of its superclass – even those named the same, as the MileMover does). So, if I say karen.move(), the object karen will interpret this to mean do whatever is in the move method that it was created with. This is what happens in a simple example.

```
require "ur_robot"

def do_many_moves(robot)
    robot.move()
    robot.move()
    robot.move()
end

class TwoMover < UrRobot
    def move()
        super()
        super()
    end
end

if __FILE__ == $0
    karel = UrRobot(1, 1, EAST, 0)
    carol = TwoMover(2, 1, EAST, 0)
    carl  = UrRobot (3, 1, EAST, 0)
    karl  = TwoMover (4, 1, EAST, 0)

    karel.move() # 1 block
    carol.move() # 2 blocks
    do_many_moves(carl)   # 3 blocks
    do_many_moves(karl)   # 6 blocks
end
```

Since we will use them in the Choreographer, let's also look at a situation in which a method has an additional parameter. We have seen this already, in fact, in the initialize methods discussed above. Here we will show only a fragment of a class to illustrate what we mean. Suppose that we have a world with exactly two robots and we want one of them to be able to find the other and give it a beeper. The class of the first can have two methods like the following to help accomplish this (omitting some details):

```
# move around to find robot
def find(robot)
        # TODO move self to the same corner as robot
end

# Precondition: must be on the same corner as robot
def exchange(robot)
    put_beeper()
    robot.pick_beeper()
end
```

There is nothing magic here. Each of the methods has a parameter. If karel is the robot that knows how do this, and mookie is another robot, then, perhaps in the main task block, we could say:

```
karel.find(mookie)
karel.exchange(mookie)
```

Note that it is karel that tells mookie to pick the beeper within the exchange method.

4.4.2 How it Fits Together

For the Choreographer plan to work we need at least two different kinds of robots. One kind of robot will be called a Choreographer, because it directs the others, which can be ordinary, standard issue UrRobot robots. The trick here is that the Choreographer will set up the others and then will guarantee that they mimic the actions of the Choreographer. A Choreographer is like a contractor except that its "workers" exactly mimic what the choreographer does. In particular, a Choreographer needs to be a robot.

For this to work, the Choreographer also needs to have references to the other robots and have complete control over them, so we will again save the "dancers" in an array owned by the Choreographer object. We will see another way to insert them, however.

This array that remembers the dancers emphasizes the second major feature of objects. Objects can **do** things. For example, robots can move, as we have already seen several times. But objects can also **remember** things. So a Choreographer can remember its helpers. The things that robots, and objects in general, can do are represented by its methods, like turn_left. The things that objects remember are called its **instance variables** or **fields**. When one object remembers a reference to another, it sets up a (one way) association between the objects. A Choreographer will know who its helpers are, but the helper may not know the Choreographer. Usually human associations are two way, of course, but it is not the same with robots, or objects in general.

Our Choreographer will also need to override all of the UrRobot methods so that, for example, if we tell the Choreographer to move, that it can direct the others to move as well. Below we show the complete Choreographer class, with some annotations.

```
require "harvester"

class Choreographer < Harvester

   def initialize(street, avenue, direction, beepers)
      super(street, avenue, direction, beepers)
      @dancers = []
   end

 . . .
```

The Choreographer will subclass Harvester so that it already knows, for example, how to harvest_two_rows, but it could be anything you like. The constructor includes all the parameters generally needed for robot initial specification, and the definition of the dancers field should be familiar. However, the first statement in the initialize method is new for us. Constructors in Ruby, like any other method, are inherited as usual. And this initialize just overrides the one inherited from Harvester, the superclass. In fact, the implementation of this method really occurs in UrRobot and was itself inherited by Harvester. We didn't need to override it in Harvester (or the other classes we've seen so far, because nothing new needed to be done beyond what the inherited version does. But because we need to define the @dancers field for each object, we need a constructor here. But it is a bit more complex than it seems.

Constructors: The usual form of a constructor is shown in the Choreographer class above. The constructor is a method with the name initialize, and for robot classes normally has four parameters: the street and avenue, the direction faced initially, and the initial number of beepers. This is the minimal Ruby definition that is required in a subclass so that our *delivery specification* makes sense when we create a robot.

```
def initialize (street, avenue, direction, beepers)
      super(street, avenue, direction, beepers)
end
```

In Choreographer, super refers to Harvester, and in general is the actual superclass. In the Robot Programming Language direction is a different kind of object with possible values NORTH, SOUTH, EAST, and WEST. You occasionally need a constructor like the above in robot classes you write, but only if you need to do something beyond what is defined in the superclass. For Contractors, we also need to create the @workers field. But contractors weren't robots, so their superclass was Object, which requires no parameters for construction. Ruby helps us here and automatically invokes a super constructor without arguments if there is such a thing. Choreographers, on the other hand derive ultimately from UrRobot, requiring parameters, and since we need a constructor for the @dancers to be created, we need a complete construction.

When we write a constructor we need to specify a complete construction, so it isn't enough to just create the dancers. We need to assure that all constructions done by superclasses, including UrRobot, are also done. If we don't do this, we won't even have access to a move method, since it was defined in UrRobot, and until that level is properly constructed we don't have a proper robot. Think of this as if the robot factory sends each model down a series of assembly lines; first for UrRobot, then for Harvester, and finally for Choreographer. We need to assure that each level is properly done, by invoking the constructor of any superclass from any constructor that we write. And when needed the super reference should be first in the initialize method. This assures that the constructions are done in the correct (top-down) order.

Next, we see an alternate way to add dancers to the list of helpers: a method specifically designed for the purpose.

```
# Add a dancer robot to the dance team
def add_dancer(dancer)
   @dancers << dancer
end
```

There is nothing unusual about this, though it is a method with an extra parameter as we discussed above.

We could have used slightly different syntax to manipulate the @dancers field. We created it in the constructor with

```
@dancers = []
```

but we could have said equivalently

```
@dancers = Array.new()
```

Likewise, we add an item to the end of the array with

```
@dancers << dancer
```

but that is just the same as

```
@dancers.push(dancer)
```

You can write it either way, but many programmers prefer the shortcuts.

Now, however, we will see what will make this a real Choreographer. The idea is that each of the dancers will do exactly what the Choreographer does. We assure that this is the case by overriding each of the basic UrRobot methods in Choreographer (not the dancer's class). For example:

```
# Move the entire team forward
def move()
   super()
   @dancers.each do |dancer|
      dancer.move()
   end
end
```

First we invoke the inherited (from UrRobot) method with super(), which refers to the move method of the superclass. Saying move() here would be a disaster, since that message brings us back to the method we are now defining, not the inherited one that we use as part of the definition. Then move would invoke move which would invoke move which... infinitely. Then we use an *each* iteration to send ordinary move messages to each of the dancers. Thus, when the choreographer moves, so will each dancer. The other four methods inherited from UrRobot are written analogously to this one. Each invokes the inherited method and each sends the message to each dancer. Here is a main task block that will exercise this class:

```
def task()
   world = RobotWorld.instance()
   world.read_world("../worlds/fig3-2.kwld")
   martha = Choreographer.new(2, 2, EAST, 0)

   martha.add_dancer(UrRobot.new(4, 2, EAST, 0))
   martha.add_dancer(UrRobot.new(6, 2, EAST, 0))
   martha.move()
   martha.harvest_two_rows()
   martha.move()
   martha.turn_off()
end
```

Notice that when asked to move, the Choreographer robot (here martha) first executes the inherited move instruction to move itself. It then sends move messages to the two helpers, which are only UrRobots, so they don't affect any other robots. This means that whenever martha moves, each of its helpers also moves "automatically." The same will be true for the pick_beeper, turn_left, and turn_off instructions. When a robot sends a message to another robot, the message passes from the sender of the message through the satellite to the other robot. The sender must then wait for the completion of the instruction by the robot it sent the message to before it can resume its own execution. Notice that the Choreographer doesn't send harvest_two_rows to the helpers. Indeed they don't know that instruction as they are just UrRobots. But when martha carries out the harvest_two_rows instruction, it does so by executing move, pick_beeper, and turn_left as we saw before.

We also snuck in another small feature of Ruby (and almost all programming languages). Instead of creating the dancer objects and assigning a variable to refer to them and then passing that object to the add_dancer method as an argument, we just used the construction expression (UrRobot.new...) as the argument directly. Since we don't otherwise need to refer to the robots by name, this is preferable as it makes our intention clearer. We want to pass a new robot to the choreographer. We could have done it more explicitly, though. In general, however, in most places in which we use a variable reference, a more general expression may be used. Not all, however. The main exception is on the left side of an assignment where we are giving a new value to something. Only certain expressions are allowed in such a context. This will become more clear as you get more experience.

Be sure to trace the execution of this program. Notice that the order of execution of this solution is very different from the solutions given in Section 3.8 or 4.1.

The reader may consider what would happen here if the helper robots were not simply UrRobots but were instead robots of some other class with new move methods of their own. The results can be very interesting. The choreographer would ask each helper to move and the helper would, of course, do what it was programmed to do when asked to move, which might be quite complex.

Finally, let us discuss a different, but inferior design. We could have created the Choreographer class without a new constructor if we had also added a method like

```
def create_dancers()
  @dancers = []
end
```

But this would be problematic. The purpose of a constructor is to make an object complete and ready for use. A Choreographer with no dancers is ok, but one with no way to add a dancer would be a serious problem. Suppose someone decides to use our revised code and does the following, forgetting to invoke create_dancers.

```
def task
    martha = new Choreographer.new(3, 3, NORTH, 0)
    martha.add_dancer(UrRobot.new(5, 5, EAST, 0))
       ...
    end
```

The program would fail, since the add_dancer method would find that the @dancers field didn't refer to anything (that it was nil). So we would be adding a requirement to a user of our program to guarantee correct behavior. In fact is is our responsibility when writing the class to assure that the objects behave correctly. Constructors help us do that.

4.5 Using Polymorphism

Here is a simple problem. Suppose we have a bunch of robots, one on each corner of a street (say first street) from some avenue to some avenue farther on and we want to ask each robot to put down one beeper. We want to write a program that will work no matter how many robots there are. To make it explicit, suppose there is a robot on first street on every corner between the origin and 10'th avenue. Each robot has one beeper and we want to ask them all to put down their beeper. We want to build a set of classes to solve this problem in such a way that it doesn't matter how many robots there are. In other words, the same program (except for the setup of the robots) should work if we have robots between first and 20'th avenues instead. The idea is that most of the robots will put down a beeper and then pass the same message to the next robot. The last one won't pass the message on, since there are no more.

To do this we need two classes of robots, one for each of the two behaviors. However, as usual with polymorphism, we will try to factor out the common behavior of our classes into an abstract superclass. In this case we will call this abstract class BeeperPutter and it will define one method: distribute_beepers. For most of the robots this method will cause the robot that receives the message to put down its own beeper and then send the same message to its neighbor robot, similar to a Choreographer. One of the robots will be different, however, and it will simply put down its beeper and nothing else. However, in order to see the effect we will also have each robot move off its corner after it puts down its beeper so that we can see the beepers.

```
# Abstract class for beeper putting robots"
class BeeperPutter < UrRobot

   def distribute_beepers()
      raise NotImplementedError.new("Implemented in Subclasses")
   end
end
```

Abstract classes, as we have said before are just a way to express programmer intentions, though in some other computer languages they have a more fundamental and necessary role. We will have two classes that implement this one as mentioned above. The simplest kind of a BeeperPutter doesn't have any neighbor to pass any message to, but still must be able to put down a beeper and move. It simply extends BeeperPutter and implements the required distribute_beepers method. In this case it just puts its own beeper and moves off of its original corner.

```
# A BeeperPutter that simply puts a beeper and moves"
class NoNeighbor < BeeperPutter

   def distribute_beepers()
      put_beeper()
      move()
   end
end
```

On the other hand, the NeighborTalker robots remember a reference to another robot and they will pass the distribute_beepers message to this robot after they have placed their own beeper and moved.

```
# A BeeperPutter that puts a robot and moves, but also asks its
# neighbor to do the same
class NeighborTalker < BeeperPutter

   def initialize(street, avenue, direction, beepers, neighbor)
      super(street, avenue, direction, beepers)
      @neighbor = neighbor
   end

   def distribute_beepers()
      put_beeper()
      move()
      @neighbor.distribute_beepers()
   end
end
```

Here we have an example of a robot remembering something. A NeighborTalker remembers a reference to another robot: its neighbor, which must understand the distribute_beepers message. Here an extra parameter of the constructor is used to get the NeighborTalker to remember a specific robot. It will remember this robot in its own instance variable called @neighbor. Each NeighborTalker can remember a different neighbor. The @neighbor *instance variable*, or *field*, becomes part of each robot of this kind. This instance variable is just a reference to some other BeeperPutter, like a local nickname. Note that the Karel-Werke must build in this ability to reference another robot. Not only that, when you create such a robot we want the one that it will reference to exist beforehand. Then the other robot can be given as part of the delivery specification of the one you create with new.

Sometimes we need to send additional information when we create a robot or send it a message. This extra information is called a parameter to a constructor or a method as we have seen before.

You have experience with parameters in your ordinary dealings in the world. Suppose you go to the post office. You want to *send a message* buyStamps to the postal worker. Since there are many kinds of stamps, you can either have a separate message for each kind, or use a parameter to make the distinction. Moreover, even if you use a different message for each kind of stamp (buyFirstClassStamps, etc.) you still need to say how many you want. These are parameters: postalWorker.buyStamps(FirstClass, 20); or postalWorker.buyFirstClassStamps(20);

In this case we want to tell a NeighborTalker which other robot (a BeeperPutter, actually) will be its neighbor when we create it. This other robot is the one that this one will tell to put down a beeper after it puts down its own. Here it is the constructor that we use to accomplish this.

Note that we first invoke the super construction to create the UrRobot and then we save the parameter named neighbor in the @neighbor field of this robot using an assignment statement. This assignment just makes the @neighbor reference refer to the BeeperPutter we are passing as a parameter. The parameter is itself a reference to some robot that is specified in the delivery specification. We have been using parameters all along, of course, in our constructors. Here we just use an additional one. Methods can have parameters as well, as we have seen.

Note that the field @neighbor is known within the robots of class NeighborTalker and can be referenced from any of the methods. But if we create several NeighborTalker robots, then each will have the ability to reference a different robot via its @neighbor field. The reference field is built into each robot separately. When the constructor references @neighbor as above, it is setting the reference for the robot being created at that moment.

On the other hand, the parameter name *neighbor* is known only within the constructor itself since that is where it is declared. It is called *local* to the constructor. Parameter names are local to the constructor or method in which they occur. Fields are known in all methods of the object.

Now we are ready to use the above classes. We define a set of NeighborTalker robots and one NoNeighbor. We let each of the NeighborTalkers know which robot we want to designate as its neighbor by naming some BeeperPutter as the argument matched with the extra parameter in the delivery specification. Notice that most of the Neighbor Talkers have another NeighborTalker for a neighbor. This works since a NeighborTalker is a BeeperPutter, and we need the method defined in BeeperPutter for this to work. However, one of the NeighborTalkers is given the NoNeighbor as in the delivery specification. This is also ok, since a NoNeighbor is also a BeeperPutter.

Then all we need to do is tell the first robot to distribute_beepers. It will place its own beeper and pass the same message to its neighbor, which in this case is another NeighborTalker. Thus the neighbor will do the same, putting a beeper and passing the message to its neighbor, and so on down the line until a NoNeighbor gets the same message. This one will put the beeper and will not pass on any message so the process stops. (Each robot also moves, of course.) Here we create only four robots, but any number will do.

```
def task()
   noname = NoNeighbor.new(1, 1, NORTH, 2)
   noname = NeighborTalker.new(1, 2, NORTH, 2, noname)
   noname = NeighborTalker.new(1, 3, NORTH, 2, noname)
   noname = NeighborTalker.new(1, 4, NORTH, 2, noname)
   noname.distribute_beepers()
end
```

The interesting thing is that it doesn't matter how many of the NeighborTalker robots we put before the final NoNeighbor robot. All of the robots will place their beepers and the process will be stopped only when the distribute_beepers message is finally sent to the NoNeighbor robot. (It also doesn't really matter where the robots are. We positioned them along first street simply for convenience.)

> **Invariants**: The purpose of a constructor is actually more than just to deliver an object. More important is to guarantee that the object (here a robot) can be used immediately: that it is properly and completely constructed. When you define a class you are really giving the definition of a set of objects that the class can create. It is a template that the factory uses to create objects of that kind. These objects may have certain requirements. Here we require that the @neighbor field actually refer to a BeeperPutter. If it does not, for whatever reason, then trying to send a message to the neighbor will result in an intent error. Normally this will halt our program. To avoid this we say that the NeighborTalker class has an object invariant that it must maintain. This is just a statement that must be true whenever we have such a robot and it must hold throughout its life. Here the invariant is the statement that the @neighbor refers to an actual BeeperPutter (or at least an object that understands distribute_beepers), rather than remaining undefined. The job of the constructor is really to establish all object invariants. While technically the word invariant means "doesn't vary," in practice it means "is always true." So the job of the constructor is to make all invariants true. The other public methods then keep them true.
>
> Actually we don't do a very good job of it here, since the delivery statement could in fact specify nil for the argument. We will think about this more in the future. It is possible to do a better job here. The value nil is a special *reference* value that points an object that does nothing.

The above code might be confusing the first time you encounter it. Note that we have used only one reference variable and at different times it points to either a NoNeighbor or a NeighborTalker. In the first statement of the task we initialize the variable to refer to a new NoNeighbor robot. In the second line the name *noname* appears twice, once on the left side of the assignment operator, =, and once as a parameter to the NeighborTalker constructor. How can this be? Note that before we can assign something to the noname variable on the left side, that object must exist. It exists because it is created on the right, so here the Robot Programming Language (Ruby) must process the right side of the = before the left side. Not only that, but the parameters themselves are all evaluated before the constructor's execution begins. Therefore, the current value of the reference noname is used, and that is the object created in the first statement. Thus the new robot is made to point to the first one, and then the name, which up to now has been pointing to the first one, is made to point to the second. Likewise in the third statement, the new robot is initialized to point to the second and the variable is made to point to the newly created third robot.

There are actually two rules at work here. The first is that parameter values are evaluated before the constructor or method is executed, using current values. The second rule is that the right hand sides of assignments are evaluated before the assignments to the left side variables are made.

The careful reader will also have noted that we constructed a specific number of robots here. It didn't matter in the operation how many it was, but we knew when we wrote the program how many it would be. In Chapter 6 we shall see a way to avoid even this limitation.

When we define a new parameter we give a local name. Later when we use the constructor or method with the new parameter, we match some value, called an argument, with the parameter.

4.6 Still More on Polymorphism -- Strategy and Delegation

So far, most of the objects we have seen have been robots, UrRobots and the robots we have built. Beepers and walls are not objects because they don't have behavior, other than implicitly. In order to take advantage of polymorphism you want to have lots of objects of different kinds. Here we will introduce some new kinds of objects that are not robots, but they can be helpful to robots. We will also learn a bit more about Ruby as we go along.

When we look back at section 4.2 we notice that we used two types (classes) of robots and several robot objects. We called them all by the same name, lisa, but there were still several objects. We did that to get different behavior. Different objects can perform different behaviors when sent the same message. That is the main message of polymorphism. Now we want to try something different and have the same robot behave differently at different times -- polymorphically. To do this we use a simple idea called *delegation*. A robot can delegate one of its behaviors to another object. We did something like this with the Contractor robot earlier in this chapter, which delegated the building tasks to its helpers which were robots. Here the object we delegate to won't be another robot, however, but a special kind of object called a *Strategy*.

If effect, a strategy is an object that helps another object carry out a task. This idea of helper objects and delegation is one of the big ideas of object-oriented programming. What other places here have you seen a robot delegate some part of a task to some other object?

You probably use strategies yourself when you do things: play games for example. A smart player will change strategies when she learns that the current one is not effective. This happens in both active games (basketball) and mental games (golf, Clue,...). To be useful, strategies need to be somewhat interchangeable, as well as flexible. You probably use a strategy to do your homework, in fact. Some strategies are more effective than others, also. Some common homework strategies are "As early as possible," and "As late as possible." I've even heard of a "Don't bother" strategy. In the robot world, as in ours, a strategy is something you use. The strategy is used to do something. We will capture strategies in objects and what they do in methods. By having a robot employ different strategies at different times, it will behave differently at different times. For example, we could have a robot with a turn method, in which sending the turn message causes the robot to turn left sometimes and the same message causes it to turn right at other times, by employing different strategies. Let's see how to do this.

First note that objects model things. Some objects model things like robots that seem concrete. Other objects can model things of pure thought, like strategies. Objects can model almost anything you can think of.

Strategy is not built in to the robot infrastructure, however. It is something you define and create yourself. There can be several kinds of strategies and several kinds of delegation also. We will explore only a simple case.

We will use a Ruby abstract class to define what we mean here by a strategy.

```ruby
# An interface to define strategies
#       Subclass this to define concrete strategies.
class Strategy
   def do_it (robot)
      raise NotImplementedError.new("Unimplemented Strategy")
   end
end
```

This just defines what strategies "look like", without defining any strategies themselves. As always, in Ruby, it is used to express our intent and nothing more. A strategy will, indirectly, form the body of one of our methods, though it could form just a part of the body. A class can inherit this interface, but to do so it should implement the do_it method of the Strategy interface (otherwise the error will occur when we try to invoke do_it). And note that the do_it message of any strategy will normally be given an argument that is a robot, as our parameter name indicates, but this isn't strictly necessary in Ruby. This is a consequence of the dynamic nature of the language. Within any do_it method it will be possible to send messages to this object and we need to assure that the messages sent from the concrete do_it method can be handled by the argument we use in the message.

For starters, it will be useful to have a concrete strategy that does nothing.

```ruby
# An implementation in which do_it does nothing at all
class NullStrategy < Strategy
   def do_it(robot)
      # nothing
   end
end
```

Not very interesting, of course, but certainly simple. This is a concrete class, but it is not a robot class. It defines objects, but not robots since we don't extend UrRobot. Classes may inherit from one other class, including abstract classes. When they inherit an abstract class, they should define the methods declared by the interface. Otherwise they are themselves abstract. In NullStrategy we implement the do_it method by giving it an empty body. Note that the parameter list must match that of the method defined in the interface exactly. And note also that we comment the fact that the body is empty, not simply leaving it empty and later wondering if we forgot to do something. Always express your intent in your programs.

This do_it method has a parameter named *robot*. The intent is to use the body of the method to do something with the robot referred to by the name *robot* by sending it some messages. The do_it method can actually send any messages it requires to the robot object. We shall see some more examples of concrete Strategies soon.

Now we will see how to use a strategy. Let's create a special kind of BeeperLayer called a StrategyLayer. Recall that BeeperLayer is an abstract class.

```
# Uses a strategy to determine how to put_beepers
class StrategyLayer < BeeperLayer


   # Initially does nothing when asked to put_beepers
   def initialize(street, avenue, direction, beepers)
      super(street, avenue, direction, beepers)
      @strategy = NullStrategy.new()
   end

   # "Change the current strategy to any other
   def set_strategy(strategy)
      @strategy = strategy
   end

   # Delegate the action to the strategy
   def put_beepers()
      @strategy.do_it(self)
   end
end
```

There are a few things to note here. First is that the constructor first invokes the superclass constructor as usual and then creates the @strategy field, initializing that with a new NullStrategy. The StrategyLayer will remember a strategy in its instance variable @strategy and we want to assure that it has a valid one at all times (an invariant). Most important, is that when we call put_beepers the StrategyLayer will delegate the action performed to whatever Strategy it currently has. In other words, when you ask a StrategyLayer to put_beepers, the StrategyLayer in turn asks its @strategy to do_it. This is *delegation*. You can think of the StrategyLayer object as a client of the Strategy in this interaction, and the Strategy as a server. Object interactions always have this basic client-server character to them. The sender of any message is the client, and the receiver is the server.

We also have a method, set_strategy, by which a StrategyLayer can learn a new strategy and remember it.

Finally, in put_beepers, when the do_it message is sent to the strategy, the robot also sends a reference to itself as the parameter. The strategy will then act on this BeeperLayer. The idea, is that the strategy will send other messages to this robot, almost as if the robot had sent messages to itself. In essence here, the StrategyLayer is delegating its put_beepers method to the strategy object that it is currently remembering.

Now it gets interesting. Suppose we create a TwoBeeperStrategy as follows.

```
# A strategy for putting two beepers on a corner
class TwoBeeperStrategy < Strategy
   def do_it(robot)
      robot.put_beeper()
      robot.put_beeper()
   end
end
```

Now we can create something that behaves like a TwoRowLayer from the StrategyLayer class with just

```
lisa = StrategyLayer.new(1, 3, EAST, INFINITY)
lisa.set_strategy(TwoBeeperStrategy.new())
```

A simple shorthand was used here also. Instead of declaring a variable to refer to the strategy, we just created it where the argument to the StrategyLayer's constructor required a strategy. We have seen this before. Since there is no need for the reference variable. We can just create a new strategy wherever a strategy is needed, without providing it a name.

Similarly we could create another StrategyLayer using a similar ThreeBeeperStrategy. However, we can do something much more interesting, which is to change lisa's strategy so that it then puts three beepers on each corner instead of two. If it was already remembering another strategy when this occurs, it will forget that strategy and now remember this one instead.

```
lisa = StrategyLayer.new(3, 4, EAST, INFINITY)
lisa.set_strategy(TwoBeeperStrategy.new())
lisa.lay_beepers()
...
lisa.set_strategy(ThreeBeeperStrategy.new())
lisa.lay_beepers();
...
```

In the above, it might be advantageous to actually name the two strategies. Since each strategy object might be needed more than once in the program. If lisa wants to go back to the two beeper strategy at the end of the above, then having a name for the one we created means that we can just reuse it and don't need to create another.

At any given time, lisa is delegating the put_beepers action to whichever strategy object it holds. It does this by simply sending the do_it message to the strategy. The strategy objects behave polymorphically, each doing what it was designed to do. The lisa robot doesn't need to know what kind of strategy it has, just that it does implement the do_it method, which we assure by inheriting the Strategy abstract class. In any case, the do_it method will behave polymorphically. And note that it is an invariant of BeeperLayers that they have a valid strategy.

Here we have had strategies only for putting down beepers. You could, however, also have strategies for moving, or for doing complicated combinations of things. All you need in order to make things useful is some way to change the strategy as needed. Here we used a set_strategy method, but there are other interesting ways as well.

For example, a robot can alternate between two known strategies. Suppose we want a robot that will walk around a rectangle that is three blocks long in one direction and two blocks long in the other. I'm sure you could write this easily, but here is another way that might give you some ideas about the possibilities of strategies. Note that it uses a feature of Ruby we haven't seen yet. It is possible to switch the values of two (or more) variables with a statement as simple as:

```
x, y = y, x
```

The object that x originally referenced (on the right hand side) is now referenced by y, and the object that y originally pointed to is now referenced by x. This is normally called swap. We will use this to swap our strategies, but to do so requires writing a long statement. Note that such multiple assignments are executed by the computer evaluating all of the expressions on the right hand side of the assignment operator before any of the assignments are done.

```ruby
class BlockWalker < UrRobot

    def initialize(street, avenue, direction, beepers)
        super(street, avenue, direction, beepers)
        @strategy = ThreeBlockStrategy.new()
        @otherStrategy = TwoBlockStrategy.new()
    end

    def walk_a_side()
        @strategy.do_it(self)
        @strategy, @otherStrategy =
                @otherStrategy, @strategy
    end

    class TwoBlockStrategy < Strategy
        def do_it(robot)
            robot.move()
            robot.move()
        end
    end

    class ThreeBlockStrategy < Strategy
        def do_it(robot)
            robot.move()
            robot.move()
            robot.move()
        end
    end
end
```

Such a robot starts out with a ThreeBlockStrategy as the one it will delegate to. (More on the ThreeBlockStrategy and the TwoBlockStrategy classes below.) However, whenever it is asked to walk_a_side, it not only performs that strategy, it also replaces that strategy with the other one it is remembering, while also remembering the current one as if it were the other.

Now, if we set a BlockWalker, say john, down in the world and execute

```ruby
john.walk_a_side()
john.turn_left()
john.walk_a_side()
john.turn_left()
john.walk_a_side()
john.turn_left()
```

```
john.walk_a_side()
john.turn_left()
```

then it will walk around a block that is three blocks in one direction and two in the other. We say that the BlockWalker changes its **state** each time it executes walk_a_side and its current state is the strategy it will use the next time it is asked to walk_a_side. The state of an object is both what it remembers and what situation it finds itself in within the world at the moment.

Now a bit on the two strategy classes we wrote above. If you notice the indentation, it should be clear that these two classes are defined within the BlockWalker class. This is perfectly allowable. We put them inside the BlockWalker class because our only purpose was to use them there. They could also be separated out and defined at top level in this file or in another. But Ruby is very flexible about where you define classes for local use. But since we have used the Strategy class more than once it is useful to put it in its own file so that we can require it generally.

4.7 Ruby Array and More on Strategies

Now that we know how to use a strategy and how to change a strategy, let's try something fun. Imagine a situation like this. Suppose we have a Spy robot that has an initial set of clues (a Strategy) to move somewhere. When it does that it meets another Accomplice robot on the final corner and gets a set of clues (another Strategy) from the accomplice. It takes that Strategy for its own and follows it, which should take it to another corner with another Accomplice. This can be repeated for as many steps as you like. The very last Strategy will direct the original Spy to some treasure, say. We can do most of this now, except the handoff. Up until now, if a robot wants to exchange things, beepers or strategies, with another, it must have a reference to the other, but this would be bad practice for spies. In fact, a Spy robot won't even know where its accomplices are until it follows the strategies.

When a robot arrives on a corner there will be a **collection** of other robots on the same corner. Usually this collection is empty. But not always. When the spy arrives on the corner with the accomplice the collection will not be empty since it will contain the accomplice. We can ask about this collection using any robot's neighbors() method, which returns a Ruby Array, a kind of collection. This method will give us information about all the other robots on the same corner. The neighbors method is part of UrRobot, but we have not yet referred to it. In fact, the neighbors method returns a Ruby Array of the robots, other than the one executing the method, that are on the same corner.

Until now, few of our methods return information to the message sender. They represent actions: things robots do. Now we need to look at the other situation. Recall that some objects remember things. Sometimes a user (client) of that object may want some of the information remembered by another object. This new kind of method is used to obtain it. When the method is defined, it determines what kind of information it provides, if any.

The neighbors method in the UrRobot class looks like this:

```
def neighbors()
   result = []
   ... # put things into result
   return result
```

```
    end
```

And the neighbors method returns an object to us of type Array.

Objects **do** things and objects **remember** things. So we have methods that don't return anything, sometimes called *procedural* so that we can ask an object to do something. We also have these other methods (called *functional*) that we use to ask an object to return information of some kind to us. These are also called *accessors*, since they access information. An object can simply remember this information, it can compute it as needed (which, in fact, is what happens in this case) or it can ask another object (delegation again) for the information that it will then return to the message sender. To the client, however, it seems like the server actually remembers the information.

Arrays are defined as part of the Ruby built in features. Actually there are two kinds of collections in Ruby: *hashes* and *arrays*. Arrays have a linear, sequential, ordering. Arrays are variable size and we have already seen the empty Array ([]) and the *push* method. Here we will also see the *pop* method, which removes an item from the sequence. In its simplest form, it just removes the most recently pushed item. It not only removes the item, but returns it to us as the return value.

The UrRobot class defines a method, neighbors(), that returns an Array containing the robots on the same corner as the one that executes it, though the one executing it will NOT be part of the Array. So a better way to say it is that neighbors() is an Array of the *other* robots on the same corner. If we can be sure that there *is* another robot on the same corner, then we can safely know that the list is not empty and we can safely send it a pop message, though that will change the list itself. We say that pop is a *mutator* on the list, since it changes or mutates the state of the list. But it is also an *accessor*, since it returns the value removed.

But if a robot executes its neighbors() method on a corner with no robots we will get an empty Array and pop will return nil. We have already seen how to process all of the elements of an Array with the each method. We shall see more of this in Chapter 6.

So, when our spy meets its accomplice on a corner, the spy can get a reference to the accomplice by executing

```
    my_neighbors = neighbors()
    my_accomplice = my_neighbors.pop()
```

Of course, my_accomplice is nil if you are on a corner with no other robots.

But doing this also implies that you know the robot on the corner is an Accomplice, and that if there are several, that they are all Accomplices, since we don't know which of them will be returned by pop if there are several. We need to know that it is an Accomplice since we intend to send it messages known to Accomplices but not necessarily to other objects.

Before we proceed, note that my_neighbors.pop() doesn't remove the neighbor from the corner, only a reference to it from an Array.

Let us put this together so that we can do our Spy's search. We need two classes. The Accomplice is simpler, so we write it first. It remembers some strategy and has a way to tell it to another robot who asks for it.

```
# Maintains a strategy object that it will hand-off to a Spy
class Accomplice < UrRobot

    def initialize(street, avenue, direction, beepers, strategy)
        super(street, avenue, direction, beepers)
        @clue = strategy
    end

    # Give the strategy to whichever object asks for it -- a Spy
    def request_clue()
        return @clue
    end
end
```

Again, we see a method returning information. request_clue is a method that returns a Strategy. The strategy held by the accomplice is set during its creation in the constructor also and remembered in the @clue field.

Now we can create several strategy classes. One to direct the robot to turn left and then move three times, or whatever you want. That is easy and we leave it to you. Next we see how the Spy robot will use the accomplices.

```
# Knows how to follow strategies given by accomplices
class Spy < UrRobot
    def initialize(street, avenue, direction, beepers,
initial_strategy)
        super(street, avenue, direction, beepers)
        @strategy = initial_strategy
    end

    # Get the next part of the puzzle from the accomplice.
    # Must be on the same corner as the accomplice to get the
strategy
    def get_next_clue()
        robot = neighbors().pop()
        @strategy = robot.request_clue()
    end

    # Follow the current strategy. Usually the one just obtained.
    def follow_strategy()
        @strategy.do_it(self)
    end
end
```

In get_next_clue we see another feature of Ruby that we haven't seen yet. The statement

```
robot = neighbors().pop()
```

does two things. First it invokes neighbors() to get an Array. There is no reference that we point to this list, however. Instead we just send that array the pop message immediately and save the reference to that robot in the robot variable. This is called *cascading* messages and you can always do this in Ruby. If a message returns an object you can send that object a message by cascading the messages. This is another example of uniformity of the language. If we can say anArray.pop() where anArray is a variable referencing an Array we can also say neighbors().pop since neighbors() is an expression returning an Array.

When you create a Spy, you must give it the strategy that will let it find the first accomplice. Each accomplice will provide one that takes it to the next, and the last "clue" will take you to the final target. If we have already created and placed some accomplices and some strategies, including one called StartStrategy, we can then say.

```
... create and place three accomplices, then
bernie = Spy.new(1, 1, EAST, 0, StartStrategy.new())
bernie.follow_strategy()
bernie.get_next_clue()
bernie.follow_strategy()
bernie.get_next_clue()
bernie.follow_strategy()
bernie.get_next_clue()
bernie.follow_strategy()
```

Again we emphasize the relationship to polymorphism here and the meaning of the word. Put simply, all it really means is that each object knows what to do when it receives a proper message. You can't force an object to do something else. We can refer to different objects at different times in the same program by a single name, and the actual behavior of a message sent through that name to an object will depend on the object to which the name actually refers. This means that each object is in complete control of what it does, depending on its class and its current state. The behavior is under the control of the (server) object and not the other program code (client) that makes requests of the object.

Finally, note that once a robot has established a reference to its neighbors list, then all the robots can move off this corner without affecting the Array that was returned. The robot that sent the neighbors() message has access to all of the robots that were neighbors at the point at which the message was sent. Thus, the Array is like a snapshot of what was the state of that corner at that moment. Likewise, even though the pop method removes a reference from the list, it doesn't affect the robots on the corner. Sending a neighbors message again will return the same list as originally if none of the robots have moved.

4.8 Decorators

Let's start writing such a Spy walk, considering what other tricks we might employ. Here is a simple situation. The Spy will start at the origin facing East. The first Accomplice will be three blocks to the East. The next will be three blocks East beyond the first. The third will be three blocks north of the second. Finally the "treasure" will be four blocks East of the last Accomplice. The Spy doesn't know all of this, of course, and only has a clue (Strategy) to reach the first. So the initial Strategy will be a ThreeStep.

```
class ThreeStep < Strategy
   def do_it(robot)
      robot.move()
      robot.move()
      robot.move()
   end
end
```

> **Mutable and Immutable Objects**: An object with no fields normally always behaves exactly the same when you send it a message. If there are fields, the behavior may depend on them. An object that has no fields (no state variables) is an example of an immutable object: one whose state cannot be changed. Robots, on the other hand, are mutable, since their state changes when they move, for example. Immutable objects can be re-used in a program and having multiple references to them cause no problems since no reference can cause a modification of the object that might get in the way of what the other reference expects. Here our ThreeStep strategies are immutable, though the robot they manipulate is not.
>
> A program with a high percentage of immutable objects is normally easier to reason about since you don't have to think about changes in such objects.

Interestingly, we can use the same Strategy for that of the first Accomplice, so that simplifies our work a bit. We not only don't need another class, we can reuse the same ThreeStep object. That will get us to the second Accomplice on 1st street and 7th avenue. Since the Spy arrives here from the West, all it needs to do from here to find the next Accomplice is to turn_left and then apply the ThreeStep strategy again, but there is no way for the Spy itself to know about the turn. It needs to be incorporated into another Strategy. We can write it simply, of course, but if we do so, we will be writing the same code (for three moves) a second time in the program.

We can, however, apply another technique that lets us modify a strategy's operation in a variety of ways without changing the code defined in the strategy. This works beyond strategies, by the way. We just employ it here for convenience. The new idea is called a Decorator. A Decorator makes something "nicer" without changing its character. Much like you decorate a cake or a house. The first thing to know about a strategy decorator is that it is itself a strategy. The second thing to know is that it knows about another strategy -- the one it decorates. It learns of this in its constructor. So here is a LeftTurnDecorator for strategies.

```
class LeftTurnDecorator < Strategy
   def initialize(decorated)
      @decorated = decorated
   end

   def do_it(robot)
      robot.turn_left()
      @decorated.do_it(robot)
   end
```

```
end
```

The constructor here is used to get a reference to another strategy, which it remembers. Thus, a decorator IS-A strategy, but it also HAS-A strategy. This is the essence of a decorator. Remember that, as a Strategy, it must implement the do_it method. A strategy decorator does something somewhere in its do_it method and then sends the same do_it message to the strategy that it is decorating. So if we create a new strategy with

```
initial_strategy = ThreeStep.new()
second_strategy = LeftTurnDecorator.new(initial_strategy)
```

then the resulting strategy is a decoration of a ThreeStep, and which also does a turn_left before it executes the ThreeStep strategy, so it turns left and then moves three blocks. Employing this strategy in the second Accomplice will get us to the third. Note that two objects are created here.

We arrive at the third Accomplice from the South, so we need to turn right and then walk four blocks. Again this could be done with an entirely new class, but we could also again decorate a ThreeStep with another decorator that turns left three times **before** applying the decorated strategy and **then** moves once afterwards. This emphasizes that the decorator can do anything it wants, before and after sending the do_it message to the Strategy it decorates.

While the situation here is somewhat simplified, this works best when the basic strategies are somewhat complex and the modifications are quite simple. And note that the decorated object's strategy's do_it is executed in full. We don't modify it. We just create a new strategy that uses it: surrounds it, actually.

The key to a Decorator is that it decorates an object of some abstract class that it also extends. In other words, it remembers another object implementing some interface and it also itself implements the same interface. Finally, some method of the inherited abstract class is implemented by doing something and also sending the same message to the object it has remembered. And it is important to remember that since a strategy decorator is itself a strategy it can itself be decorated by another StrategyDecorator. Quite complex behavior can be built up in parts from a sequence of decorators on a basic strategy. Each decorator can do some simple thing. When well done, decorators can also be generally useful. For example, our left turn decorator could be applied to other strategies than just walk strategies.

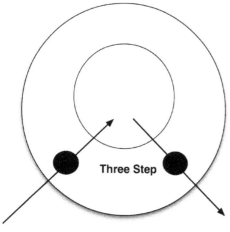

Figure 4.2 A Decorator and the Object it Decorates

One way to think of decorators is as if the decorated object is *inside* the decorator. A message sent to it has to pass through the decorator to get to it. Likewise, if you have a strategy with an action method that returns a value, then that value has to pass back out through the decorator to get back to the original client. The decorator can make modifications both as the message passes in, and as the returned value passes back out. While this may not be a precisely accurate picture, it is helpful to pretend that it is.

Here the arrows represent a message moving through the decorator and the object it decorates, and the two bullet points are places where the decorator can make changes and additions.

4.9 Observers

In this section we will see another means of building and using robot teams. The idea is that a controller robot will perform some basic actions that will cause another controlled robot to automatically do something. We will also provide a flexible way for the controller robot to learn about the controlled robot. In general, the first robot could control several this way, but first we will show the case of one controlled robot. The controlling robot is called *observable* and the one controlled is called an *observer*. This is because the one controlled does nothing until it *observes* the other signaling, by doing the thing that causes it to carry out its action.

Actually, the common notion of the meaning of the word observer might be misleading here. Usually, the observed takes no action to cue the observer and may not even know of the existence of the observer. Imagine yourself at a sporting event in which your friend is a participant and you are a spectator. At various times you decide to take a picture of your friend in competition. This is the normal meaning, but not the one we intend here. Instead, imagine yourself at the same sporting event, but you have prearranged with your friend that you will only take her picture when she waves to you. So, the observed actually signals the observer. Note that you could arrange to do this for several friends at the same event. Likewise your friend could have the same arrangement with several observers.

4.9.1 The Simple Case of a Single Observer

Here we will show a single Observed robot and a single Observer In the next section we will show the general situation, and the one implemented in UrRobot.

First we will need an agreement or *protocol* that the two robots can agree upon to set up their cooperation. We do this in the form of an interface (defined by an abstract class, as usual) that is implemented by the observer.

```
class RobotListener
    def update()
        raise NotImplementedError.new("Listener update undefined")
    end
end
```

Update will be invoked when the event of interest occurs. Next we need a version of this that does nothing at all.

```
class NullListener < RobotListener
    def update()
        # nothing
    end
end
```

We will create a very simple example here, of a robot that just walks one block when the robot it is observing does the key thing that causes the update action to occur. Nothing yet has specified what that key event is.

```
class WalkListener < UrRobot # < RobotListener (see note below)
    def update()
        move()
    end
end
```

> **Multiple Inheritance, Modules, and Dynamic Languages**: Some languages permit a class to extend multiple parent classes. Ruby does not. Much of what those languages can do in combining functionality from different sources, Ruby does with Modules. This is a clean design, but it depends on the dynamic nature of Ruby. In a Module you can write a statement that invokes a non-existent method, or even a non-existent instance variable. All will be well if the module is included into a class that, itself, has the missing parts.
>
> Likewise, Ruby has no real notion of an interface, or inheriting from an interface. That is just a mental trick we use to express our intent in a program and try to get some help when we intend to do something while designing, but forget to do it when implementing.
>
> Any language designer makes choices that guide programmers in developing a style.
>
> In the definition of the WalkListener, we would have liked to inherit from two different classes: UrRobot and RobotListener. Ruby only allows inheritance from a single superclass so that was impossible. The comment we wrote is just to register our intent here. But we draw on the dynamic aspects of Ruby also, which makes such *multiple inheritance* here unneeded. In fact, Ruby doesn't care what *type* of object you pass as a parameter anywhere, or what type of thing it is that receives a message. All that matters is that the thing passed or the thing receiving the message understand the messages. Since our WalkListener has the required update method with a suitable parameter it doesn't matter at all that it doesn't really subclass RobotListener. This is called *duck typing*. The joke is that if something walks like a duck and quacks like a duck, then it IS a duck for all purposes. This isn't true in many other languages (such as Java, which has different solutions to such problems). On the other hand, it is good to document your intent and your design decisions, hence the comment in WalkListener.

So, whenever such a robot is sent the update message, it just moves, but it could do anything you like. If you look carefully at the definition of RobotListener, you will notice that it doesn't actually require that a RobotListener be another Robot. This is intentional. Any object can observe a robot by implementing this interface. On the other hand, a WalkListener is an UrRobot that also observes another robot. However, it doesn't know which robot it observes and in fact, can observe many. We will see how next.

Now we will build a robot that can have one observer and whenever it picks up a beeper, it signals to its observer to do whatever action the observer is prepared to do. Note that the action performed by the observer (perhaps a WalkListener) is defined there, not here.

```
class ObservablePicker < UrRobot
    def initialize(street, avenue, direction, beepers)
        super(street, avenue, direction, beepers)
        @listener = NullListener.new()
    end

    def add_observer(listener)
        @listener = listener
    end

    def pick_beeper()
        super()
        @listener.update()
    end
end
```

Again, note that the observable does not define the action of the observer, but only arranges for it to be executed. The add_observer method is used to let an observable robot know who wants to observe it. Finally note that we protect against the possibility of forgetting to register any observer, by initializing @listener with one that does nothing. The pick_beeper method is overridden here to also signal our observer to perform its action.

We create such robots as follows.

```
tom = WalkListener.new(1, 1, NORTH, 0)
jerry = ObservablePicker.new(2, 3, EAST, 0)
jerry.add_observer(tom)
```

Now, whenever jerry picks a beeper, tom moves one block. An observable knows very little about its observer, only that it implements the update method. The observer knows nothing at all of the object it is observing. This *decoupling* between the definitions of the two robot classes allows for great flexibility. We can create complex observers. We can create complex observables. We can do both, independently. All that we need is an agreed upon method in the observer and a registration mechanism in the observable logically held together by an interface. In a sense, it is the interface that forms a glue between these two kinds of objects.

Observers, like strategies, can use any of the techniques we have discussed so far and will discuss later in the book. In particular, they can create additional robots and send them instructions. This can be used to create extremely complex behavior.

4.9.2 Multiple Observers

The Robot Programming Language (and Ruby in general) actually has something like our simple observers in its libraries but it is much more sophisticated there. In particular it permits an observable to have several observers. We shall examine this now. While the following is just our way of documenting requirements, suppose an abstract class like the following (which isn't strictly correct, but gives the right idea).

```
# Defines an interface showing how the observable will call back to
# the observer. It is implemented by observers.
class Observer

    # Called by the observable(s) with which this observer
    #   is registered whenever changes occur. Parameter observable
    #   points to the changed item and data tells what has changed.
    def update(observable, data1, data2, …) #not valid syntax
        raise NotImplementedError.new("Unimplemented observer")
    end
end
```

Within the Ruby libraries there is a module in observer.rb that you can include. It has approximately the following structure (simplified here):

This is really the same as the version above, except that it has an additional parameter in which arbitrary data can be passes as long as the observer and observable objects agree on its form. The module also exports a rather sophisticated ordinary Module Observable. Here is a small part of that class. Again it isn't exactly valid, though Ruby has features to do what is intended here. It is conceptually accurate.

```
# Observers register with observable objects and then
# get notified whenever the observable changes state
module Observable

    @observers = []

    # Add an observer to the set of objects to be notified of changes
    def add_observer(observer)
        @observers << observer
    end

    # Notify all observers
    def notify_observers(self, data1, data2, …)
        @observers.each do |observer|
            observer.update(data1, data2, …)
        end
    end

    ...
end
```

Note a few things. First this doesn't extend UrRobot, and is intended as a mixin. Next, the register method, named *add_observer* actually adds the observer to a collection. So an Observable will admit many Observers, not just one. When the event of interest occurs, the object that this is part of (via the include command) will just send the *notify_observers* message to itself, sending any data it likes. Our simplification hides the fact that several different data items may be sent, but we can ignore that for now. The real module has other methods as well, such as *remove_observer*. And we emphasize that UrRobot includes the real definition as a module. So an UrRobot knows how to add_observer and will send notify_observers whenever its state changes.

Here is an example of how we can take advantage of this. We are getting ahead of ourselves a bit here, since we need to use a feature that will be discussed in detail in the next Chapter, but you should be able to follow it ok. The class UrRobot includes Observable (as a module) so all robots may be observed. Moreover, any UrRobot will send itself the *notify_observers* message whenever it executes any primitive action. The data it sends as an argument is an object that forms a snapshot of the state of the robot immediately after executing the primitive. For example, if the robot has just been sent pick_beeper(), it will send itself the notify_observers message with an object whose action is PICK_BEEPER_ACTION and whose state variable include the location and direction, etc. With that background the following should be (more or less) clear. In the following constructor, any robot can be passed as the observed parameter. It tells the WalkListener object that it wants to be observed by it. Here a WalkListener will observe only one robot, but we could extend that also. This fragment uses actual Ruby syntax.

```
# Moves whenever the observed robot picks a beeper
# Note that these objects are both robots and observers (of robots).
class WalkListener < UrRobot  # < Observer - implements update

    def initialize(street, avenue, direction, beepers, observed)
       super(street, avenue, direction, beepers)
       observed.add_observer(self)
    end

    # Message sent by the observed robot
    def update(robot, action, state)
       if action == PICK_BEEPER_ACTION
          move()
       end
    end
end

def task()
   world = RobotWorld.instance()
   world.place_beepers(1, 1, 9)
   james = UrRobot.new(1, 1, EAST, 0)
   # james will be observed. Any robot is Observable
   gloria = WalkListener.new(2, 1, EAST, 0, james)
   # gloria is observing james and will walk when james picks a
   # beeper
   james.pick_beeper() # gloria moves
```

```
    james.pick_beeper()  # gloria moves
    james.pick_beeper()  # gloria moves
    james.pick_beeper()  # gloria moves
    james.pick_beeper()  # gloria moves
    james.move()
end
```

4.10 Final Words on Polymorphism

Polymorphism is both simple and profound. Simply stated it just means that each robot (or object) does what it knows how to do when sent any message. However, the consequences of this are quite deep. In particular, it means that when you as a programmer send a message to a robot referred to by a reference, you don't know in general what will happen. You have a reference, but you may not know with precision the kind of object it points to. You don't decide. The object to which the reference points will decide. You might think you have a simple UrRobot, since the reference variable once pointed to an object of that type, but the variable might now point to a robot in some other class instead. So even if you say something as simple as

```
mary.move()
```

you can't be sure what will happen. In particular, the following is legal

```
mary = MileMover.new(1, 1, NORTH, 0)
```

in which case mary.move() will move a mile, rather than a block. Combining this with the ability to write a method that has a robot parameter to which you can pass any robot type, and again with the possibility of changeable strategies in robots, means that what happens when you write a message, may not be precisely determinable from reading the program, but only from executing it. Moreover, the same variable can refer to different robots of different types at different times in the execution of the program.

This doesn't mean that all is chaos, however. What it does mean is that you need to give meaningful names to methods and parameters, and also guarantee that when that kind of robot receives that message, it will do the right thing for that kind of robot. Then, when some programmers decide to use that kind of robot, they can be assured that sending it a message will do the right thing, even if they don't know precisely what that will be. The main means of achieving this is to keep each class simple, make its name descriptive of what it does, and make it internally consistent and difficult to use incorrectly.

Perhaps even more important are two rules: one for interfaces and one for inheritance. When you define an interface (with an abstract class) you need to have a good idea about what the methods defined there mean logically, even though you don't implement them. When you do inherit the interface in a concrete class, make sure that your implementation of the methods is consistent with your logical meaning. If you do this consistently, then the interface will have a logical meaning that a programmer can depend upon, even though they don't know what code will be executed. You should also include explanatory comments with class declarations and method defs. Document your intent.

The rule for inheritance is a little more precise. Think of inheritance as meaning specialization. If class SpecialRobot extends class OrdinaryRobot, for example, make sure that logically speaking a special robot is really just a specialized kind of ordinary robot. So it wouldn't make sense for an IceSkaterRobot to extend Carpenter, for example, since ice skaters are not specialized carpenters, but a different kind of thing altogether. If you do this faithfully, then the logic of your program will make sense to users of your classes. Our shorthand for this is called the IS-A rule. Ask "IS-A skater a carpenter?" The answer is no, so skater classes should not be subclasses of any Carpenter class. On the other hand a "Carpenter IS-A UrRobot" and has all of its capabilities and more, so it is appropriate to make Carpenter a subclass of UrRobot. Note that a strategy is not a robot at all, but it is an object. If you create a class and don't specify what it extends, then it automatically extends the built-in Object class.

You may have noticed that we have been careful to initialize all of our instance fields when we declare them. This helps avoid problems. We have also used null strategies and listeners to make sure that every class that requires these has a default version available even if the user doesn't supply a more useful one. All of this is necessary to guarantee that every class you write can be guaranteed to **do the right thing** when used.

Finally, we note that we have two different kinds of decomposition of programs. Stepwise refinement takes a complex method and breaks it into simpler methods. Polymorphism, on the other hand, takes related tasks and puts them into different objects, perhaps strategies or similar things. If you have two distinct behaviors possible for a robot (or other object) put each behavior into a different object. This makes each object simple, but you need to use the right object at the right time, of course.

4.11 Important Ideas From This Chapter

polymorphism
abstract class
interface
import
delegation
strategy
null strategy
decorator
duck typing
observer
client, server
observable
instance variable (field)
parameter
object invariant
iteration
list
iterator
return value
IS-A and HAS-A
constructor
assignment
reference
invariant
mutable, immutable

4.12 Problem Set

1. Re-do problem 3.12-5, but this time use five robots; one for each letter to be written. You may choose each robot's starting position.

2. Re-do problem 3.12-5, but this time use 5 robots; one for each street.

3. Re-do problem 3.12-5, but this time use 17 robots; one for each avenue.

4. Re-do Problem 3.12-6, using 5 robots, one for each digit and one for the colon.

5. Re-do Problem 3.12-7 with four robots. You may choose the starting positions of each robot.

6. Re-do Problem 3.12-7 with eight robots. You may choose the starting positions of each robot.

7. Re-do Problem 3.12-7 with a Choreographer and 3 helpers. You may choose the starting positions of each robot.

8. Solve the harvester problem of Chapter 3 again using a team of six robots. Each robot can harvest a single row.

9. There is a simpler kind of strategy in which the robot is not passed to the do_it method.

```
class Controller
    def control_it()
        raise NotImplementedError.new("Undefined controller")
    end
end
```

For this to work, however, the class that implements the interface needs to remember a robot on which it will act. One way to do this is to provide a constructor that is passed a robot, which is saved within the strategy object in a @robot instance variable. When a controller is sent the control_it message, it applies the strategy to its own saved robot. This is quite nice, except that such strategies can't be exchanged between robots as easily, since if a robot john passes its strategy to george, then the strategy still refers to john and so if george sends control_it to the strategy, it will manipulate john and not george. This can be useful, actually, and makes george something like a choreographer or a contractor for john. This is why we called the interface Controller. Try to exploit this in a fun and interesting way.

10. What happens if a Spy chase causes a Spy to return to an Accomplice for the second time? Are there situations in which this is OK? Are there situations in which this is dangerous? Demonstrate each situation with a separate program for each.

11. Actually, it is possible for robots to adopt strategies of other robots even if the version of Problem 9 is used. Explain how. Write a program to test your ideas.

12. Write a beeper layer program, using strategies, that allows a single robot to place a beeper on every other corner of a 5 by 5 field. Do this by alternating strategies as you go along a single row, but starting each row with the "one beeper" strategy.

13. A class that implements an interface must implement the methods defined in that interface, but it can implement additional ones as well. Build three interesting controller classes. Give each one an additional method un_do_it, that will do just the opposite of the do_it method. The meaning of this is that if you do_it and then immediately un_do_it, the robot using the strategy will return to its original location and orientation. Moreover, if it placed any beepers on the way, it will pick them up, etc. Note that if you do this correctly and

if you apply (say) three strategies and then immediately undo each in the opposite order, they should all be undone.

14. Develop a set of rules that you can use to make writing un_do_it methods easier. For example, how do you undo the following?

```
self.move()
self.move()
self.turn_left()
self.move()
self.turn_right()
self.move()
self.turn_left()
```

15. Write and test a new observer that normally sits on First street and Second avenue. Whenever its observable sends it an action message it leaves a beeper at the origin and returns to its original location.

16. Write and test an observer that turns left whenever its observed robot moves, puts a beeper, picks a beeper, or turns left. The allowable values of action are MOVE_ACTION, PICK_BEEPER_ACTION, TURN_LEFT_ACTION, PUT_BEEPER_ACTION, TURN_OFF_ACTION, and NO_ACTION. They are defined in robota.rb and are constants as the names imply.

17. Two Spy robots who don't know each other's name, meet on a pre arranged corner and exchange clues (Strategy objects). Each then follows the strategy it was given. Test this.

18 (hard). Revisit Problem 14. Will your rules still work if the programmer overrides some of the UrRobot primitives? Suppose, for example, that move has been defined as:

```
def move()
    super()
    super()
    turn_right()
    super()
    turn_left()
end
```

Would it also work if we had omitted the final turn_left()? What do you need to do to fix this, so that undo still works in such a class?

19. A Contractor is standing at the origin with one Roofer, one Carpenter, and one Mason. The Contractor gives each of them a strategy telling where a house is supposed to be constructed and sends them off to build it. Write this program. It should be one strategy for all, probably. Note that the same Strategy object can be shared by all. (Why?)

20. Here is an example of a fairly common problem. You want an object to behave one way the first time it gets a message and a second way each time thereafter that it gets the same message. For example,

suppose you want something like a beeper layer to lay down two beepers on each corner of the first row of a rectangular field, but three beepers on each corner of all the other rows. Use strategies to solve this so that the robot automatically changes its strategy at the right time.

21. Create a beeper laying robot that starts somewhere in the world with an infinite number of beepers in its beeper bag and begins to lay down beepers in a "left handed" spiral pattern until it eventually runs into one of the bounding walls. Use a strategy that you modify at each turn by adding a decorator. The idea is if you walk in one direction for a certain number of steps, turn left, and then walk in the new direction for one greater than the old number of steps, and repeat this over and over, you will walk in a widening spiral. At each step you lay down one beeper. Except for the fact that the robot must eventually come to one of the boundary walls, this would be an infinite program. This can be done with a single basic strategy class and a single decorator class, in addition to a robot that uses a strategy and knows just the right way to modify its own strategy. Hint. You many need a lot of objects, but only these few classes.

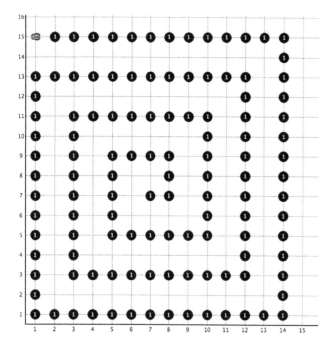

Figure 4.3 A Spiral Walk

22. Here we want to run a robot relay race using Observers. Imagine three robots at different avenues along first street. Starting from the West, the first two are observable robots and the last two are observers. Each observer observes the robot to its West. Note that the middle one both observes the one to the West and is observed by the one to its East. The robot to the West will carry a beeper to the one in the middle and then put it down and signal the one in the middle. When signaled, the one in the middle will pick up the beeper and carry it to the one to the east and put it down. It will then signal the one on that corner which will then pick up the beeper and carry it farther along. Suppose the robots start on first, fifth, and ninth avenues and the finish line is at thirteenth. Note that the robots should come from different classes. (How many classes are required? Would an abstract superclass help here? How much harder would it be to have four robots instead of three?)

23. Suppose you have a class of robots, say TurnTrue that inherits from UrRobot and includes Turner, so that robots of the class know how to turn_right as well as left. Suppose you create a subclass of TurnTrue in which you override turn_left as follows:

```
def turn_left()
    super()
    super()
    super()
end
```

What happens when robots of the new class are sent turn_left? And what happens to such robots when you send them the turn_right message? What do they do, and how do they do it? If you truly understand this you have a pretty good grasp of how polymorphism works.

24. In the distribute_beepers method of NeighborTalker, what happens if you rearrange the three statements in various ways. Watch the simulation carefully to see if you have predicted correctly.

5 Conditionally Executing Instructions

In the preceding chapters, a Robot's exact initial situation was known at the start of a task. When we wrote our programs, this information allowed karel to find beepers and avoid running into walls. However, these programs worked only in their specific initial situations. If a robot tried to execute one of these programs in a slightly different initial situation, the robot would almost certainly perform an error shutoff. Polymorphism gave us a way around this restriction, but now we shall study another.

What a robot needs is the ability to survey its local environment and then decide from that information what to do next. The IF instructions are discussed in this chapter. There are two versions of the IF statement, the IF and the IF/ELSIF. Both of these forms may also end with an ELSE clause, making four possibilities in all. They provide robots with their decision ability. Both allow a robot to test its environment and, depending on the result of the test, decide which instruction to execute next. The IF instructions enable us to write much more general programs for our robots that accomplish the same task in a variety of similar, but different, initial situations. These instructions are especially suited for letting robots deal with things like walls and beepers that are not objects. If they were objects, we could interact with them polymorphically as we saw in the last chapter. We will mostly discuss the IF and IF/ELSE forms.

Robot programs contain several different kinds of instructions. The first, and most important, is the message to a robot. These messages are sent to robots, either by the pilot (when they appear in the main task block) or by another object (when they occur in a method of some class). The action associated with this kind of instruction is defined by the corresponding method in the class of the robot to which the message is directed.

Another kind of instruction is the delivery specification, which is sent to the factory to construct a new robot and have the helicopter pilot deliver it. The assignment is a third kind of instruction.

The IF instruction is yet another different kind of instruction. It provides a way to structure the program itself. The rest of this chapter and the next are going to add to this list of kinds of instructions.

5.1 The IF Instruction

The IF instruction is the simpler of the IF variants. It has the following general form.

```
if <test>
   <instruction-list>
end
```

The IF instruction introduces the new reserved word *if* (spelled in lowercase). The reserved word *if* signals a program reader that an IF instruction is present, and the header line is followed by a list of instructions and an end. The <instruction-list> is known as the THEN clause of the instruction. We indent the instruction list of the IF instruction as shown (normally two to four spaces), to highlight the fact that <instruction-list> is a component of the IF instruction. An IF instruction is not a message to any robot.

In general the if statement is executed by some client. It could be a robot (if it is within a method), or the helicopter pilot (if it is in the main task block). A client executes the IF instruction by first checking whether <test> is true or false in the current situation. If <test> is true, the client executes <instruction-list>; if <test>

is false, the client skips <instruction-list>. In either case, the client is then finished executing the entire IF instruction. For an example, let's look at the program fragment below, which consists of an IF instruction followed by a turn_left message. Assume that this fragment is contained in a method of some robot class. Some robot of that class will be executing the code[6]. The robot is the client.

```
if next_to_a_beeper?()
    pick_beeper()
end
turn_left()
```

When this IF instruction is executed by the robot, it first checks whether it is next to (on the same corner as) a beeper. If it finds that **next_to_a_beeper**? is true, the robot executes the THEN clause, which instructs it to execute pick_beeper. The robot is now finished executing the IF instruction, and continues by executing the rest of the instructions, starting at the turn_left message.

Now suppose that there are no beepers on the corner when the robot executes this program fragment. In this case **next_to_a_beeper**? is false, so the robot does not execute the THEN clause. Instead, it skips directly to the turn_left message and continues executing the program from there. The result of this second case is that the robot executes the IF instruction by doing nothing more than asking itself to check whether or not it is next to a beeper. An error shutoff cannot occur in either case because the robot executes the pick_beeper message only if it confirms the presence of at least one beeper on the corner.

It is also possible to use IF statements in the main task block, but here we must be careful to ask a particular robot about its state. We ask about a robot's state by sending messages, just as we ask robots to perform instructions using messages. If we want to know about the state of a particular robot we must send a message to that robot. When we send the message to self we are asking about the state of the robot actually executing the current instruction. Since the main task block is not a method of any particular robot, we must use a robot's reference there.

```
if  karel.next_to_a_beeper?()
    karel.pick_beeper()
end
karel.turn_left()
```

5.2 The Conditions That Robots Can Test

In Chapter 1 we briefly discussed the sensory capabilities of robots. We learned that a robot can see walls, hear beepers, determine which direction it is facing, and feel if there are any beepers in its beeper-bag or other robots on its current corner. The conditions that a robot can test are divided according to these same four categories.

Below is a new module that defines the several conditions that robots of this class can test. The module is called SensorPack since it is like a package (or pack) of options that can be added to a robot to get a fancier model. Here we show the structure only, since the actual implementation depends on the simulator.

---

[6]To conserve space, we often demonstrate a programming idea without writing a complete robot program or new method. Instead, we just write the necessary instruction, which is called a program *fragment*.

```
# Adds sensing facilities to robots,
module SensorPack

    # Return true if there are beepers carried by this robot.
    def any_beepers_in_beeper_bag?()
        # Implementation dependent on simulator, so omitted
    end

    # Return true if there are beepers on the current corner.
    def next_to_a_beeper?()
        # Implementation dependent on simulator, so omitted
    end

    # Return true if this robot is facing north.
    def facing_north?()
        # Implementation dependent on simulator, so omitted
    end

    # Return true if this robot is facing east.
    def facing_east?()
        # Implementation dependent on simulator, so omitted
    end

    # Return true if this robot is facing south.
    def facing_south?()
        # Implementation dependent on simulator, so omitted
    end

    # Return true if this robot is facing west.
    def facing_west?()
        # Implementation dependent on simulator, so omitted
    end

    # Return true if there is no wall immediately in front
    # of this robot.
    def front_is_clear?()
        # Implementation dependent on simulator, so omitted
    end

    # Return true if there are any other robots on
    # the current corner."
    def next_to_a_robot?()
        # Implementation dependent on simulator, so omitted
    end
end
```

The Robot class inherits UrRobot and it includes the SensorPack module and so can serve as the parent class of many of your own classes for the remainder of your visit to karel's world. The class is so important, in fact, that the Karel-Werke makes its definition available to all robot purchasers. Therefore, you may use this class in the same way that you use UrRobot. You don't need to create it. Since these are the most common type of robot, the name of the class is simply Robot. These robots will be able to make good use of IF and other similar statements. Here is the complete definition. If you *require "robot"* instead of ur_robot in your own programs you can use them easily.

```
require "sensor_pack"

# A class of robots with sensing abilities
class Robot < UrRobot
    include SensorPack
end
```

The items in the instruction list name the tests that a robot of the Robot class may perform using its sensors. They return true or false values to the robot mechanism and so call them *Boolean* methods. These methods are also called *predicates*. They provide the means by which robots can be queried (or can query their own internal state) to decide whether certain conditions are true or false. On the other hand, actions like **move** and **turn_off** provide no feedback information when invoked. In computer programming languages, parts of a program that have a value are called *expressions*. Expressions are usually associated with a type, giving the valid values of the expression. A predicate represents a *Boolean expression*, meaning that its value is either true or false[7].

In the Robot Programming Language there are defined two Boolean values true and false. In actuality Ruby will consider any value (say 42) that is not nil or an explicit false, as if it is true. We prefer to use the names as a way of documenting our intent. But ruby actually has many values considered "true", but not the same as the actual value true.

So, in fact Ruby treats *nil* as false and (almost) anything else as true. The rules are a bit strange, due to the dynamic nature of the language. But a non-empty list serves for true. This leads to some quite interesting programs, but we won't pursue the details in this book. You won't want to be bored after leaving the Robot Programming Language, so we will leave you plenty to learn.

Methods that return information are called *functional* and those that do not are called *procedural*. The terminology is historic, going back to a time in which the distinction was thought more important than it is today. Predicates are just one kind of functional method. Other things can be returned from methods besides truth values. Even functions may be returned, in fact. Robot programmers can create new predicates in their own classes, just as they can create new procedural methods such as move_mile. It is traditional in Ruby to spell the names of predicates ending in a question mark since they seem to answer a question: "Is the robot next to a beeper?" for example. (The question mark is only legal at the end of a name.)

Recall that robots have a microphone that they can use to listen and determine if there are any beepers present on their current corner. This action is activated by the **next_to_a_beeper?** message. If a robot, say carol, is sent the message **carol.next_to_a_beeper?()** it will activate the microphone, and will respond to the message with true or false and then turn the microphone off again. The state of the robot doesn't change, but the sender of the message will obtain information about the state of the robot. This information can be put to use by statements like the IF instruction and others in this and the next chapter. The **next_to_a_beeper?** test is true when a robot is on the same corner as one or more beepers. A robot cannot hear beepers any farther away, and it cannot hear beepers that are in the sound proof beeper-bag.

[7]Note that since there are two behaviors here, you might want to look for a polymorphic solution to this problem, but our purpose here is to demonstrate the IF statement.

The **next_to_a_robot?** predicate is similar and returns whether or not there is another robot on the same corner. This predicate momentarily activates the robot's arm, which is used to feel about for other robots.

Remember that each robot has a TV camera for eyes, focused to detect a wall exactly one half of a block away to the front. This camera is facing directly ahead. The **front_is_clear?** predicate tests this condition. If a robot needs to test if its right is clear, it will need to proceed by first turning to the right to check for the presence of a wall. It can then return to its original orientation by turning back to its left.

A robot consults its internal compass to decide what direction it is facing. Finally, a robot can test whether or not there are any beepers in the beeper-bag by probing it with the mechanical arm. This condition is returned by the **any_beepers_in_beeper_bag?** predicate.

We will often want both positive and negative forms of many predicates. For example, we would probably want a predicate front_is_blocked? as the negative form of **front_is_clear?**. Only the positive forms are provided by the Robot class, however. To aid in the writing of such negative forms, we will rely on the logical negation operator. In English and in Ruby, it is written **not**. For example, we have **next_to_a_beeper?**. If we also want to act if karel is "**not next_to_a_beeper?**", what we write is "**not karel.next_to_a_beeper()**". Any message evaluating a predicate can be "negated" by preceding it with the negation operator, "not". Thus, if robot karel has beepers in its beeper-bag, then it could respond to the instruction

```
if not karel.next_to_a_beeper?()
# Read: "If it is not true that karel is next to a beeper... "
   karel.put_beeper()
end
```

Alternatively we could create our own subclass of the Robot class and provide a new predicate **not_next_to_a_beeper?**, as shown in the next section. In this case we could use:

```
if karel.not_next_to_a_bceper?()
   karel.put_beeper()
end
```

It is probably not worth doing so in such a simple case, but for complex predicates it may be. We shall explore this next.

5.2.1 Writing New Predicates

While the eight predicates defined above are built into the language, the user can also write new predicates. Predicates return Boolean values, true and false. Therefore, in the block of the definition of a new predicate we need to indicate what value is to be returned. For this we need a new kind of instruction: the RETURN instruction. The form of the RETURN instruction is the reserved word **return**, followed by an expression. In a Boolean method the value of the expression must evaluate to true (non nil) or false (nil). There are also functional methods that are not predicates and these will return something other than Boolean values. We shall see some of that in Chapter 7.

We might want predicates that are negative forms of the Robot class predicates. They can be defined using the not operator. For example, in a class CheckerRobot, we might want the following as well as some others.

```
class CheckerRobot < Robot
   def front_is_blocked?()
      return not front_is_clear?()
   end
   ...
```

Then, when a CheckerRobot is asked if its **front_is_blocked?**, it executes the return instruction. To do this it must first evaluate the **front_is_clear?** predicate, receiving an answer of either true or false. It then returns the negative of this because of the logical negation operator. Therefore, if **front_is_clear?** returns false, and if this is negated, then **front_is_blocked?** returns true. We can similarly write **not_next_to_a_beeper?**. We show just the predicate here. Of course, it has to be written within its class.

```
def not_next_to_a_beeper?()
   return not next_to_a_beeper?()
end
```

We might also want to "extend" a robot's vision by providing a test for **right_is_clear?**. This instruction is much more complicated since robots have no sensor to their right. One solution is to face towards the right so that the forward sensor may be used. However, we shouldn't leave the robot facing that new direction, since the name of the method, **right_is_clear**?, doesn't seems to imply any change in direction. Therefore, we should be sure the robot faces the original direction before returning. Therefore, **right_is_clear**? must execute turn instructions in addition to returning a value.

```
def right_is_clear?()
   turn_right()
   if  front_is_clear?()
      turn_left()
      return true
   end
   turn_left()
   return false
end
```

The **return** instruction immediately terminates the predicate it is contained within. Therefore, if *front_is_clear*? is true then the robot will turn left and return true. This method will have then terminated (returned). It won't reach or execute the second *turn_left* or the *return false* instruction. On the other hand, if the *front_is_clear*? test returns false, then the robot skips the THEN clause of the IF, and so it executes the second *turn_left* and the *return false* instruction. Notice that we were careful here to leave the robot facing the same direction that it was facing before this predicate was executed. Therefore the programmer using *right_is_clear*? can ignore the fact that the robot executes turns in order to evaluate this predicate, since any turn is undone. We can say that the turn is *transparent* to the user. Said another way, *right_is_clear*? is *directionally invariant*. Viewed from outside, the robot executing it faces the same direction after executing it as it did before. More precisely, the direction of the robot is invariant under this instruction.

By the way, this method would be an excellent candidate to add to our Turner mixin, since it seems pretty generally useful. You could discuss whether Turner is the correct mixin for it, but some mixin class would make it available in other problems you might want to solve.

Notice that in the *right_is_clear*? method, if we reverse the order of the last two messages in the body, then the *return* instruction will be executed before the *turn_left* (only when **front_is_clear**?() is false of course).

But since the return will terminate the predicate, we won't ever execute the *turn_left*. This would be an intent error, since it wouldn't leave the robot facing the original direction as was intended.

It is a fact that in Ruby, every method returns something. In the absence of anything else, it will return nil or the value of the last expression evaluated in the body of the method. The basic five methods of UrRobot actually return a reference to the robot that just executed the method: self.

5.3 Simple Examples of the IF Instruction

This section examines three new methods that use the IF instruction. During our discussion we will also discuss how IF instructions are checked for correctness.

5.3.1 The harvest_one_row Method

Let's give karel a new task similar to the harvesting task discussed in Section 3.8.1. Karel's new task still requires the robot to harvest the same size field, but this time there is no guarantee that a beeper is on each corner of the field. Because karel's original program for this task would cause an error shutoff when it tried to execute a pick_beeper on any barren corner, we must modify it to avoid executing illegal pick_beeper instructions. Karel must harvest a beeper only if it determines that one is present.

Knowing about the new IF instruction, we can now write a program for this slightly more general task. One sample initial situation is illustrated in Figure 5-1.

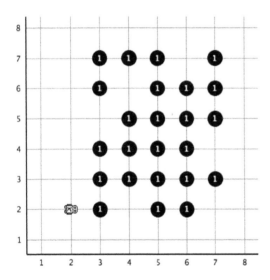

Figure 5-1: A Modified Harvest Task-not all corners have beepers

Please notice that this is only one of many possible initial situations. Our program must be able to harvest this size field (six by five) regardless of which corners have beepers and which corners do not.

Luckily for us, most of our previously written harvesting program can be reused -- another advantage of object-oriented programming with classes. All we need to do is to create a new version of the harvest_corner method in a new subclass of Harvester. The new version of harvest_corner only picks up a beeper if it knows there is one on the current corner. To do this we create a new class, SparseHarvester, whose parent class is Harvester. We will also, however, need to either modify Harvester so that its parent class is Robot rather than UrRobot OR, have the SparseHarvester include the SensorPack as well. With either of these options we can take advantage of the predicates defined in class Robot. We prefer the second option, since changing existing programs that once worked often lead to error.

```
class SparseHarvester < Harvester
    include SensorPack

    def harvest_corner()
        if next_to_a_beeper?()
            pick_beeper()
        end
    end
end
```

5.3.2 The face_north_if_facing_south Method

This section will demonstrate how we decide when to use the IF instruction and how we decide what condition we want a robot to check in <test>. As part of this and future discussions, let's assume we are planning and implementing the solution to a large problem where a robot named karel is on a treasure hunt for the "Lost Beeper Mine" which is a very large pile of beepers.

Let's further assume that we have developed an overall plan and are working on one small task within this plan. This task requires that karel face to the north only if it is currently facing south. In Chapter 3 we introduced a question and answer format to show how we might plan and analyze possible ways to solve a problem. The same format also works well in the implementing phase of problem solving.

Question: What does karel have to do?

Answer: Karel must turn to face north only if it is currently facing south.

Question: How many alternatives does the robot have to choose from?

Answer: Two.

Question: What are these alternatives?

Answer: Alternative #1 is to turn to the north if it is facing south. Alternative #2 is to do nothing if it is facing any other direction.[8]

Question: What instruction can we use to allow karel to decide which alternative to choose?

Answer: The IF instruction allows karel to decide which alternative to choose.

―――――――――――――――

[8]Note that since there are two behaviors here, you might want to look for a polymorphic solution to this problem, but our purpose here is to demonstrate the IF statement.

Question: What test can karel use in the IF instruction?

Answer: Since karel is supposed to turn to the north only if it is facing to the south, the facing_south? test can be used.

Question: What does karel do if it is facing south?

Answer: Karel will turn_left twice.

Question: What does karel do if it is not facing south?

Answer: Karel does nothing.

The thought process for implementing each instruction definition in our program must be as careful and detailed as it was when we were developing our original plan for the solution. Each step must be carefully analyzed for its strengths and weaknesses. If we ask a question and we cannot answer it satisfactorily, then either we have asked the wrong question or our plan for the instruction's definition is flawed. The longer we spend thinking about the implementation, the less time we will spend correcting errors. Having taken the time to analyze our answers, our instruction implementation looks like this. We assume here that we are building a new class, Prospector, of robots that can search for the Lost Beeper Mine.

```
def face_north_if_facing_south()
    if  facing_south?()
        turn_left()
        turn_left()
    end
end
```

5.3.3 The face_north Method

Here is a new problem to solve. Let's assume we are planning the definition of another part of the Lost Beeper Mine problem. We must implement an instruction definition that faces a robot north regardless of the direction it is currently facing. Using the question/answer format, we approach this solution by first thinking about karel's situation. Can we use the information about the direction karel is currently facing to solve the problem?

Question: What does karel have to do?

Answer: It must determine which direction it is facing to decide how many turn_lefts to execute so it will be facing north.

Question: How many different alternatives does the robot have?

Answer: Karel has one alternative for each direction it could be facing. Therefore, it has four alternatives.

Question: What are these alternatives?

Answer: Alternative #1 facing north - do nothing.

Alternative #2 facing east - turn left once.

Alternative #3 facing south - turn left twice.

Alternative #4 facing west - turn left three times.

Question: What test(s) can karel use to decide which direction it is facing?

Answer: Karel can check to see if it is **facing_east**?, **facing_south**?, **facing_west**?--since karel does not have to do anything when it is facing north, we do not have to use that test.

We can use these questions and their answers to aid us in implementing the new method, **face_north**.

```
def face_north()
    if facing_east?()
        turn_left()
    end
    if facing_south?()
        turn_left()
        turn_left()
    end
    if facing_west?()
        turn_left()
        turn_left()
        turn_left()
    end
end
```

Compare this method to the set of questions preceding it. Did we ask all of the necessary questions? Did we answer them correctly? Trace this method for execution and simulate it four times, one for each direction karel could initially be facing. Does it work in all cases?

There is another way to solve this problem. Examine this set of questions.

Question: What does karel have to do?

Answer: Karel must turn_left until it is facing north.

Question: How many alternatives does the robot have?

Answer: Two.

Question: What are they?

Answer: Alternative # 1 is to turn_left if it is not facing north.

Alternative # 2 is to do nothing if it is already facing north.

Question: How can we use this information?

Answer: Karel can never be more than three turn_lefts away from facing north so we can use a sequence of three IF instructions; each one will check to see if karel is not facing_north?. If the test is true, karel will turn_left and be one turn_left closer to facing north.

Question: What happens when karel starts out facing north?

Answer: All three tests will be false and karel does nothing.

Question: What happens when karel is facing east?

Answer: The first test is true and karel executes a turn_left. The remaining two tests are false and karel does nothing.

Question: What happens when karel is facing south?

Answer: The first two tests are true so karel executes two turn_lefts. The third test is false and its THEN clause is skipped.

Question: What happens when karel is facing west?

Answer: All three tests will be true so karel will execute three turn_lefts.

Here is our resulting new instruction.

```
def face_north()
    if not facing_north?()
        turn_left()
    end
    if not facing_north?()
        turn_left()
    end
    if not facing_north?()
        turn_left()
    end
end
```

Trace this instruction for execution and simulate it four times, one for each direction karel could initially be facing. Does it work in all cases? We will see alternatives later in the Chapter.

The question must be asked as to which of these two face_north instructions is better. For now, either is perfectly acceptable.

5.3.4 Determining the correctness of the IF Instruction

Checking an IF instruction is similar to checking a dictionary entry, since both are *meaningful* components of a program. Both IF instructions and method definitions use reserved words and indentation to separate their different parts. You check the IF instruction by first checking the <test>, making sure it is correct and is addressed to some robot. You then check the instructions inside the indented list. Make sure you have what you need, but only what you need. Check for the end delimiter. Finally, you check the entire IF instruction, examining it as a whole.

Note that an IF instruction IS an instruction, but it also contains instructions. There is usually at least one instruction in the indented instruction list but there may be none at all.

Study, for example, the version of capture_the_beeper that follows.

```
def capture_the_beeper()
   move()
   if next_to_a_beeper?()
      pick_beeper()
      turn_around()
   end
   move()
end
```

This definition contains three instructions: the first move, the IF and the second move. The two messages inside the block of the IF are properly indented and there is an end. The predicate is correct (addressed to self, of course). It seems OK. Notice, however, that it leaves us in one of two different places, facing in one of two different directions, depending on whether it finds a beeper or not. It might be important in some problems to avoid this difference since other instructions will be executed after this one. If we are not careful, the robot could wander away from the desired path. We try to be careful to pick a name for a method that describes all that the robot will do when executing it. We also generally try to leave the robot in the same state regardless of how it executes the instruction when that makes sense in the overall problem. We at least try to be specific about the final situation: the post-condition. Section 5.4 will help in this.

5.3.5 A Ruby Shortcut

Ruby has a shortcut that you can use in simple situations. If you have a single statement that should be executed only conditionally you can replace this:

```
if next_to_a_beeper?()
   pick_beeper()
end
```

with this:

```
pick_beeper() if next_to_a_beeper?()
```

Notice that both phrasings are similar to constructions used in ordinary language. The latter is a bit more compact and makes the intent just as clear. But don't try to over use this, especially in complex situations or with long and complex tests, such as we will see soon. The *if* must appear on the same line as the command that it modifies, but the test can extend over more than one line if necessary, but it is usually ugly if you need to do so, and might be better with an ordinary IF statement. The part of the command that begins with the token if is called a statement modifier. Others are possible as well. For example, if you have a front_is_blocked? predicate it is legal to say

```
move() unless front_is_blocked?()
```

The word unless is like "if not"

5.4 The IF/ELSE Instruction

In this section we discuss the ELSE variation of the IF instruction built into the robot vocabulary. The IF/ELSE instruction is useful when, depending on the result of some test, a robot must execute one of two alternative instructions. The general form of the IF/ELSE is given below.

```
if <test>
    <instruction-list-1>
else
    <instruction-list-2>
end
```

The form of the IF/ELSE is similar to the IF instruction, except that it includes an ELSE clause. A robot executes an IF/ELSE in much the same manner as an IF. It first determines whether <test> is true or false in the current situation. If <test> is true, the robot executes <instruction-list-1>; if <test> is false, it executes <instruction-list-2> instead. Thus, depending on its current situation, the robot executes either <instruction-list-1> or <instruction-list-2>, but not both. By the way, the first instruction list in an IF/ELSE instruction is called the *THEN clause* and the second instruction list is called the *ELSE clause*. Note that there is only one end here.

Let's look at a task that uses the IF/ELSE instruction. Suppose that we want to program a robot to run a one mile long hurdle race, where vertical wall sections represent hurdles. The hurdles are only one block high and are randomly placed between any two corners in the race course. One of the many possible race courses for this task is illustrated in Figure 5-2. Here we think of the world as being vertical with down being south. We require the robot to jump if, and only if, faced with a hurdle.

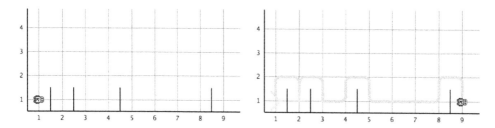

Figure 5-2: A Hurdle Jumping Race (before and after)

The robot could easily run this race by jumping between every pair of corners, but although this strategy is simple to program, it doesn't meet the requirements. (Perhaps it would slow the robot down too much.) Instead, we must program the robot to move straight ahead when it can, and jump over hurdles only when it must. The program implementing this strategy consists of a main task block that contains eight race_stride messages followed by a turn_off. The definition of race_stride can be written using stepwise refinement as follows.

```
class Racer < Robot

    def race_stride()
        if front_is_clear?()
            move()
        else
            jump_hurdle()
        end
    end
```

We continue our refinement by writing jump_hurdle.

```
    def jump_hurdle()
        jump_up()
        move()
        glide_down()
    end
```

Finally, we write jump_up and glide_down, the methods needed to complete the definition of jump_hurdle.

```
    def jump_up()
        turn_left()
        move()
        turn_right()
    end

    def glide_down()
        turn_right()
        move()
        turn_left()
    end
  end # of Racer
```

But now we notice that we also need to turn_right, so we include our Turner mixin in the class as usual. To verify that these methods are correct, complete and assemble the program. Then simulate a Racer robot running the race in Figure 5-2.

5.5 Nested IF Instructions

Although we have seen many IF instructions, we have ignored an entire class of complex IF'S. These are known as nested IF instructions because they are written with an IF instruction nested inside the THEN or ELSE clause of another IF. No new execution rules are needed to simulate nested IF's, but a close adherence to the established rules is required. Simulating nested IF instructions is sometimes difficult because it is easy for us to lose track of where we are in the instruction. The following discussion should be read carefully and understood completely as an example of how to test instructions that include nested IF's.

To demonstrate a nested IF instruction, we propose a task that redistributes beepers in a field. This task requires that a robot named karel traverse a field and leave exactly one beeper on each corner. The robot must plant a beeper on each barren corner and remove one beeper from every corner where two beepers are present. All corners in this task are constrained to have zero, one, or two beepers on them. One sample initial and final situation is displayed in Figure 5-3. In these situations, multiple beepers on a corner are represented by a number. We can assume that karel has enough beepers in its beeper-bag to replant the necessary number of corners.

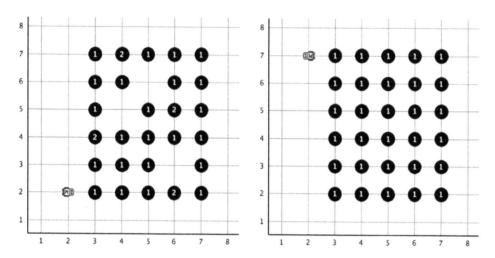

Figure 5.3: A Beeper Replanting Task (before and after)

```
class Replanter < FieldHarvester
   include SensorPack

   def harvest_corner()
      if not next_to_a_beeper?()
         put_beeper()
      else
         pick_beeper()
         if not next_to_a_beeper?()
            put_beeper()
         end
      end
   end
end
```

The heart of the program that solves this task is the method above that enables karel to satisfy the one-beeper requirement for each corner. We provide an override method for the harvest_corner method of the Harvester class.

The outer IF statement in this definition is an IF/ELSE and the nested IF statement is an ordinary IF. The nested IF instruction is inside the ELSE clause of the outer IF. Next, we simulate karel in the three possible corner situations: an empty corner, a corner with one beeper, and a corner with two beepers.

In the empty corner situation, karel executes the outer IF and determines that the test is true. The robot executes the put_beeper message in the THEN clause placing one beeper on the corner. Karel has now finished executing the outer IF instruction and thus has finished executing harvest_corner.

Next we assume that there is one beeper on karel's corner. Karel first executes the outer IF. The test is false so the robot executes the ELSE clause. This clause consists of two instructions, pick_beeper and the nested IF instruction. Karel picks the beeper and performs the test associated with the nested IF. The test is true so karel executes the THEN clause of this IF instruction and puts a beeper back on the empty corner. Karel is now finished with the nested IF, the ELSE clause, the outer IF, and the entire harvest_corner instruction.

Finally, we assume that karel is on a corner with two beepers. Karel executes the outer IF, finds the test is false, and then executes the ELSE clause. Karel picks up one of the two beepers on the corner. Up to this point karel has duplicated its actions in the one-beeper situation, but now comes the difference in execution. Karel executes the nested IF instruction, finds the test is false, and skips the nested IF'S THEN clause. Once again, karel is now finished with the nested IF, the ELSE clause, the outer IF, and the entire harvest_corner instruction.

We want to emphasize that when nested IF instructions seem too intricate we should try replacing the nested IF with a new message instruction. The definition of the associated method must command karel to perform the same actions as the nested IF and may help us better understand what karel is doing. Because nesting also makes an instruction less readable, a good rule of thumb is to avoid nesting IF instructions more than one level deep. The harvest_corner method, which has one level of nesting, is rewritten below using an auxiliary method. Simpler methods are easier to understand and, therefore, easier to use.

```
class Replanter < FieldHarvester
    include SensorPack

    def harvest_corner()
        if not next_to_a_beeper?()
            put_beeper()
        else
            next_to_one_replant_one()
        end
    end
end
```

We write the next_to_one_replant_one method by copying the ELSE clause from our original definition of harvest_corner.

```
    def next_to_one_replant_one()
        pick_beeper()
        if not next_to_a_beeper?()
            put_beeper()
        end
    end
```

We can use the shortcut introduced in Section 5.3.5 to help us here and increase the readability of our program somewhat. We replace the nested if instruction with a command modified with unless.

```
def harvest_corner()
  if not next_to_a_beeper?()
    put_beeper()
  else
    pick_beeper()
    put_beeper() unless next_to_a_beeper?()
  end
end
```

We still have a nested if, but it isn't so obvious and the reduced "clutter" of the if...end is helpful. But there are a lot of negatives expressed in this (not, unless). Section 5.9 will show a way to reduce it somewhat.

Given the entire program from Section 3.9.1 along with any of these new definitions of the harvest_corner method, do we have a correct solution for the beeper replanting task? We may consider using our old method of verification and test the program with karel in every possible initial situation, but there are more than 200 trillion[9] different fields that this program must be able to replant correctly! Attempting verification by exhaustively testing karel in every possible initial situation would be ludicrous.

Instead, we will try to establish correctness based on the following informal argument: (1) we have verified that harvest_corner works correctly on any corner that is empty or contains one or two beepers, and (2) we can easily verify that our program commands karel to execute this instruction on each corner of the field. Therefore, we conclude that the program correctly replants the entire field.

This argument further enhances the claim that karel's mechanism for instruction definition is a powerful aid to programming. Usually, we can informally conclude that an entire program is correct by verifying that: (1) each new instruction in the program works correctly in all possible situations in which it can be executed, and (2) the program executes each new instruction at the appropriate time. This method allows us to verify a program by splitting it into separate, simpler, verifications, just as stepwise refinement allows us to write a program by splitting it into separate, simpler instructions.

Suppose that a robot is in a situation in which it must determine if there are exactly two beepers on the current corner. We would like to write a predicate to return true if this is so, and false otherwise. We imagine that this is needed in some replanting task, so we will add it to the Replanter class. We can write such a predicate if we pick up beepers one at a time and then ask if there are any more. We must remember to put back any beepers that we pick up, however. Otherwise it will be more than just a predicate, having modified the current situation. Note that if we have picked two beepers up, we still need to ask if there are any more to determine if there are exactly two beepers on the current corner.

```
def exactly_two_beepers?()
  if next_to_a_beeper?()        # one or more beepers
    pick_beeper()
    if next_to_a_beeper?()      # two or more beepers
      pick_beeper()
      if next_to_a_beeper?()    # more than two
        put_beeper()
        put_beeper()
```

[9]There are 3 different possibilities for each corner; and there are 30 corners in the field. The total number of different fields is thus 3 multiplied by itself 30 times. For you mathemagicians, the exact number of different fields is 205,891,132,094,649.

```
                    return false
             else  # exactly two beepers
                put_beeper()
                put_beeper()
                return true
             end
        else  # only one beeper
           put_beeper()
           return false
        end
     else  # no beepers
        return false
     end
  end
```

This is about the limit of how far we should nest such statements, or perhaps over the limit. Any more than this and they become very difficult to understand. Actually two levels is much better than three. You should always define a new instruction for the inner IF statement and if you name it well, the entire structure will be much easier to understand. Try it yourself for the above instruction.

5.6 More Complex Tests

It may not be a trivial matter to have a robot make two or more tests at the same time. Programming languages provide the capability to make multiple tests within an IF or an IF/ELSE instruction. We can do this but we must be careful in our thinking as illustrated by the following example.

Let's assume we are still working on the Lost Beeper Mine problem introduced earlier. Recall that the Lost Beeper Mine is a very large pile of beepers. We have another assignment from that problem--a very important landmark along the way is found where all of the following are true:

* karel is facing west,

* karel's right side is blocked,

* karel's left side is blocked,

* karel's front is clear, and

* there is at least one beeper on the corner.

Following these requirements we must plan an instruction that will test all of these conditions simultaneously. If we do what seems logical we might try to write something like this:

```
if    facing_west?()
      and right_is_blocked?()
      and left_is_blocked?()
      and front_is_clear?()
      and next_to_a_beeper?()
   <instruction>
end # not quite legal - see below
```

This seems very logical, but there is one problem. However, if we use a sequence of nested IF instructions to do the job the result will be very ugly.

```
if facing_west?()
   if not right_is_clear?()
      if not left_is_clear?()
         if front_is_clear?()
            if next_to_a_beeper?()
               <instruction>
            end
         end
      end
   end
end
```

If we trace this, we will find that all of the tests must evaluate to true before karel can execute <instruction>.

Fortunately, Ruby and the robot programming language have an operator for AND, and it is spelled *and* (lower case). So the original form can be made to work, but we also need to tell the language processor that we have an expression written on more than one line. The way to tell Ruby that an expression spreads over several lines is to put a backslash character, "\", at the end of each line except the last. This gives us the following:

```
if    facing_west?() \
      and right_is_blocked?() \
      and left_is_blocked?() \
      and front_is_clear?() \
      and next_to_a_beeper?()
   <instruction>
end
```

The entire five clause "and" expression is just an expression and an IF test requires an expression, so it is legal, but they do get rather long. But of course the right_is_blocked? and other predicates must also be defined.

Another way to build complex tests is to define new predicates. Suppose we would like to write

```
if next_to_a_beeper?() and left_is_blocked?() # which is legal
   ...
```

We could, if we like, write the following predicate, which is equivalent. There is no real need for this, given the and operator, but it is instructive to examine it. For example:

```
def next_to_a_beeper_AND_left_is_blocked?()
    if next_to_a_beeper?()
        if not left_is_clear?()
            return true
        else
            return false
        end
    end
    return false
end
```

This can be simplified to:

```
def next_to_a_beeper_AND_left_is_blocked?()
    if next_to_a_beeper?()
        return not left_is_clear?()
    end
    return false
end
```

One way to help determine if a predicate with two or more conditions is correct is to look at the truth table, which gives all possible combinations of the parts of the predicate. The truth table for AND is shown below.

next_to_a_beeper?	left_is_blocked?		AND
T	T		T
T	F		F
F	T		F
F	F		F

The IF instruction in the predicate says that when **next_to_a_beeper**? is true we should return the negation of left_is_clear?, which is the same as left_is_blocked?. Note that the first two lines of the truth table also say this. On these two lines **next_to_a_beeper**? is true and the **left_is_blocked**? lines exactly match the AND lines here. Likewise, the predicate says that when next_to_a_beeper? is false we should return false. Again, this matches the truth table exactly, since on the last two lines, where **next_to_a_beeper**? is false, we return false.

Note that in the next_to_a_beeper _AND_left_is_blocked? instruction there is no need to check that the left is clear if we have already determined that we are NOT next to a beeper. We can simply return false in this case. We only need to check the second part of the AND when the first part is true. This is known as *short-circuit evaluation* of the predicate, and it is very useful. To use it wisely when you write your own predicates, however, so that a user isn't misled, you must check the leftmost part (**next_to_a_beeper**?) first. The Ruby *and* operator also uses this short circuit evaluation. In short-circuit evaluation of a complex predicate only enough of the expression is evaluated (starting at the left, or inside parentheses) to establish the truth of the value and remaining clauses are not evaluated at all.

Similarly we can say

```
if next_to_a_beeper?() or left_is_blocked?()
    ...
```

using the Ruby *or*. The truth table for an OR is as follows. Notice that when **next_to_a_beeper**? is true the OR is also true, and when **next_to_a_beeper**? is false the result is the same as left_is_blocked?.

```
next_to_a_beeper?    left_is_blocked?    |    OR
       T                    T            |    T
       T                    F            |    T
       F                    T            |    T
       F                    F            |    F
```

The or expression above is equivalent to the following, which also demonstrates the short-circuit evaluation.

```
def next_to_a_beeper_OR_left_is_blocked?()
    if next_to_a_beeper?()
        return true
    end
    return not left_is_clear?()
end
```

Note also that the *and* and the *or* operators have the same precedence in Ruby. This means that in a sequence of terms separated by these operators the operators are applied left to right. If you wish it otherwise, you can use parentheses, just as in arithmetic expressions using addition and multiplication. The rules are that you apply the operators in parentheses first, otherwise apply the higher precedence operators before lower, and also work left to right among operators of the same precedence. The *or* operator also uses short-circuit evaluation. If the left expression (**next_to_a_beeper**?, here) is true the result is already known to be true. Ruby has two additional operators && and ‖ that are similar to *and* and *or* respectively, but && has higher precedence than ‖ (and both are higher than *and* and *or*). Operator precedence can get somewhat complex in Ruby so we mostly avoid it here and use *and* and *or* when necessary.

5.7 The IF/ELSIF and IF/ELSIF/ELSE Instructions

We will give only a brief introduction to this instruction. It is really just a shorthand for things we can already do. Let's look again at the first of our face_north instructions and suppose our robot is initially facing East:

```
def face_north()
    if facing_east?()
        turn_left()
    end
    if facing_south?()
        turn_left()
        turn_left()
    end
    if facing_west?()
        turn_left()
```

```
            turn_left()
            turn_left()
        end
    end
```

Note that after we finish the first IF, the robot is facing North so the second and third IF tests will fail. There is, therefore, no need to execute them. So we could re-write the above as:

```
def face_north()
    if facing_east?()
        turn_left()
    else
        if facing_south?()
            turn_left()
            turn_left()
        else
            if facing_west?()
                turn_left()
                turn_left()
                turn_left()
            end
        end
    end
end
```

This is a bit more efficient for the robot, but ugly for us to read. Nesting really seems to get in the way. Therefore Ruby provides another solution: elsif. This is really a run-on of else and if. So a final form would look like this.

```
def face_north()
    if facing_east?()
        turn_left()
    elsif facing_south?()
        turn_left()
        turn_left()
    elsif facing_west?()
        turn_left()
        turn_left()
        turn_left()
    end
end
```

Here we have the efficiency along with the readability. Note the indentation. The ELSIF clauses line up with the IF and their statement blocks are indented as usual. Such a structure can also have a final else clause. The execution of it is as follows. The first IF test is checked and if true, the first instruction block is executed after which the instruction is finished and nothing more is checked or done. If the first is false, the next (the first ELSIF test) is checked, and if true the corresponding statement block is executed and the entire statement is then done, etc. If none of the tests are true then nothing is done if there is no ELSE clause at the end. If there is an ELSE clause in this case, then the block after ELSE is executed, but none of the others. We could add a dummy ELSE part above, just to show it as:

```
def face_north()
    if facing_east?()
        turn_left()
    elsif facing_south?()
        turn_left()
        turn_left()
    elsif facing_west?()
        turn_left()
        turn_left()
        turn_left()
    else
        # nothing
    end
end
```

Notice that we comment the "do nothing" Sometimes it is useful to write such an empty else block to make explicit that there is nothing to do in this case. Otherwise, you might come back to it in the future and wonder if you really meant to put something there and just forgot it. You will then spend time figuring out the logic again.

And notice that the elsif comes in to play when you have more than two possibilities for what is required in your problem. You may have as many ELSIF clauses as your problem may require, but ELSE, if present, is always last and each ELSIF has an additional test. And remember, the tests are checked in order.

5.8 When to Use an IF Instruction

Thus far we have spent most of our time and effort in this chapter explaining how the IF and the IF/ELSE instructions work. It is at this point that students are usually told, "Write a program that uses the IF and the IF/ELSE instructions so that a robot can..." It is also at this point that we hear the following question being asked by students, "I understand how these work but I don't understand when to use them." It is "understanding when to use them" that is the focus of this section.

Let's review what the IF and the IF/ELSE instructions allow robots to do in a robot program:

* The IF instruction allows a robot to decide whether to execute or skip entirely the block of instructions within the THEN clause.

* The IF/ELSE instruction allows a robot to decide whether to execute the block of instructions in the THEN clause or the ELSE clause.

* The IF/ELSIF /ELSE instruction allows a robot to try a series of tests in order and execute the block of instructions associated with the first true test.

* Nesting these instructions allows karel to make more complex choices if required.

We can use these statements to build a decision map. A decision map is a technique that asks questions about the problem we are trying to solve. The answers to the questions determine the branch we follow through the map. Here is the section of the decision map that a programmer would use for choosing between an IF and an IF/ELSE.

To use this part of the decision map we must be at a point during our implementation where a robot needs to choose from among alternatives. We use the map by asking each question as we encounter it and following the path that has the answer. If done correctly, we eventually arrive at an implementation suggestion. If the map does not work, we probably do not need to choose between alternatives or have not correctly thought out our plan. By the way, we say we choose from among one alternative as a shorthand for the situation where the choice is simply to do something or not.

Suppose a robot must face north if there is a beeper on the current corner and face south otherwise. How many tests does the robot have to make? One-either *next_to_a_beeper?* or *not next_to_a_beeper?*. This answer directs us down the left path to the next question, how many alternatives does the robot have available? Two-the robot must either face north or face south. This takes us down the path to the IF/ELSE instruction. Our implementation looks like this.

```
if next_to_a_beeper?()
    face_north()
else
    face_south()
end
```

5.9 Transformations for Simplifying IF Instructions

This section discusses four useful transformations that help us simplify programs containing IF instructions. We start by observing that when two program fragments result in a robot's performing exactly the same actions, we call this pair of fragments *execution equivalent*. For a simple example, turn_left(); put_beeper() is execution equivalent to put_beeper(); turn_left().

In general, we can create one execution equivalent IF/ELSE instruction from another by replacing <test> with its opposite and interchanging the THEN and the ELSE clauses as illustrated below. We call this transformation *test reversal*. Notice that if we perform test reversal twice on the same instruction, we get back to the instruction with which we started.

```
if front_is_clear?()           if not front_is_clear?()
    move()                         jump_hurdle()
else                           else
    jump_hurdle()                  move()
end                            end
```

Generally speaking we prefer the positive, rather than the negative forms of tests, so we prefer the first of the above forms over the second. This is not an absolute rule, but it is the reason why the built in predicate is called **front_is_clear**? rather than front_is_blocked?. The first seems to be stated more positively.

What does the robot need to do at this point in the program?

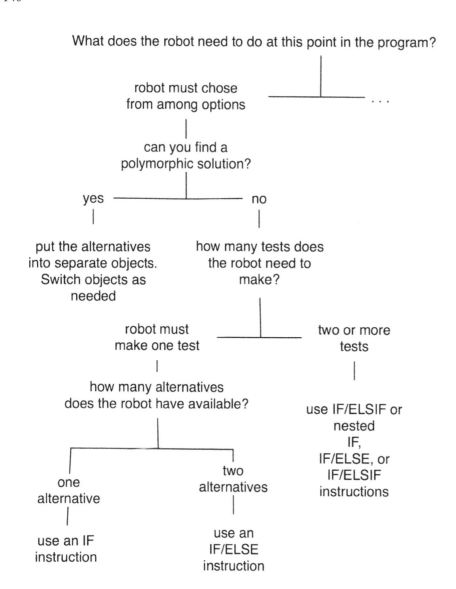

Figure 5-4 Part of the Decision Map

Test reversal can be used to help novice programmers overcome the following difficulty. Suppose that we start to write an IF instruction and get ourselves into the dilemma illustrated below on the left. The problem is that we want a robot to do nothing special when its front is clear[10] but when its front is blocked we want karel to execute <instruction >. We would like to remove the THEN clause. The solution to our problem is illustrated on the right.

```
if front_is_clear?()        if not front_is_clear?()
    do_nothing()                <instruction>>
else                        end
    <instruction>
end
```

To transform the IF on the left into the IF on the right, we use test reversal. First we change <test> to its opposite, then switch the doNothing instruction into the ELSE clause and bring <instruction> into the THEN clause. By the previous discussion of test reversal, execution equivalence is preserved. Finally, the new ELSE clause (which contains the doNothing instruction) can be removed, resulting in the simpler IF instruction on the right.

The second transformation we discuss is *bottom factoring*. Bottom factoring is illustrated below, where we will show that the IF/ELSE instruction on the left is execution equivalent to the program fragment on the right. We have kept the bracketed words in these instructions because their exact replacements do not affect this transformation.

```
if <test>                   if <test>
    <instruction_1>             <instruction_1>
    <instruction_3>         else
else                            <instruction_2>
    <instruction_2>         end
    <instruction_3>         <instruction_3>
end
```

In the program fragment on the right, we have factored <instruction _3> out of the bottom of each clause in the IF. We justify the correctness of this transformation as follows: If <test> is true, the instruction on the left has the robot execute <instruction_1> directly followed by <instruction_3>. In the program fragment on the right, if <test> is true the robot executes <instruction_1> and then, having finished the IF, it executes <instruction_3>. Thus, when <test> is true, these forms are execution equivalent. A similar argument holds between the left and right fragments whenever <test> is false.

In summary, <instruction _3> is executed in the IF on the left regardless of whether <test> is true or false. So we might as well remove it from each clause and put it directly after the entire IF/ELSE instruction. Moreover, if the bottoms of each clause were larger, but still identical, we could bottom factor all of the common instructions and still preserve execution equivalence. Think of this process as bottom factoring one instruction at a time until all common instructions have been factored. Since execution equivalence is preserved during each factoring step, the resulting program fragment is execution equivalent to the original.

---

[10]We can define the method do_nothing as four left turns. Executing this instruction would leave karel's position unchanged, and this instruction is also immune to error shutoffs. This would be wasteful of the Robot's battery capacity, however. We can also use just a comment as we have done before: # nothing

The third transformation we discuss in this section is *top factoring*. Although this transformation may seem as simple and easy to use as bottom factoring, we will see that not all instructions can be top factored successfully. We divide our discussion of this transformation into three parts. First, we examine an instruction that can safely be top factored. Then we show an instruction that cannot be top factored successfully. Finally, we state a general rule that tells us which IF instructions can safely be top factored.

Top factoring can safely be used in the following example to convert the instruction on the left into the simpler program fragment on the right. These two forms can be shown to be execution equivalent by a justification similar to the one used in our discussion of bottom factoring.

```
if facing_north?()          move()
    move()                  if facing_north?()
    turn_left()                 turn_left()
else                        else
    move()                      turn_right()
    turn_right()            end
end
```

In the next example, we have incorrectly used the top factoring transformation. We will discover that the program fragment on the right is not execution equivalent to the instruction on the left.

```
if next_to_a_beeper?()      move()
    move()                  if next_to_a_beeper?()
    turn_left()                 turn_left()
else                        else
    move()                      turn_right()
    turn_right()            end
end
```

To show that these forms execute differently, let's assume that a robot named karel is on a corner containing one beeper, and that the corner in front of the robot is barren. If karel executes the instruction on the left, the robot will first find that it is next to a beeper, and then will execute the THEN clause of the IF by moving forward and turning to its left. The program fragment on the right will first move karel forward to the next corner and then will instruct it to test for a beeper. Since this new corner does not contain a beeper, karel will execute the ELSE clause of the IF, which causes the robot to turn to its right. Thus, top factoring in this example does not preserve execution equivalence.

Why can we correctly use top factoring in the first example but not in the second? The first instruction can be top factored safely because the test that determines which way karel is facing is not changed by having it move forward. Therefore, whether karel moves first or not, the evaluation of the test will remain unchanged. But in the second example, the move changes the corner on which karel checks for a beeper, so the robot is not performing the test under the same conditions. The general rule is that we may top factor an instruction only when the conditions under which the test is performed do not change between the original and factored versions of the instruction. This is complicated, of course, if some of the methods have been overridden.

The fourth and final transformation is used to remove redundant tests in nested IF instructions. We call this transformation *redundant-test-factoring* and show one application of this rule.

```
if facing_west?()              if facing_west?()
   move()                         move()
   if facing_west?()              turn_left()
      turn_left()              end
   end
end
```

In the instruction on the left, there is no need for the nested IF instruction to recheck the condition **facing_west**?. The THEN clause of the outer IF is only executed if karel is facing west, and the move inside the THEN clause does not normally change the direction that karel is facing. Therefore, facing_west? is always true when karel executes this nested IF instruction. This argument shows that karel always executes the THEN clause of this nested IF. So, the entire nested IF instruction can be replaced by turn_left, as has been done in the instruction on the right. Once again, this transformation preserves execution equivalence. Of course, if we have given move a new meaning in the class of which this is a member, then we cannot guarantee that move doesn't change the direction. In this case the two fragments would not be equivalent. A similar transformation applies whenever we look for a redundant test in an ELSE clause. Remember, though, in an ELSE clause <test> is false.

This transformation is also a bit more subtle than bottom factoring, and we must be careful when trying to use it. The potential difficulty is that intervening instructions might change karel's position in an unknown way. For example, if instead of the move message we had used a **turn_around_if_next_to_a_beeper** message, we could not have used redundant-test factoring. Here we cannot be sure whether karel would be facing west or east when it had to execute the nested IF.

These four transformations can help us make our programs smaller, simpler, more logical, and--most important--more readable. Readability is a very important property of programs since we spend so much time trying to understand programs and modify them. This may not seem too important to you now, but programs that do something significant are usually built by teams of people who need to communicate effectively through the programs they write.

We said above that we prefer the positive form of a test when possible. There are some other tricks that you can use to make your programs more readable. One is not to use deeply nested structures, defining new predicates as necessary. Another is, when writing an IF-ELSE statement to arrange things so that if one of the clauses (THEN or ELSE) is very short and the other long, then choose a predicate so that the short one comes first as the THEN clause. This lets you read and understand it and move on to the other before you forget what the predicate is.

5.10 Polymorphism Revisited (Advanced Topic)

Since polymorphism is in many ways the most important topic of this book, we would like to say a few more things about it and see how it can be used in conjunction with IF statements to do some wonderful things. In a certain sense IF statements achieve a measure of polymorphism, called ad-hoc polymorphism, since the program must make explicit (or ad-hoc) decisions to provide alternate behavior. In some circumstances we don't have a choice of using IF statements or polymorphism to achieve an end, but when we do, polymorphism gives a more satisfactory result. This is because problems change and when they do, IF statements usually need to be modified. When a program contains a large number of IF statements and only some of them need to be changed for the new problem, it can be a major task keeping the updates consistent. In this section we will solve a few problems that use both IF statements and polymorphism to get a sense of the difference.

The situations in which we cannot use polymorphism in the robot language involve those things that cannot behave polymorphically. Beepers and walls are not objects, so we can't use polymorphism to deal with them. Robots on the other hand can behave (and always behave) polymorphically when sent messages, so with robot behavior we prefer polymorphism.

Here is a simple problem that we looked at in Chapter 4, but can extend here. Suppose we have a bunch of robots, one on each corner of first street from some avenue to some avenue farther on and we want to ask each of them to put down one beeper. We want to write a program that will work no matter how many robots there are. To make it explicit, suppose there is a robot on first street and n'th avenue and we want a robot with one beeper on each corner between the origin and this robot and then we want to ask them all to put down their beepers. We will use IF statements to set up the situation and then use polymorphism to get the robots to put down their beepers. Back in Chapter 4 we had to do the setup manually. Here we can automate it.

To do this we need at least two classes of robots, just as before. We will make a few changes to our BeeperPutter hierarchy of classes that we built in the previous chapter. We will make these classes a bit more polymorphic as well as illustrating how we can use IF statements to set up later polymorphic actions. Previously, BeeperPutter was an abstract class, with one method. We will add a method to it here.

```
# Abstract class for beeper putting robots"
class BeeperPutter < Robot
    include Turner

    def distribute_beepers()
       put_beeper()
       move()
    end

    def create_neighbor()
       raise NotImplementedError.new("Implemented in Subclasses")
    end
end
```

So, every subclass will need a create_neighbor instruction. In Chapter 4 we used the constructor to tell a robot who its neighbor is. Here we will not need to do that since each robot will create its own neighbor. Therefore, we want a *create_neighbor* method with no parameters. We will also want this method to be polymorphic. Since a NoNeighbor robot has no neighbor it needs to do nothing at all when it performs *create_neighbor*. Therefore we will implement a "no action" version of *create_neighbor* in the NoNeighbor subclass of BeeperPutter. The body of this version of *create_neighbor* is just the an empty instruction list.

In the *create_neighbor* method of NeighborTalker we will have a robot create its own neighbor. We want to be able to do this so that the neighbor is one street to the left of the given robot. Furthermore, if the robot is standing on second avenue then the neighbor it creates (on first avenue) will be a NoNeighbor robot rather than a NeighborTalker robot. If it creates a NeighborTalker, then it will send the *create_neighbor* message to the newly created neighbor.

We have a problem with this, however. No robot knows the corner on which it is standing, so it can't create this neighbor with a simple delivery specification. To do so would require knowing the street and avenue on which to place it. We will therefore need to use another way to create this neighbor.

Any robot can ask the factory to create a robot exactly like itself. When it does so, the newly created robot will be delivered to the corner on which the robot sits when it makes the request and will be set up in the same state as the existing robot: facing the same direction, with the same number of beepers. To do this we send the robot the *clone* message. A robot can even send this message to itself, of course, as it can with any other message. The clone message takes no parameters, but returns a new robot of the same class as the original. Thus, we see again that methods can return things other than Boolean values. Note that the meaning of clone is "faithful copy" and the built in UrRobot method will do this properly. It will even work for most of your robot classes as well, though we will discuss some exceptions in Section 6 of the Appendix.

Note that the clone method itself is highly polymorphic. When properly implemented it can be executed in any robot class and it always returns a robot of the same class and in the same state as the original.

Since we want the neighbor on the adjoining corner, we will move to that corner before sending the clone message. Then we can return to the original corner and send the newly-created neighbor the create_neighbor message. The exception will be when we discover that after the first move we find that front is blocked, meaning that we are about to create a robot on first avenue. In this case we want to create a NoNeighbor robot instead of a clone.

```ruby
class NeighborTalker < BeeperPutter

    def create_neighbor()
        move()
        if front_is_clear?()
            @neighbor = clone() # Create the copy
            @neighbor.create_neighbor()
        else
            @neighbor = NoNeighbor.new(1, 1, WEST, 1)
            @neighbor.turn_right()
        end
        back_up()
        turn_right()
    end

    def distribute_beepers()
        super()
        @neighbor.distribute_beepers()
    end
end
```

More on Ruby Cloning can be found in Section 6 of the Appendix.

With these changes our main task block becomes especially simple.

```ruby
def task()
    albert = NeighborTalker(1, 5, WEST, 1)
    albert.create_neighbor()
    albert.distribute_beepers()
end
```

When a robot is sent the create_neighbor message it creates the neighbor, but also sends that robot the create_neighbor message, which creates another, etc. This only ends when we reach a noNeighbor robot since its create_neighbor does nothing.

Let's focus for a moment on why we needed IF statements here and why the solution couldn't be entirely polymorphic. In the robot world the walls and beepers are not objects so we cannot build subclasses of them. They are just primitive data. Therefore, they cannot act polymorphically (or act at all, actually). The robots CAN be polymorphic but in this situation the robot needs to interact with a wall to find out if its front is clear. We therefore use the non-polymorphic tool, the IF statement, to set up the situation in which polymorphism can then act. Note that aside from clone the only method of interest here was distribute_beepers which was polymorphic. However, we could also have other polymorphic methods in these classes and, once the situation was set up, all of them would work without additional IF statements. Thus, if our problem changes, we can either add a new class for a new kind of robot that must behave differently from these, or we can add a new polymorphic method to each of these classes. We do not have to visit a large number of *if* statements and add a new part for each new part of the problem. At most we have to do the create_neighbor differently.

5.11 Important Ideas From This Chapter

selection
nested instructions
predicate
condition
statement transformation
execution equivalent
clone
if, else, elsif, unless

5.12 Problem Set

The problems in this section require the use of the IF instruction in its two forms. Try using stepwise refinement on these problems, but no matter what instruction you use to obtain a solution, write a clear and understandable program. Keep the nesting level small for those problems requiring nested IF instructions. Use proper punctuation and grammar, especially within the THEN and ELSE clauses of the IF instructions. Carefully simulate each definition and program that you write to ensure that there are no execution or intent errors.

1. Write a new predicate left_is_blocked? that determines if there is a wall exactly one half block away on a robot's left. Be sure that when it terminates, the robot is on the same corner and facing in the same direction.

2. Look at the following instruction. Is there a simpler, execution equivalent instruction? If so, write it down; if not, explain why. Hint: A simplifying transformation for the IF may prove useful. Common sense helps too.

```
if not next_to_a_beeper?()
   move()
else
   move()
end
```

3. Assume that a Prospector robot is on a corner with either one or two beepers. Write a new method that commands the robot to face north if it is started on a corner with one beeper and to face south if it is started on a corner with two beepers. Besides facing the robot in the required direction, after it has executed this method there must be no beepers left on the corner. Name this method find_next_direction.

4. Write another version of find_next_direction (see the previous problem). In this version the robot must eventually face the same directions, but it also must leave the same number of beepers on the corner as were there originally.

5. Write an instruction that turns a robot off if the robot is completely surrounded by walls, unable to move in any direction. If the robot is not surrounded, it should execute this instruction by leaving itself turned on, and by remaining on the same corner, facing the same direction in which it started. Name this instruction turn_off_if_surrounded. Hint: To write this instruction correctly, you will need to include a turn_off inside it. This combination is perfectly legal, but it is the first time that you will use a turn_off instruction outside the main task block.

6. Program a robot to run a mile long steeplechase. The steeplechase course is similar to the hurdle race, but here the barriers can be one, two, or three blocks high. Figure 5-5 shows one sample initial situation, where the robot's final situation and path are shown on the right. Call the class of this new robot Steeplechaser. It should have Racer as a parent class. Override appropriate instructions of Racer to implement the new behavior.

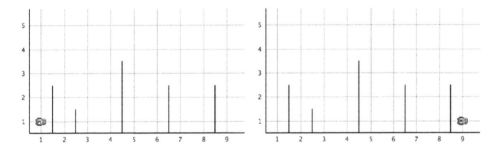

Figure 5-5 Steeplechase Race Task

7. Rewrite and check the following new instruction, taking care to interpret all of the robot programming grammar rules correctly. This instruction uses nested IF 's to face a robot toward the east; verify that it is correct by simulation.

```
def face_east( )
    if not facing_east?()
        if facing_west?()
            turn_left()
            turn_left()
        else
            if facing_north?()
                turn_right()
            else
                turn_left()
            end
```

```
        end
      end
  end
```

8. The current version of mysteryInstruction is syntactically correct, but very difficult to read. Simplify it by using the IF transformations.

```
def mystery_instruction()
    if facing_west?()
      move()
      turn_right()
      if facing_north?()
        move()
      end
      turn_around()
    else
      move()
      turn_left()
      move()
      turn_around()
    end
end
```

9. Write an instruction for the MazeWalker class named follow_wall_right, assuming that whenever a robot executes this instruction there is a wall directly to the right. Figure 5-6 shows four of the different position changes that the robot must be able to make. This instruction is the cornerstone for a program that directs a robot to escape from a maze (this maze-escape problem is Problem 6.11-17).

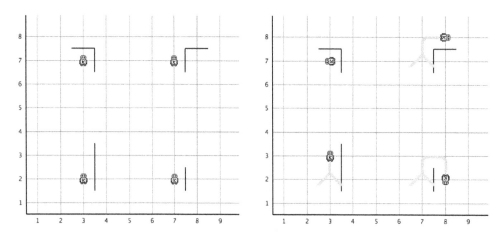

Figure 5-6 The follow-wall-right Specification

10. Program a robot to run a mile-long steeplechase where the steeples are made from beepers instead of wall segments. The robot must jump the steeples in this race by picking the beepers that make up the steeples. Each steeple is made from beepers that are positioned in columns that are one, two or three blocks long. Corners have either zero or one beeper. There are no gaps in any of the steeples. Figure 5-7 shows one sample initial situation.

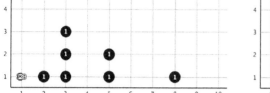 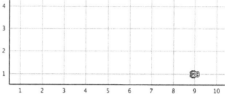

Figure 5-7 Different Steeplechase

11. A robot named karel has been hired to carpet some "small rooms" along a one mile section of its world. A "small room" is a corner that has a wall segment immediately to the west, north, and east. The door is to the south. Karel is to put a single beeper in only the "small rooms" and on no other corners. Figure 5-8 shows one set of initial and final situation s. You may assume that karel has exactly eight beepers in its beeper-bag.

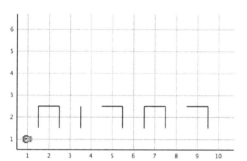 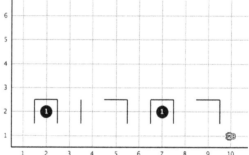

Figure 5-8 Carpeting Some Small Rooms

12. Karel did so well on the job in Problem 5.10-11 that the robot has been hired for a more complex carpeting task. The area to be carpeted is still one mile long. The rooms are now one, two or three blocks long. The room must have continuous walls on its west and east side and at its northern end. If any walls are missing, the area must not be carpeted. Also, karel must not reuse beepers. This means that once a beeper has been put down, it must not be picked up. Figure 5-9 shows one set of initial and final situations. You give karel exactly twenty-four beepers during construction and delivery.

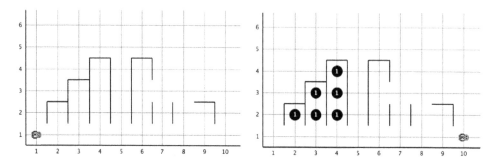

Figure 5-9 More Complex Carpet Laying

13. Write a predicate that will return true if and only if the robot executing it is both next to a beeper AND its left is blocked. Write another predicate that will return true if the robot executing it is either next to a beeper OR its left is blocked. In this latter case if the robot is next to a beeper with its left blocked it should also return true. Recall that nested IF 's can be used to implement AND. Similarly, a sequence of IF's can be used to implement OR. What general conclusions can you draw from this exercise?

14. Write a predicate that will return true if and only if the robot executing it is has exactly two beepers in its beeper-bag. Can we write a predicate that will return true if and only if the robot executing it is on a corner with exactly two other robots? Why or why not? Write another predicate that will return true if and only if the robot executing it is on a corner with at most two beepers.

15. We are used to writing tests to be sure that a robot doesn't get into trouble. For example:

```
if karel.front_is_clear?()
    karel.move()
end
```

However, there is a situation in some robot programs in which this is not safe. For example, if we override move. Suppose we do override move to do something other than move one block. What can we also do in the same class to make the above safe again?

16. Modify your solution to Problem 4.12-21 so that the spiral walking robot properly shuts off when it reaches a wall.

17. Rewrite the exactly_two_beepers? predicate to simplify it and make it easier to read and use. Write additional predicates as usual. Try to think of really good names for the parts.

6 Instructions That Repeat

This chapter completes our discussion of the instructions built into the robot programming language vocabulary. The two new instructions we will learn are FOR-LOOP and WHILE. Both instructions can repeatedly execute any instruction that a robot understands, including nested FOR-LOOP and WHILE instructions. These additions greatly enhance the conciseness and power of the robot programming language. In Section 6.8 we will construct a complex robot program by using stepwise refinement and all of the instructions we have learned. We also look again at iterators and blocks in this chapter.

Since we are becoming experienced robot programmers, an abbreviated view of the robot world will be used for some figures. To reduce visual clutter, the street and avenue labels and, occasionally, the southern or western boundary walls will not be shown. As usual, our examples will use a single robot, often named karel. Since most of our examples will involve manipulation of beepers, we suppose that we are building a class named BeeperController.

6.1 The FOR-LOOP Instruction

When we program a robot, having it repeat an instruction a certain number of times is sometimes necessary. We previously handled this problem by writing the instruction as many times as needed. The FOR-LOOP instruction gives us a mechanism which allows karel to repeat another instruction a specified number of times. More generally, it allows us to process all elements of a *sequence*. A sequence in Ruby is some linear arrangement of some kind of data. We have already seen arrays, though only simple forms of that. It is a sequence because you can go through the elements of it one after another. In fact the For-Loop is one of the major techniques for processing sequences of all kinds.

One especially simple kind of sequence is a *range*. A simple form of a range in Ruby is just a sequence of integer values. For example, 0..4 consists of the numbers 0 through 4 in order. Note that this range has five values in it. There are more complex forms of range, but this is all we shall need here.

In Ruby and in the Robot Programming Language, a simple FOR-LOOP has the following structure.

```
for <variable-name> in <sequence> do
    <instruction-list>
end
```

This instruction introduces the reserved words **for** and **in**. The elements in the <sequence> will determine how many times to execute the instruction list that replaces <instruction-list>. We refer to <instruction-list> as the *body* of the FOR-LOOP instruction. The instance of <variable-name> is to be replaced with any convenient name and the variable may be used within the body of the loop. This instruction is called FOR-**LOOP** because one can imagine the instructions of the <instruction-list> arranged in a circle. If we execute them one after the other, we will come to the first one just after the last one. Our first example of a FOR-LOOP instruction is an alternate definition of turn_right. Here we have used i as the <variable-name>.

```
class BeeperController < Robot
   def turn_right()
      for i in 0..2 do
         turn_left()
      end
   end
   ...
```

The body of the FOR-LOOP will be executed three times, once when i is 0, once when it is 1, and again when it is 2. We emphasize, however, that any range can be used in a FOR-LOOP, such as a 10..15. Ruby has a number of different sequence types that you might want to explore. The range we have used here is an inclusive one and includes both of its end points. With three dots however, as in 0...10, the range excludes 10 and so has only values 0 through 9. We won't need to use this fact, but ranges in Ruby are not limited to having integer limits. For example 'a'.. 'z' is the lower case alphabet as a range. You may also have noticed that the FOR-LOOP as we present it here includes a block (do...end) as part. This makes the FOR-LOOP more general than we shall need, also. While it isn't necessary to start with 0, it is traditional to do so for a variety of reasons and it will be helpful for you to become accustomed to it for when you go beyond the robot world. So to do things 10 times, the customary range is 0..9 rather than 1..10.

As a second example, we rewrite the harvest_one_row method that was written in Section 3.8.3. This definition originally comprised nine primitive instructions, but by using FOR-LOOP we can define the method more concisely. With this new, more general version of harvest_one_row, we can now easily increase or decrease the number of beepers harvested per row; all we need to change is the size of the range we use in a FOR-LOOP instruction.

```
class Harvester < Robot
   def harvest_one_row()
      harvest_corner()
      for corner in 0..3 do   # 4 iterations
         move()
         harvest_corner()
      end
   end
   ...
```

Remember that the robot is originally on a corner with a beeper, so we need to harvest the first corner before we move. The above is equivalent to the following version, however. In this version we must remember to harvest the last corner after the loop completes, since we ended with a move and have only harvested the first four corners in this row.

```
def harvest_one_row()
   for corner in 0..3 do
      harvest_corner()
      move()
   end
   harvest_corner()
end
```

Finally, we show one FOR-LOOP instruction nested within another. Carefully observe the way that the inner loop both begins and ends within the outer loop. The <variable-name> of the control variable must be different for each nested loop. Here we have four *sides* and each side is six *blocks*.

```
def walk_square_of_length_6()
    for side in 0..3 do
        for block in 0..5 do
            move()
        end
        turn_left()
    end
end
```

If we assume no intervening walls, this instruction moves the robot around the perimeter of a square whose sides are six blocks long. The outer FOR-LOOP instruction loops a total of four times, once for each side of the square. Each time the outer FOR-LOOP's body is executed, the robot executes two instructions. First the robot executes the nested FOR-LOOP, which moves it six blocks. Then it executes the turn_left, which prepares it to trace the next side. Thus, the robot executes a total of twenty-four moves and four left turns, which are arranged in an order that makes it travel in a square.

The range is actually more sophisticated than what we have seen here. Nor have we seen a case in which the integer value is actually used, other than to count how many times we execute the body of the loop.

An array is also a kind of sequence (there are others in Ruby as well). So we can apply our for loop to process all of the elements of an array, one at a time. For example, to ask all of the neighbors of karel to move, we can say

```
for robot in karel.neighbors() do
    robot.move()
end
```

Each neighbor at that point will move one block. Note that this is somewhat more general than the above, since we don't know exactly how many neighbors karel has at this moment. But it is still a fixed number.

But note, that whenever we loop over a range, the number of times we execute the body is well determined before we begin. We will consider a more general situation in the Section 6.3.

6.2 Iterators

Ruby programmers write few FOR-LOOPs in fact. Ruby *iterators* are more convenient. In Ruby integers are objects (as is everything), and so they respond to messages. One of the methods of class Integer is *times*, which is an iterator. So we could write walk_square_of_length_6 more simply as follows:

```
def walk_square_of_length_6()
   4.times do
      6.times do
         move()
      end
      turn_left()
   end
end
```

We will prefer to use iterators here rather than writing FOR-LOOPS. Even this simplified form can be generalized, but we won't need it here.

A *block* in Ruby is a sequence of instructions that can be treated as a unit. It either begins with the keyword *do* and ends with *end*, or is enclosed in curly braces {, and }. It is actually a modifier of a method invocation like *times*. In the above method, the block modifies the *times* message, and times has caused the block to be executed (with the *yield* statement, actually) several times. A block must begin on the same line as the method invocation it modifies. We don't intend to go deeply in to this here, but it is commonly used in Ruby programming. Blocks can also have parameters, but the syntax is a bit different. Ruby iterators, which are part of some classes that define collections, use blocks. In particular, we can make all of karel's neighbors move as follows.

```
karel.neighbors().each do |robot|
   robot.move()
end
```

Here the parameter of the block is named *robot* and the iterator is each. The names of iterators vary, depending on the class of the *collection*. However, the idea is the same. Each element of the collection will be processed and will be assigned to the parameter before the iteration begins (for each iteration) if the parameter is present. The iterator yields to the block (executes it) once for each element of the collection. The order of iteration will be whatever is natural to the sequence. For a range, it is first value to last. For an array it is first element to last, etc.

We have only touched on a deep and important topic here. Iterators are an elegant solution to a general problem: how to process all of a collection, one item at a time. There is much to learn.

6.3 The WHILE Instruction

In this section we explain the WHILE instruction and analyze many of its interesting properties. It is the most powerful single instruction that is built into the robot programming language.

6.3.1 Why WHILE is Needed

To motivate the need for a WHILE instruction, we look at what should be a simple programming task. Assume that a robot is initially facing east on some street, and somewhere east of it on that same street is a beeper. The robot's task is to move forward until it is on the same corner as the beeper, and then pick it up. Despite this simple description, the program is impossible to write with our current repertoire of instructions[11]. Two attempts at solving this problem might be written as follows.

---

[11]Unless we use the technique called recursion that is discussed in Chapter 7.

```
if not next_to_a_beeper?()           for i in 0..???
   move()                               move()
end                                   end
if not next_to_a_beeper?()           pick_beeper()
   move()
end

   . . .

if not next_to_a_beeper?()
   move()
end
pick_beeper()
```

We can interpret what is meant by these instructions, but robots understand neither "..." nor "???". The difficulty is that we do not know in advance how many move instructions the robot must execute before it arrives at the same corner as the beeper; we do not even have a guaranteed upper limit! The beeper may be on the robot's starting street corner, or it may be a million blocks away. The robot must be able to accomplish this task without knowing in advance the number of corners that it will pass before reaching the beeper. We must program our robot to execute move instructions repeatedly, until it senses that it is next to the beeper. What we need is an instruction that combines the repetition ability of the FOR-LOOP instruction with the testing ability of the IF instruction.

6.3.2 The Form of the WHILE Instruction

The WHILE instruction commands a robot to repeat another instruction as long as some test remains true. The WHILE instruction is executed somewhat similarly to an IF instruction, except that the WHILE instruction repeatedly executes itself as long as <test> is true. The general form of the WHILE instruction is given below.

```
while  <test>
   <instruction-list>
end
```

The new reserved word **while** starts this instruction, <test> is a predicate, and body, <instruction-list>, is indented in the usual way. The **end** completes the statement. The conditions that can replace <test> are the same ones used in the IF instructions.

A robot executes a WHILE loop by first checking <test> in its current situation. If the <test> is false, the robot is finished with the WHILE instruction, and it continues by executing the instructions following the entire WHILE loop. On the other hand, if the <test> is true, the robot executes <instruction-list> and then re-executes the entire WHILE loop. Here is a sample WHILE instruction that solves the problem that began this discussion.

```
class BeeperController < Robot
   def go_to_beeper()
      while not next_to_a_beeper?()
         move()
      end
      pick_beeper()
   end
```

. . .

This method moves a robot forward as long as **next_to_a_beeper**? is false. When the robot is finally next to a beeper, it finishes executing the WHILE loop. After the loop terminates, the robot picks up the beeper. The following method is another simple example of a WHILE loop, and we will examine its behavior in detail.

```
def clear_corner_of_beepers()
   while next_to_a_beeper?()
      pick_beeper()
   end
end
```

Suppose we have a robot named karel in class BeeperController and send it the message karel.clear_corner_of_beepers(). This method commands karel to pick up all of the beepers on a corner. Let's simulate karel's execution of this instruction on a corner containing two beepers. Karel first determines whether **next_to_a_beeper**? is true or false. Finding the test true, it executes the body of the WHILE loop, which is the pick_beeper message. Karel then re-executes the entire WHILE loop. The robot finds <test> is true (one beeper is still left), and executes the body of the WHILE loop. After picking up the second beeper, karel re-executes the entire WHILE instruction. Although we know that no beepers are remaining, karel is unaware of this fact until it rechecks the WHILE loop test. Now karel rechecks the test and discovers that **next_to_a_beeper**? is false, so the robot is finished executing the WHILE loop. Because the entire definition consists of one WHILE loop, karel is finished executing clear_corner_of_beepers. It appears that no matter how many beepers are initially on the corner, karel will eventually pick them all up when this instruction is executed.

But what happens if karel executes clear_corner_of_beepers on a corner that has no beepers? In this situation, <test> is false the first time that the WHILE instruction is executed, so the loop body is not executed at all. Therefore, karel also handles this situation correctly. The key fact to remember about a WHILE instruction is that until karel discovers that <test> has become false--and it may be false the first time--karel repeatedly checks <test> and executes the loop's body if it is true. Also note that when a WHILE terminates, its <test> must be false.

6.3.3 Building a WHILE Loop - the Four Step Process

In the previous chapter on IF's we discussed the problems novice programmers frequently face when introduced to a new programming construct. We are in a similar situation with the WHILE loop. We have seen the form of a WHILE loop, looked at an example, and traced the execution of the example. Before using a WHILE loop in a robot program, it would be helpful to have a framework for thinking about the WHILE loop.

We should consider using a WHILE loop only when a robot must do something an unknown number of times. If we are faced with such a situation, we can build our WHILE loop by following the four step process shown below. To illustrate these steps, we will again consider the problem of having a robot named karel pick all beepers from a corner without knowing the initial number of beepers on the corner.

Step 1: Identify the one test (predicate) that must be true when karel is finished with the loop.

In the above problem, karel must pick all beepers on the corner. If we consider only tests that involve beepers we have four from which to choose: **any_beepers_in_beeper_bag**?, **next_to_a_beeper**?, and their opposites. Which one is the test we want? When karel is finished, there should be no beepers left on the corner, so the test we want to be true is **not next_to_a_beeper?**().

Step 2: Use the opposite (negated) form of the test identified in step 1 as the loop <test>.

This implies we should use **next_to_a_beeper**?. Does this make sense? The WHILE instruction continues to execute the loop body as long as the test is true and stops when it is false. As long as karel is next to a beeper it should pick them up. When it is done, there will be no beepers on the corner.

Step 3: Within the WHILE, make progress toward completion of the WHILE. We need to do something within the WHILE to ensure that the test eventually evaluates to false so that the WHILE loop stops. Often it is helpful to do the minimum amount of work that is necessary to advance toward the completion of the task.

Something within the body of the loop must allow the test to eventually evaluate to false or the loop will run forever. This implies that there must be some instruction (or sequence of instructions) within the loop that is related to the test. In this problem, what must be done to bring us closer to the test being false? Since we are testing for **next_to_a_beeper**?, we must pick one (and only one) beeper somewhere in the loop. We can argue that if karel keeps picking one beeper, it must eventually pick all the beepers leaving none on the corner. Why pick only one beeper during each iteration? Why not two or three? If there is only one beeper on the corner, and we instruct karel to pick up more than one, an error shutoff will occur. Picking just one beeper during each iteration of the loop is the minimum needed to guarantee that all the beepers are eventually picked up.

Step 4: Do whatever is required before or after the WHILE instruction is executed to ensure we solve the given problem.

In this example, we have to do nothing before or after the loop. However, there are times when we may miss one iteration of the loop and have to "clean things up" which can be done either before or after the WHILE. Also, we sometimes need to execute an instruction or two before the WHILE loop to get our robot into the correct position.

If we follow these four steps carefully, we reduce the chance of having intent errors and infinite repetition when we test our program. Infinite execution is the error that occurs when we begin to execute a WHILE instruction, but it never terminates. This is discussed in Section 6.4.2.

6.3.4 A More Interesting Problem

Let's apply the steps presented above to a new problem. A robot named karel is somewhere in the world facing south. One beeper is on each corner between karel's current position and the southern boundary wall. There is no beeper on the corner on which karel is currently standing. Write a new method, clear_all_beepers_to_the_wall, to pick all of the beepers.

As before, let's ask ourselves some questions:

Question: What do we know about karel's initial situation?

Answer: Karel is facing south.

Karel is an unknown distance from the southern boundary wall.

Each corner between karel and the southern boundary wall has one beeper.

Question: Does any of this information provide insight toward a solution?

Answer: Karel can travel forward until it reaches the southern boundary wall. It can pick a beeper from each corner as it travels.

We have the beginnings of a plan. We continue the process below.

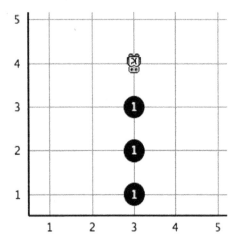

Figure 6-1 Pick All Beepers

Question: What robot instruction can we use to keep karel traveling southward until it reaches the southern boundary wall?

Answer: Since traveling to the southern boundary wall requires an unknown number of move instructions, we can use a WHILE loop.

Question: How do we actually use the WHILE loop?

Answer: We can use the four step process as follows:

Step 1: Identify the one test that must be true when karel is finished with the loop. Karel will be at the southern boundary wall, so the test, *front_is_clear?()*, will be false, so *not front_is_clear?()* will be true.

Step 2: Use the opposite form of the test identified in step 1 as the loop <test>: *front_is_clear?()* is the opposite form.

Step 3: Do the minimum needed to ensure that the test eventually evaluates to false so that the WHILE loop stops. Karel must move forward one block within the loop body, but we must be careful here. Karel is not yet standing on a beeper so it must move first before picking the beeper. We can use a single pick_beeper instruction because there is only one beeper on each corner.

Step 4: Do whatever is required before or after the WHILE is executed to ensure we solve the given problem. Since karel is already facing south, we do not have to do anything.

Based on the above discussion we can write the following new method:

```
def clear_all_beepers_to_the_wall()
    while front_is_clear?()
        move()
        pick_beeper()
    end
end
```

Our work is not finished. We must carefully trace the execution before we certify it as correct. Can we test all possible situations that karel could start this task in? No! We cannot test all possible situations but we can test several and do a reasonable job of convincing ourselves that the method is correct. One method of informally reasoning about the instruction follows.

First: Show that the method works correctly when the initial situation results in the test being false. That would mean that the initial situation would look like this:

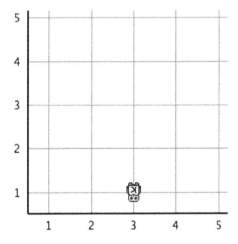

Figure 6-2 The Same Task Without Beepers

Second: We must show that each time the loop body is executed, karel's new situation is a simpler and similar version of the old situation. By simpler we mean that karel now has less work to do before finishing the loop. By similar we mean that karel's situation has not radically changed during its execution of the loop body (in this example a non-similar change could mean that karel is facing a different direction). If our new method is correct, we should see these changes in the following karel world:

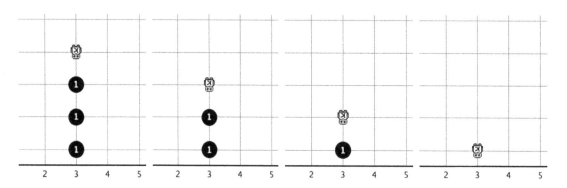

Figure 6-3 Tracing karel's Progress Executing the Loop

After each iteration of the loop, the current corner should have no beepers. Take some time and trace the robot's execution of the loop and verify that it is correct.

6.4 Errors to Avoid with WHILE Loops

The WHILE loop provides a powerful tool for our robot programs. Using it wisely, we can instruct robots to solve some very complex problems. However, the sharper the ax, the deeper it can cut. With the power of the WHILE loop comes the potential for making some powerful mistakes. This section will examine several typical errors that can be made when using the WHILE loop. If we are aware of these errors, we will have a better chance of avoiding them or, at least, an easier time identifying them for correction.

6.4.1 The Fence Post Problem

If we order five fence sections, how many fence posts do we need? The obvious answer is five! But it is wrong. Think about it.

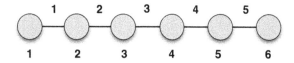

Figure 6-4 The Fence Post Problem

This diagram should help us to understand why the correct answer is six. We can encounter the fence post problem when using the WHILE loop. Let's take the previous problem with a slight twist and put a beeper on karel's starting corner.

Since this is a slight modification of the clear_all_beepers_to_the_wall task of the class BeeperController, it would be advantageous to have solutions to both problems available. One good way to do this is to build a new class, say BeeperSweeper, derived from BeeperController, in which to implement this new method, which is just an override of clear_all_beepers_to_the_wall.

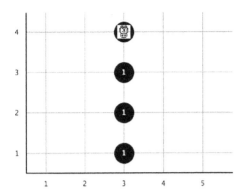

Figure 6-5 Initial Situation

Suppose we decide to solve this problem by reversing the order of the messages in the original loop body and have karel pick the beeper before moving:

```
class BeeperSweeper < BeeperController
   def  clear_all_beepers_to_the_wall()
      while front_is_clear?()
         pick_beeper()
         move()
      end
   end
. . .
```

If we trace the method's execution carefully, we will discover that the loop still finishes--there is no error shutoff --however, the southernmost beeper is not picked.

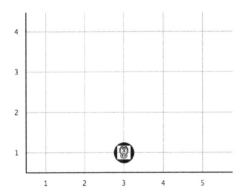

Figure 6-6 Final Situation

In this example the beepers were the fence posts and the moves were the fence sections. The WHILE loop executes the same number of pick_beeper and move messages. Consequently, there will be one beeper left when the loop finishes. This is where step 4 in the four step process comes in. We now have a situation where we must do something before or after the loop to make sure we solve the given problem. There are at least two ways to handle this. Here is one.

```
def clear_all_beepers_to_the_wall()
    while front_is_clear?()
        pick_beeper()
        move()
    end
    pick_beeper()
end
```

Our solution is simply to pick the final beeper after the WHILE loop stops executing. What is the other way to solve this fence post problem? Ah yes. We could pick up the beeper on the start corner first. This would put us in the initial position of clear_all_beepers_to_the_wall. This means that we can actually use that instruction to write this one.

```
def clear_all_beepers_to_the_wall()
    pick_beeper()
    super()
end
```

This works since we are in a subclass. We could also use a decorator, of course.

6.4.2 Infinite Execution

Having looked at step 4 in the four step process, let's now refocus our attention on step 3: do what is needed to ensure that the test eventually evaluates to false so that the WHILE loop stops. Sometimes we forget to include an instruction (or sequence of instructions) that allows the test to eventually become false. Here is an example:

```
while facing_north?()
    pick_beeper()
    move()
end
```

Look at this loop carefully. Is there any instruction within the loop body that will change the robot's direction? Neither pick_beeper nor move does so. The loop will iterate zero times if the robot is initially facing any direction other than north. Unfortunately, if it is facing north we condemn the robot to walk forever (since the world is infinite to the north) or to execute an error shutoff if it arrives at a corner without a beeper[12]. We must be very careful when we plan the body of the WHILE loop to avoid the possibility of infinite repetition.

---

[12] Of course, if we have overridden pick_beeper or move, then anything is possible. One of the new versions could change the direction, and then the robot would exit the WHILE.

6.4.3 When the Test of a WHILE is Checked

Section 6.3.2 explained how a robot executes a WHILE instruction, yet unless the instruction is read carefully, there may be some ambiguity. In this section we closely examine the execution of a WHILE instruction and explain a common misconception about when a robot checks <test>. Let's examine the following instruction carefully.

```
def harvest_line()
    while next_to_a_beeper?()
        pick_beeper()
        move()
    end
end
```

This method commands a robot to pick up a line of beepers. The robot finishes executing this method after moving one block beyond the final corner that has a beeper.

Let's simulate this new method in detail for a line of two beepers. Karel starts its task on the same corner as the first beeper. The robot is again named karel. Karel executes the WHILE instruction and finds that the test is true, so it executes the body of the loop. The loop body instructs karel to pick up the beeper and then move to the next corner. Now karel re-executes the loop; the test is checked, and again karel senses that it is next to a beeper. The robot picks up the second beeper and moves forward. Karel then executes the loop again. Now when the test is checked, the robot finds that its corner is beeperless, so it is finished executing the WHILE loop. The definition of harvest_line contains only one instruction--this WHILE loop--so harvest_line is also finished.

The point demonstrated here is that karel checks <test> only before it executes the body of the loop. Karel is totally insensitive to <test> while executing instructions that are inside the loop body. A common misconception among novice programmers is that karel checks <test> after each instruction is executed inside the loop body. This is an incorrect interpretation of when karel checks <test>.

Let's see what would happen if karel used the incorrect interpretation to execute the harvest_line method in the two-beeper situation. This interpretation would force karel to finish the WHILE loop as soon as it was not next to a beeper. Karel would start by determining if it were next to a beeper. Finding the test true, karel would execute the loop body. This is fine so far but, after executing the pick_beeper, karel would not be next to a beeper anymore. So, according to this incorrect interpretation, karel would now be finished with the loop and would be limited to picking up only one beeper regardless of the length of the beeper line.

Recall again the fence sections and fence posts. Notice that the body of a while is like a fence section and the test is like a fence post. The number of test evaluations is always one more than the number of executions of the body of the WHILE instruction.

6.5 Nested WHILE Loops

We have already discussed nesting, or the placing of one instruction within a similar instruction. Nesting WHILE loops can be a very useful technique if done properly and in this section we will look at both a good and a bad example of nesting.

6.5.1 A Good Example of Nesting

We will use a modification of a previous problem. A robot named karel is somewhere in the world facing south. Between its current location and the southern boundary wall are beepers. We do not know how many beepers are on each corner (some corners may even have no beepers). Write a new method that will direct karel to pick all the beepers between its current location and the southern boundary wall.

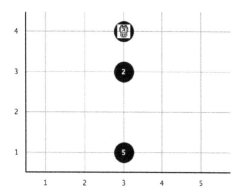

Figure 6-7 A Problem to Move and Pick Beepers

We can use our question/answer format to plan a solution to this problem.

Question: What is the problem?

Answer: We must move karel an unknown distance and have karel pick an unknown number of beepers from each corner it passes.

Question: What does karel have to do?

Answer: Karel must perform two tasks:

- First, karel must walk an unknown distance to the southern wall.

- Second, karel must pick all the beepers on each corner it encounters. There may be from zero to a very large number of beepers on each corner.

Let's concentrate on the first task and save the second task for later.

Question: What instruction can we use to keep karel moving forward to the southern boundary wall?

Answer: Since this requires an unknown number of iterations of the move instruction, we can use the WHILE loop.

We can apply the four step process for building WHILE loops and write the following code for karel to test.

```
while front_is_clear?()
   move()
end
```

If karel executes this instruction correctly, then our plan is on the right track. However, if karel stops before arriving at the boundary wall or executes an error shutoff when it tries to move through the wall, we must reanalyze our plan. This instruction works properly so we now consider the second task--the picking of all beepers on each corner karel encounters as it travels to the boundary wall.

Question: What instruction will allow karel to pick all the beepers that might be on a corner?

Answer: Since this requires an unknown number of iterations of the pick_beeper instruction, we can use the WHILE instruction to do this task also.

We can apply the four step process for building WHILE loops and write the following implementation.

```
while next_to_a_beeper?()
   pick_beeper()
end
```

We simulate this and it appears to work. We now have to decide which loop to nest inside which loop. Do we put the loop that moves karel to the southern boundary wall inside the loop that picks beepers or do we put the beeper picking loop inside the loop that moves karel to the wall?

Question: Can we interchange these two actions?

Answer: No, we cannot. Arriving at the wall should stop both karel's moving and picking. Running out of beepers on one corner should NOT stop karel's moving to the wall. As we move to the wall we can clean each corner of beepers if we nest the beeper picking loop inside the loop that moves karel to the wall.

Our new method definition will look like this.

```
def clear_all_beepers_to_the_wall()
   while front_is_clear?()
      while next_to_a_beeper?()
         pick_beeper()
      end
      move()
   end
end
```

To solve the problem of deciding which WHILE loop is to be the outer loop, we can apply the each test. Do we need to pick up all of the beepers for each single step we take to the wall, or do we need to walk all the way to the wall for each single beeper that we pick up? Here, the answer is the former and the outer loop is the stepping (move) loop.

When we nest WHILE loops we must be very sure that the execution of the nested loop (or inner loop) does not interfere with the test condition of the outer loop. In this problem the inner loop is responsible for picking beepers. The outer loop is responsible for moving the robot. These two activities do not affect each other so the nesting seems correct.

We are not done. We must now test this new method. Take some time and trace karel's execution of it using the initial situation shown in Figure 6.7. As much as we would like to believe it is correct, it isn't. We appear to have forgotten the fence post discussion of section 6.4.1. The way we have written the new method, the last corner will not be cleared of beepers; this last corner is our forgotten fence post. To ensure the last corner is cleared of beepers, we must make one more modification.

```
def clear_all_beepers_to_the_wall()
    while front_is_clear?()
        while next_to_a_beeper?()
            pick_beeper()
        end
        move()
    end
    while next_to_a_beeper?()
        pick_beeper()
    end
end
```

This third loop is outside the nested loops and it will clear the last corner of beepers.

One note here about overall design of our new method: As a rule we prefer to perform only one task (e.g., moving to a wall) in a new method and move secondary tasks (e.g., picking the beepers) into a different new method. We believe the following represents a better programming style for the previous problem.

```
def clear_beepers_this_corner()
    while next_to_a_beeper?()
        pick_beeper()
    end
end

def clear_all_beepers_to_the_wall()
    while front_is_clear?()
        clear_beepers_this_corner()
        move()
    end
    clear_beepers_this_corner()
end
```

This programming style is easier to read and, if we suddenly find that clearing the beepers requires a different strategy, we only have to make a change in one place, clear_beepers_this_corner.

6.5.2 A Bad Example of Nesting

A robot named karel is facing south in the northwest corner of a room that has no doors or windows. Somewhere in the room, next to a wall, is a single beeper. Instruct karel to find the beeper by writing the new method, find_beeper.

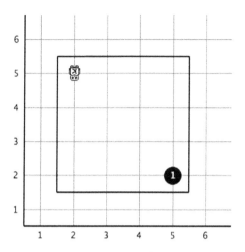

Figure 6-8 Initial Situation

We begin with our usual question/answer planning.

Question: What is the problem?

Answer: We must instruct karel to find a beeper that is somewhere in the room next to the wall. We do not know how far away it is, and we do not know how big the room is.

Question: What instruction can we use to move karel to the beeper?

Answer: Since the distance karel must travel is unknown, we can use a WHILE loop.

Using the four step process to build a WHILE loop we develop the following new method.

```
def find_beeper()
    while not next_to_a_beeper?()
        move()
    end
end
```

If we carefully analyze this new method, we find, as shown in Figure 6-9, that karel executes an error shutoff when it arrives at the southern wall.

Question: What happened?

Answer: We forgot about turning karel at the corners.

Question: How can we fix this problem?

Answer: Let's walk karel forward until it detects a wall.

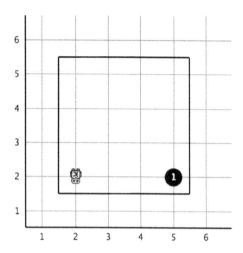

Figure 6-9 Karel Executes an Error Shutoff

Question: What instruction can we use to do this?

Answer: Since the distance karel must travel is unknown, we can use a WHILE loop.

Again we use the four step process to build a nested WHILE loop and develop the following new method.

```
def find_beeper()
   while not next_to_a_beeper?()
      while front_is_clear?()
         move()
      end
      turn_left()
   end
end
```

We must test this to see if it works. Since this problem is somewhat involved, we should use several different initial situations. Will the following situations be sufficient to test our code completely?

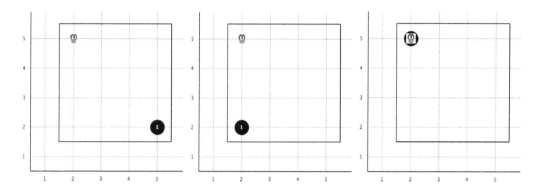

Figure 6-10 Three Different Initial Situations

If we trace our program using these situations, it appears that our method is correct. However, does the original problem statement guarantee that the beeper will always be in a corner? It does not. The original problem statement says that the beeper is somewhere next to a wall. Our three test situations each put the beeper in a corner. We should try an initial situation such as this.

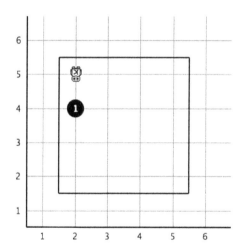

Figure 6-11 Another Situation With Which to Test Our method Definition

Let's see what happens here: karel makes the outer test, not **next_to_a_beeper**?, and it is true so it begins to execute the outer loop body.

Karel makes the inner test, **front_is_clear**?, which is true, so karel moves forward one block coming to rest on the corner with the beeper. What happens now? Karel remains focused on the inner loop. It has not forgotten about the outer loop but its focus is restricted to the inner loop until the inner loop stops execution. Karel is required to make the inner test, **front_is_clear**?, which is true and moves one block forward away from the beeper. This is now karel's situation.

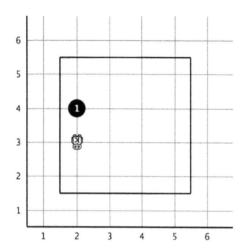

Figure 6-12 Karel Misses the Beeper

Karel remains focused on the inner loop and makes the inner test again. It is true so karel executes the move and is now in this situation:

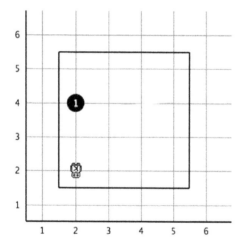

Figure 6-13 Karel Arrives at the Wall

The inner test is false, so karel ceases execution of the inner loop, executes the turn_left and is done with the first iteration of the outer loop. Now karel makes the outer test, not **next_to_a_beeper**?, which is true. Karel has no memory of once standing next to a beeper, consequently, karel will continue to walk around this room and keep going and going and going... Our method will execute infinitely in this case!

There must be something wrong with our initial reasoning. Let's look at the initial planning segment.

Question: What is the problem?

Answer: We must instruct karel to find a beeper that is somewhere in the room next to a wall. We do not know how far away it is, and we do not know how big the room is.

Question: What instruction can we use to move karel to the beeper?

Answer: Since the distance karel must travel is unknown, we can use a WHILE loop.

We then found that karel performed an error shutoff because we instructed karel to move forward when the front was blocked by a wall. Our next planning segment appears below.

Question: What happened?

Answer: We forgot about turning karel at the corners.

Question: How can we fix this problem?

Answer: Let's walk karel forward until it detects a wall.

Question: What instruction can we use to do this?

Answer: Since the distance karel must travel is unknown, we can use a WHILE loop.

This is where our plan began to go wrong. We decided to walk karel forward until the front was blocked. We reasoned that we could use a WHILE loop to move karel forward and that was the mistake. If the robot moves more than one block forward without allowing the test of the outer WHILE loop to be checked, it will violate step 4 of the four step process--"Do whatever is needed to ensure the loop stops." Karel should only move one block forward within the outer WHILE loop. We should not use an inner WHILE loop to move karel toward the wall! The reason is that karel's execution of the inner WHILE loop can cause the outer WHILE loop to never stop. Both the outer and inner WHILE loops require karel to execute the move instruction so both loops will eventually terminate. Unless both tests, not **next_to_a_beeper**? and **front_is_clear**?, are false at the exact same time, the outer loop will never stop. We must discard the inner WHILE loop and find a different way to keep karel from trying to move through the wall.

Question: How can we move karel forward without the WHILE loop?

Answer: Karel should only move forward one block inside the WHILE loop so we must use an IF/ELSE statement to check for a wall. Karel will move when the front is clear and turn left when a wall is present.

Following our new reasoning, we have the following new method.

```
def find_beeper()
   while not next_to_a_beeper?()
      if front_is_clear?()
         move()
      else
         turn_left()
      end
   end
```

```
   end
```

Nesting WHILE loops is a powerful programming idea, but with this increased power comes the increased need for very careful planning and analysis.

An alternate way to solve this is to start as we did previously with a simple while loop, but suppose the existence of a method move_toward_beeper.

```
def find_beeper()
   while not next_to_a_beeper?()
      move_toward_beeper()
   end
end
```

What do we have to do to move toward the beeper? If we don't interpret it literally, but rather as "make one step of progress toward the goal of finding the beeper" then we easily arrive at:

```
def move_toward_beeper()
   if front_is_clear?()
      move()
   else
      turn_left()
   end
end
```

6.6 WHILE and IF Instructions

Novice programmers frequently use WHILE and IF instructions in a conflicting, unnecessary, or redundant manner. Examine the following program fragments to find improperly used tests.

```
if facing_south?()
   while not facing_south?()
      turn_left()
   end
end
```

In this fragment there are conflicting tests. When the IF's test is true the WHILE's test must be false. This fragment will do nothing.

Let's try another one.

```
while not front_is_clear?()
   if front_is_clear?()
      move()
   else
      turn_left()
   end
```

```
    end
```

In this fragment there is an unnecessary test. When the WHILE's test is true, the IF's test must be false so the ELSE is the only part of the loop body that is ever executed.

Here is another.

```
while next_to_a_beeper?()
    if next_to_a_beeper?()
        pick_beeper()
    end
end
```

In this fragment there are redundant tests. The WHILE's test is the same as the IF's test. When the WHILE's test is true so is the IF's.

Problems such as these usually enter our programs when we attempt to fix execution or intent errors. We sometimes get so involved in the details of our program that we forget to take a step back and look at the overall picture. It is often very helpful to take a break and come back to the program with fresh eyes.

6.7 Reasoning about Loops

In section 6.3.3 we discussed the four step process for building a WHILE loop.

Step 1. Identify the one test that must be true when the robot is finished with the loop.

Step 2. Use the opposite form of the test identified in step 1 as the loop <test>.

Step 3. Do what is needed to make progress toward solving the problem at hand and also ensure that the test eventually evaluates to false so that the WHILE loop stops.

Step 4. Do whatever is required before or after the WHILE is executed to ensure we solve the given problem.

We also presented an informal way to reason about the correctness of WHILE loops.

1. Show that the instruction works correctly when the initial situation results in the test being false.

2. Show that each time the loop body is executed, the robot's new situation is a simpler and similar version of the old situation.

We'd like to spend a little more time discussing this last concept of correctness. Remember that a robot will do exactly what it is told and only what it is told. It is up to us to make sure that it is provided with a correct way to solve a given problem. At the same time, we need a way to *prove* (in some sense) that our solution is correct. It will be impossible for us to simulate every possible situation, so we need a way to think through our solution in a formal way to verify that it does what it is supposed to do.

In order to reason about WHILE loops, we will need to understand a key concept called a *loop invariant*. A loop invariant is an assertion (something that can be proven true or false) which is true after each iteration of the loop. For our purposes, loop invariants will be assertions about the robot's world. In particular, the items that we need to be concerned about after ONE iteration are the following:

* How has the robot's direction changed, if at all?

* How has the robot's relative position in the world changed, if at all (this may involve thinking about wall segments as well)?

* How has the number of beepers in the robot's beeper-bag changed, if at all?

* How has the number and location of other beepers in the world changed, if at all?

Let's look at these items using the example given in section 6.3.4, clear_all_beepers_to_the_wall. After one iteration of the following loop,

```
while front_is_clear?()
    move()
    pick_beeper()
end
```

What can we say (assert) about the items mentioned above? We can assert the following:

* The robot's direction is unchanged,

* The robot's position has been advanced one corner,

* That corner has one less beeper, and

* The robot's beeper-bag has another beeper.

Which of these statements are "interesting?" By "interesting" we mean which item is important in terms of the problem being solved. Since we're removing beepers from the world as the robot moves forward, we're interested in the second and third assertions. A loop invariant captures the interesting change during one iteration of the loop. Thus, for this problem, the loop invariant is that "there is still a beeper on each corner between the current position and the wall." But, we have reduced the size of the problem.

What else have we learned? Let's look at our loop test, **front_is_clear**?. When the loop ends, it will be false, thus the front will be blocked. So we know that when the loop terminates, the robot has removed one beeper from each corner it has passed and the robot's front is now blocked. We have learned that as long as each corner had one beeper on it, our loop must have solved the problem of picking up beepers to the wall.

Let's look at the fence post problem presented in section 6.4.1. What is the loop invariant for the first attempt at solving that problem? Here's the loop:

```
while front_is_clear?()
    pick_beeper()
    move()
end
```

What can we assert about this loop?

* The robot's direction is unchanged.

* The robot's position has been advanced forward one corner.

* The previous corner has one less beeper.

* The robot's beeper-bag has one more beeper.

What do we know about the robot and the world when the loop finishes? We know that any previous corners have had one beeper removed from them. Finally, we know that the robot's front is blocked. And the invariant is still true: each corner the robot has visited (previous corners) has one less beeper.

What about the robot's current corner? Since the loop invariant only mentions previous corners, we know nothing about the corner on which the robot is standing when the loop terminates--it may have a beeper, it may not. How we choose to remedy this situation is up to us, but at least in reasoning about the loop we have become aware of a potential problem with our loop--the fencepost problem.

Loop invariants can be powerful tools in aiding our understanding of how a loop is operating and what it will cause a robot to do. The key lies in determining how executing the loop changes the state of the world during each iteration and capturing that change as succinctly as possible. Once we've discovered the loop invariant, we can use it and the loop's termination condition to decide if the loop solves the problem. If not, we must look back over the steps for constructing a WHILE loop to see where we might have gone wrong.

Another use of loop invariants is to help us determine what instructions we want to use in the loop body. So far we've used the loop invariant as an after-the-fact device, to verify that a loop we've written solves a specific problem. If we decide what we want the invariant to be before we write the body of the loop, it can help in deciding what the body should be. As an example, consider the following problem: A robot is searching for a beeper that is an unknown distance directly in front of it and there may be some one-block high wall segments in the way.

What do we want to be true when the loop terminates? Since the robot is looking for a beeper, we want it to be next to a beeper. Thus, our test is not **next_to_a_beeper**?. What do we want to be invariant? It should be that there is a beeper on some corner directly in front of the robot (including possibly the current corner). The robot must move one (and only one) block forward during each iteration of the loop to ensure that each corner is examined. Otherwise we might skip over the beeper, making the invariant false. Our first pass at a loop might look like this:

```
while  not next_to_a_beeper?()
   move()
end
```

Unfortunately, this will cause an error shutoff if we happen to run into one of those intervening wall segments before reaching the beeper. How can we maintain our invariant and still avoid the wall segment? A little insight might suggest the following modification:

```
while not next_to_a_beeper?()
   if front_is_clear?()
      move()
   else
      avoid_wall()
   end
end
```

where avoid_wall is defined as:

```
def avoid_wall()
   turn_left()
   move()
   turn_right()
   move()
   turn_right()
   move()
   turn_left()
end
```

In defining avoid_wall, we must keep the loop invariant in mind. We want to make progress toward our goal, but as little progress as possible so that we don't accidentally miss something. We should spend some time convincing ourselves that this loop maintains the initial invariant: the robot moves exactly one block forward during each iteration of the loop. Then we can also convince ourselves that this loop does solve the problem.

6.8 A Large Program Written by Stepwise Refinement

In this section we will write a complex program by using stepwise refinement. Suppose that we need to patrol the perimeter of a rectangular field of beepers. Imagine that there has been theft of the beepers and we need a robot guard to walk around the edge of the field. Let us build a class of Guard robots with a method walk_perimeter. The robot will initially be positioned somewhere in the field, but not necessarily on an edge.

To make the problem more definite, let's suppose that the field is at least two beepers wide and two beepers long. The path we want the robot to follow is one that walks along corners that actually contain the beepers marking the outer edge of the field. In the sample initial situation shown in Figure 6.14, the path should include 2nd and 9th Streets and 3rd and 7th Avenues.

As an initial strategy suppose that we walk our robot, say tony, to the south-east corner and have it walk the perimeter from there. We may need other methods to help us build these, but a first approximation to our class definition is as follows.

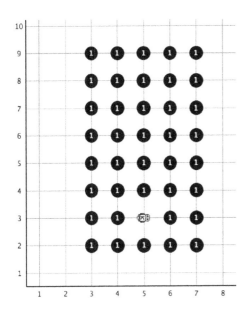

Figure 6.14 Initial Situation

```
class Guard < Robot
   include Turner

   def move_to_southeast_corner()
      # TODO
   end

   def walk_perimeter()
      # TODO
   end
end
```

First, lets attack the `walk_perimeter` method, assuming that we can begin it at the south-east corner. Since it is easier for a robot to turn left (faster anyway) than to turn right, lets program the robot to walk around the field in a counter-clockwise direction, turning left at each corner. Since there are four edges to be walked we can use a for loop instruction or an iterator. For each execution of the body of the loop we should walk one edge and then turn left at the end of it.

```
def walk_perimeter()   # Robot begins at a corner of the field
   4.times do
      follow_edge()
      turn_left()
   end
end
```

This solution, of course, requires that we add an additional method, `follow_edge`, to the Guard class. What does it take to follow an edge? Since the edge is marked by beepers the robot can simply move along it until there is no beeper on the current corner.

```
def follow_edge()
    while next_to_a_beeper?()
        move()
    end
end
```

If we try to simulate this by hand we find an error. After executing follow_edge, tony is left on a corner without any beepers. Since turn_left doesn't change the corner, we find that after executing follow_edge and then turn_left once, we are not in a legal position to execute follow_edge again. What actually happens when we execute follow_edge, is that tony walks outside the field and then turns completely around in place. Well, suppose that we have tony back-up as the last step in follow_edge, so that it is left on a corner with a beeper. Backing up requires that the robot be able to turn around. Thus we need the following but they are already in the Turner class that we mix in.

```
def turn_around()
    turn_left()
    turn_left()
end

def back_up()
    turn_around()
    move()
    turn_around()
end
```

Now we can correct follow_edge.

```
def follow_edge()
    while next_to_a_beeper?()
        move()
    end
    back_up()
end
```

Now our simulation seems to be correct, so we turn to move_to_southeast_corner. To do this we can have the robot face south and then move until it is on the edge of the field, turn left and then walk until it reaches the corner. Facing south is not especially difficult since we have a test for facing south.

```
def face_south()
    while not facing_south?()
        turn_left()
    end
end
```

But let's note that this seems like a good candidate to include in the Turner mixin that we need anyway. It will probably be useful in many projects.

To move to the south edge of the field tony now just needs to walk until there is no beeper on the current corner and then backup. But that is exactly what follow_edge does.

```
def move_to_southeast_corner()
    face_south()
    follow_edge() # Now at south edge of field
    turn_left()
    follow_edge() # Now at south-east corner of field
end
```

Well, we have carried out our plan, but when we execute it we find that the robot only walks around three sides of the field, not all four, though it does walk part of the fourth side while it is moving to the south-east corner. What is wrong? Each instruction seems to do what it was designed to do, but they don't fit together very well. The problem is that after executing move_to_southeast_corner, the robot is left facing east. Then, when we ask it to walk_perimeter it begins by walking immediately outside the field. The first execution of follow_edge has taken us outside the field. and then back to the corner, "wasting" one of our four executions of follow_edge. We should make the post-conditions of one instruction match up better with the pre-conditions of the next. A pre-condition for a method is a predicate that the caller of an instruction is required to establish before executing the method to guarantee its correct behavior. For example, a pre-condition for the pick_beeper method is that the robot be on a corner with a beeper. A post-condition for a method is the predicate that is guaranteed to be true when a method completes, if all of its pre-conditions were true before it was executed. The post-condition of the pick_beeper method is that the robot has at least one beeper in its beeper-bag.

Suppose that we add an additional post-condition to move_to_southeast_corner and require that it turn at the end of its walk to put the field to the left of the robot. We can establish this by adding requirement that it face to the North at the end of move_to_southeast_corner.

```
def move_to_southeast_corner()
    face_south()
    follow_edge() # Now at south edge of field
    turn_left()
    follow_edge() # Now at south-east corner of field
    turn_left()   # Now at south-east corner facing North
end
```

Now, when we simulate our robot, it will correctly follow all four edges of the field of Figure 6.14. When we try it in other legal fields, however, we find that we have trouble. For example, we find that tony will execute an error shutoff in trying to patrol the field of Figure 6.15.

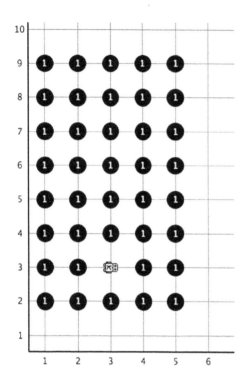

Figure 6.15 Another Initial Position

We call this type of situation a *beyond-the-horizon situation*. Normally, we write a program guided by a few initial situations that seem to cover all interesting aspects of the task. Although we would like to prove that all other situations are not too different from these sample situations, frequently the best we can do is hope. As we explore the problem and learn more about the task, we may discover situations that are beyond our original horizons--situations that are legal, but special trouble-causing cases. Once we suspect a beyond-the-horizon situation, we should immediately simulate a robot's execution in it. If our suspicions are confirmed, and the robot does not perform as we intended, we must modify our program accordingly.

We must reprogram the robot to realize that it is at the edge of a field as soon as it contacts a wall, as well as when it is no longer at a beeper. Since all of our edge sensing is in follow_edge, we look there for a solution.

Here is a solution in which we need stop moving when either not **next_to_a_beeper?**() OR **not front_is_clear?**() become true. Therefore, the opposite of this is our condition for continuing to move. The opposite is: **while next_to_a_beeper?**() **and front_is_clear?**()

This is, of course, equivalent to the predicate below, though the form above is perfectly good.

```
def next_to_a_beeper_and_front_is_clear?()
   if next_to_a_beeper?()
        return front_is_clear?()
   end
   return false
end
```

It will be instructive, however, to try to use nested constructs as in Chapter 5. Here, however, we have WHILE instructions and not IF instructions. Often the correct solution to this is to nest an IF instruction inside of a WHILE instruction. Suppose we try each of the following to see if they might help us here.

```
while next_to_a_beeper?()        while front_is_clear?()
    if front_is_clear?()             if next_to_a_beeper?()
        move()                           move()
    end                              end
end                              end
```

The second one seems clearly wrong, since once a robot begins executing, execution will continue until it encounters a wall. Since walls aren't necessarily part of the problem, the robot will walk too far afield.

The first also seems to be ok until we simulate it in our beyond-the-horizon situation, in which it will continue to execute forever. The problem is that when we encounter the wall we are still on a corner with a beeper and so we don't exit from the while. We can solve this, however, by picking up the beeper in this situation.

```
while next_to_a_beeper?()
    if front_is_clear?()
        move()
    else
        pick_beeper()
    end
end
```

Now we will exit, but must replace the beeper that we may have picked up. After we exit this while loop, we know that there is no beeper on the current corner, but we don't know if we picked one up or not. We could simply ask the robot to put a beeper if it has any, but this requires that the robot begin with no beepers in its beeper-bag. What else do we know? Well, we know that if we picked up a beeper it was because our front was blocked and we haven't moved or turned so its front must still be blocked in that case. If it is not blocked, it is because we have walked off the edge of the field to an empty corner.

```
def follow_edge()
    while next_to_a_beeper?()
        if front_is_clear?()
            move()
        else
            pick_beeper()
        end
    end
    if not front_is_clear?()
        put_beeper()
    else
        back_up()
    end
end
```

Our robot starts out fine and this works in many worlds, but now another beyond-the-horizon situation pops up. In the world of Fig 6-15, there is a wall exactly one block away from the lower edge of our field. When our guard, tony, reaches this wall its front will be blocked, but not in the same way as it would be along the left edge. So there are two ways the front can be blocked at this point in the program (the second check for **front_is_clear**?): either the robot has encountered the wall while still in the field, or just after walking off the edge. The robot will try to put a beeper here, but doesn't have one. Even if it did, it would be putting one outside the field, complicating later actions, perhaps.

The solution is to carefully examine these possibilities and provide different situations for each of them. If we can assume (a precondition) that tony starts with no beepers, then at this point, if it has a beeper it is still in the field, having just picked it up, and otherwise it is just off the edge. So if it has a beeper it can put it down, but otherwise needs to back up. So we finally arrive at the following solution, but at a cost of requiring tony to start with no beepers. Perhaps you can think of a way to relax this restriction, making it more general.

```
def follow_edge()
    while next_to_a_beeper?()
        if front_is_clear?()
            move()
        else
            pick_beeper()
        end
    end
    if not front_is_clear?()
        if any_beepers_in_beeper_bag?()
            put_beeper()
        else
            back_up()
        end
    else
        back_up()
    end
end
```

Well, as it often happens in programming, just when we think we have a solution to a programming problem, the problem changes. When the owner of the field saw our above solution in action, she observed that the robot wasn't going to be especially effective in preventing beeper theft, since, while tony was walking along one edge, someone could steal beepers by entering from the opposite edge. To prevent this, she has changed the specification of the problem to require four robots, starting at the four corners of the field, all walking in unison, to keep better watch. We will look at this problem in Chapter 7 (exercises).

Note that in the solution above, we could improve the structure somewhat by doing test-reversal on the if that follows the while. This would both give us a positively stated test, but also make the shorter (and easier to understand) case first. Try it and see if you agree.

6.9 When to Use a Repeating Instruction

As explained at the end of the last chapter, a decision map is a technique that asks questions about the problem we are trying to solve. The answers to the questions determine which path of the map to follow. If we have done a thorough job of planning our implementation, the decision map should suggest an appropriate instruction to use. Take some time and examine some of the discussions presented in this chapter and see how the complete decision map, which is presented below, might have been useful.

Note especially the distinction between the situations in which you use a FOR LOOP and those in which you use a WHILE instruction. The FOR LOOP is based on being able to count the number of iterations. The WHILE is much more flexible, being based on an arbitrary predicate.

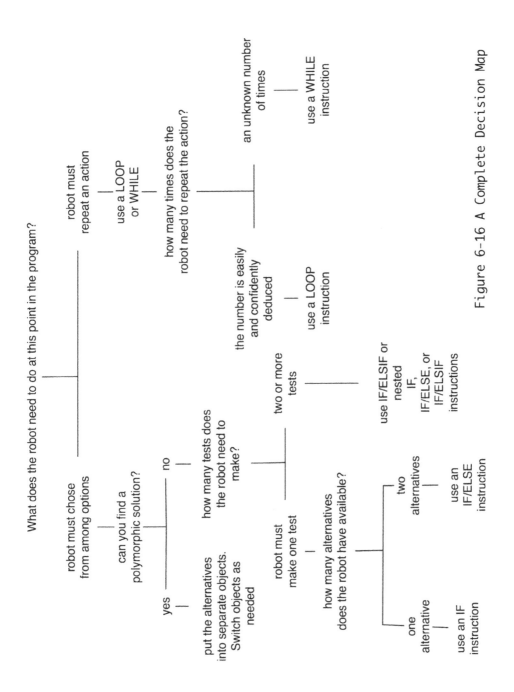

Figure 6-16 A Complete Decision Map

6.10 Important Ideas From This Chapter

repetition
iteration
fence post problem
infinite execution
loop invariant

6.11 Problem Set

The problems in this section require writing definitions and programs that use FOR-LOOP, iterator, and WHILE instructions. Try using stepwise refinement and the four step process discussed in Section 6.3.3 when writing these definitions and programs. Test your solutions by simulating them in various initial situations, and try to find beyond-the-horizon situations too. Take care to write programs that avoid error shutoffs and infinite loops.

A common mistake among beginning programmers is trying to have each execution of a while loop's body make too much progress. As a rule of thumb, try to have each execution of a WHILE loop's body make as little progress as possible (while still making some progress toward terminating the loop).

1. Write a new method named empty_beeper_bag. After a robot executes this method, its beeper-bag should be empty. What is the correct pre-condition for this method?

2. Write a new method called go_to_origin that positions a robot on 1st Street and 1st Avenue facing east, regardless of its initial location or the direction it is initially facing. Assume that there are no wall sections present. Hint: Use the south and west boundary walls as guides.

3. Study both of the following program fragments separately. What does each do? For each, is there a simpler program fragment that is execution equivalent? If so, write it down; if not, explain why not.

```
while not next_to_a_beeper?()        while not next_to_a_beeper?()
   move()                               if next_to_a_beeper?()
   if next_to_a_beeper?()                 pick_beeper()
     pick_beeper()                      else
   else                                   move()
     move()                             end
   end                               end
end
```

Describe the difference between the following two program fragment s:

```
while front_is_clear?()        if front_is_clear?()
   move()                         move()
end                            end
```

4. There is a menace in Karel's world--an infinite pile of beepers. Yes, it sounds impossible but occasionally one occurs in the world. If Karel accidentally tries to pick up an infinite pile of beepers, it is forever doomed to pick beepers from the pile. karel's current situation places the robot in grave danger from such a pile. The robot is standing outside two rooms: one is to the west and one is to the east. Only one of these rooms has a

pile of beepers that karel can pick. The other room has the dreaded infinite pile of beepers. Karel must decide which room is the safe room, enter it and pick all of the beepers. To help the robot decide which room is safe, there is a third pile of beepers on the corner at which karel is currently standing. If this third pile has an even number of beepers, the safe room is the eastern room. If the pile has an odd number of beepers, the safe room is the western room. There is at least one beeper in the third pile. Program karel to pick the beepers in the safe room. This simulator shows an infinite pile of beepers by marking it with an N instead of a number.

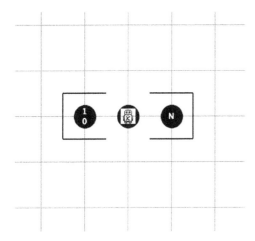

Figure 6-17 A Very Dangerous Task

5. A robot must place beepers in the exact arrangement shown below. Assume that it starts with exactly enough beepers for the task and always starts on the bottom-left corner of the square. Yes, there is a beeper on karel's current corner in the figure.

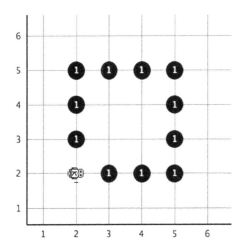

Figure 6-18 A Beeper Arranging Task

186

Chapter 6

6. Instruct a robot to escape from any rectangular room that has an open doorway exactly one block wide. After escaping from the room, the program must command the robot to turn itself off. Watch out for beyond the horizon situations. This problem is surprisingly sophisticated.

7. Program a robot to escape from a rectangular room if it can find a doorway. If there is no doorway, the robot must turn itself off. We may not be able use the program written in Problem 6 for this task, because executing this program in a door-less room could cause the to run around inside the room forever. Hint: There is a slightly messy way to solve this problem without resorting to beepers. You can write the program this way, or you can assume that the robot has one beeper in the beeper-bag, which it can use to remember if it has circumnavigated the room. This program may require a separate turn_off instruction for the completely enclosed situation in addition to a turn_off instruction for the situation with a door.

8. Karel is working once again as a gardener. Karel must outline the wall segment shown in Figure 6-19 with beepers. One and only one beeper is to be planted on each corner that is adjacent to a wall. You may assume that karel always starts in the same relative position and has exactly enough beepers to do the task. A simple variation can be programmed in which karel has infinitely many beepers rather than exactly the right number.

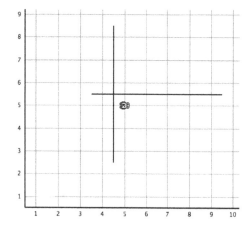

Figure 6-19 Another Gardening Job

9. Karel's beeper crop failed again. The robot is back to carpeting hallways. The hallways always have the same general shape as shown in Figure 6-20 and are always one block wide. To ensure there are no lumps in the carpet, only one beeper can be placed on a corner. Karel has exactly enough beepers to do the job and always starts in the same relative location. Can you write a single program that solves both problems 8 and 9 of this section?

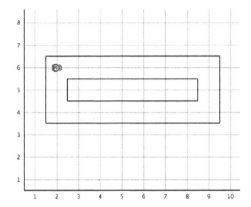

Figure 6-20 Another Carpeting Job

10. Program a robot to run a super steeplechase. In this race the hurdles are arbitrarily high and the course has no fixed finish corner. The finish of each race course is marked by a beeper that the robot must pick up before turning itself off. Figure 6-21 illustrates one possible course. Other courses may be longer and have higher hurdles. Should you modify the class you built in Problem 6 of Chapter 4 or build a new class?

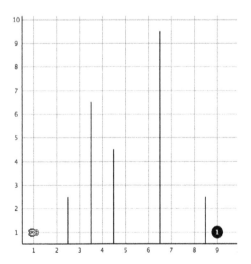

Figure 6-21 A Super Steeplechase

11. Program a robot to run a super-duper steeplechase. In this race the hurdles are arbitrarily high and arbitrarily wide. In each race course the finish is marked by a beeper, which the robot must pick up before turning itself off. Figure 6-22 illustrates one possible race course. The best way to do this exercise, of course, is to build a subclass of the Steeplechaser class you built in Problem 10. If you built an awkward or ill-structured program for problem 10, it might be worth improving it first, to make this one easier.

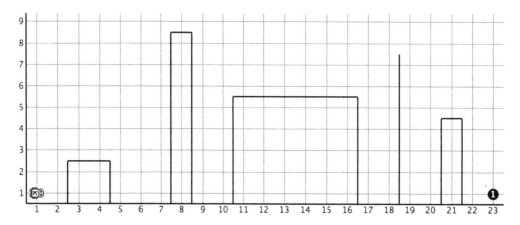

Figure 6-22 A Super-Duper Steeplechase

12. Write an instruction that harvests a rectangular field of any size. The field is guaranteed to be bordered by beeper-less corners. Also, assume that every corner within the field has a beeper on it and that our robot starts facing east on the lower left-hand corner of the field. Should we use a class derived from Harvester?

13. Karel has returned to the diamond shaped beeper field to harvest a new crop. Write a new program for karel that harvests the beepers. The beeper field is always the same size and there is always one beeper on each corner of the field.

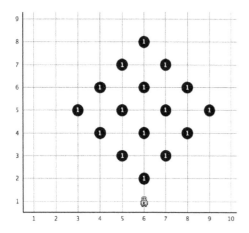

Figure 6-23 Return to the Diamond Shaped Beeper Field

14. A robot named karel is building a fence. The fence will be made of beepers and will surround a rectangular shaped wall segment. The size of the wall segment is unknown. Karel is at the origin facing an unknown direction. The fences (beepers) are stacked somewhere next to the western boundary wall. There are exactly enough beepers in the pile to build the fence. The beeper pile is on the street that is adjacent to the southern edge of the wall segment as shown in the Figure 6-24. The distances to the beeper pile and to the wall segment are unknown. Program karel to build the fence and return to the origin. Assume that there are no beepers in karel's beeper-bag at the start of the program.

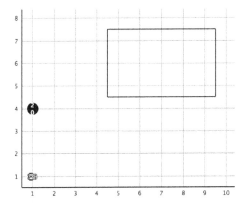

Figure 6-24 Building a Fence

15. A robot named karel likes to take long meandering walks in the woods in the world, and even though it has a built-in compass, the robot sometimes cannot find its way back home. To alleviate this problem, before karel walks in the woods the robot fills its beeper-bag and then it leaves a trail of beepers. Program karel to follow this path back home. There are many questions one can ask about this task. Ignore the possibility that any wall boundaries or wall sections interfere with karel, and assume that the end of the path is marked by two beepers on the same corner. Each beeper will be reachable from the previous beeper by the execution of one move. Also, the path will never cross over itself. See Figure 6-25 for a path that karel must follow. Hint: karel must probe each possible next corner in the path, eventually finding the correct one. It might prove useful to have karel pick up the beepers as it follows the path; Otherwise it may get caught in an infinite loop going backward and forward. How difficult would it be to program karel to follow the same type of path if we allowed for a beeper to be missing occasionally (but not two missing beepers in a row)?

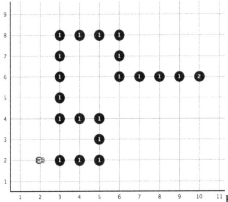 Figure 6-25 A Path of Beepers

16. Assume that a robot is somewhere in a completely enclosed rectangular room that contains one beeper. Program the robot to find the beeper, pick it up, and turn itself off.

17. Program a robot named karel to escape from a maze that contains no islands. The exit of the maze is marked by placing a beeper on the first corner that is outside the maze, next to the right wall. This task can be accomplished by commanding karel to move through the maze, with the invariant that its right side is always next to a wall. See Problem 5.11-9 for hints on the type of movements for which karel must be programmed. Figure 6-26 shows one example of a maze. (Islands are portions of wall sections that are not connected to the outer boundary of the maze.)

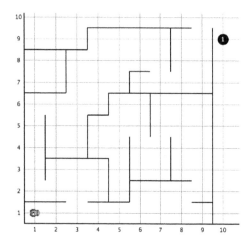

Figure 6-26 A Maze

There is a simpler way to program this task without using the instructions written in Problem 5.11-9. Try to write a shorter version of the maze-escaping program. Hint: Program karel to make the least amount of progress toward its goal at each corner in the maze.

Finally, compare the maze escape problem with Problem 6.10-11, the Super-Duper Steeplechase. Do you see any similarities? Are there any similarities to the room-escaping problem? What class should we build to solve this problem? What should the parent class be?

18. This problem is inspired by the discussion on the verification of WHILE loops (Section 5.6). Simulate a robot's execution of the following instruction in initial situation s where the robot is on a corner with 0, 1, 2, 3, and 7 beepers.

```
def will_this_clear_corner_of_beepers()
    10.times do
        if  next_to_a_beeper?()
            pick_beeper()
        end
    end
end
```

State in exactly which initial situation s this instruction works correctly. What happens in the other situations?

19. Program a robot named karel to go on a treasure hunt. The treasure is marked by a corner containing five beepers. Other corners (including the corner on which karel starts) contain clues, with each clue indicating in which direction karel should proceed. The clues are as follows: 1 beeper means karel should go north, 2 means west, 3 means south, and 4 means east. Karel should follow the clues until it reaches the treasure corner where the robot should turn itself off. Figure 6-27 shows one possible treasure hunt.

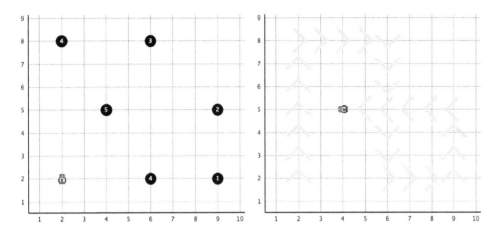

Figure 6-27 A Treasure Hunt

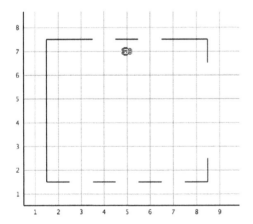

Figure 6-28 Closing the Windows (problem 20)

20. A robot named karel is inside a room that has a number of open windows. There are no windows in the corners of the room. Karel is next to the northern wall facing east. Program karel to close the windows by putting one beeper in front of each window. You may assume that karel has exactly enough beepers to complete the task. Variation: put the beepers outside the windows, rather than inside. Can you solve the variation by overriding exactly one method in the original solution?

21. A robot named karel is at the origin facing east. In front of karel, somewhere along 1st Street, is a line of beepers (one beeper is on each corner, with at least one beeper in the line). The length of the line of beepers is unknown but there are no gaps in the line. Karel must pick up and move the beepers north a number of streets

equal to the number of beepers in the line. For example, if there are five beepers in the line, the beepers must be moved to 6th Street. The beepers must be moved directly north. If the first beeper is on 4th Avenue, it must be on 4th Avenue when the program is finished.

22. A robot named karel is inside a completely enclosed room with no doors or windows. The robot is in the southeast corner facing south. There is one wall segment inside the room with karel. The wall segment blocks north/south travel and does not touch the walls that form the room. On one side of the wall segment is a beeper (which side is unknown). Program karel to find and move the beeper to the opposite side of the wall segment.

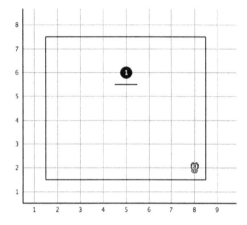

Figure 6-29 Finding and Moving a Beeper

23. Once again karel is working as a carpet layer. Before carpeting a room karel must ensure that the room has continuous walls to the west, north, and east. Only these rooms must be carpeted. The doors to the rooms are always to the south. All rooms are one block wide and there is always a northern wall at the end of each room. Karel's task ends when the robot arrives at a blocking wall segment on 1st Street. Figure 6-30 shows one possible set of initial and final situation s.

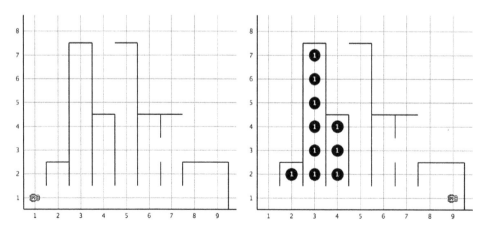

Figure 6-30 A More Complex Carpet Laying Task

24. What will be the effect of executing the following instruction?

```
while facing_north? ()
   turn_left ()
end
```

25. Program a robot named karel to arrange vertical piles of beepers into ascending order. Each avenue, starting at the origin, will contain a vertical pile of one or more beepers. The first empty avenue will mark the end of the piles that need to be sorted. Figure 6-31 illustrates one of the many possible initial and final situation s. (How difficult would it be to modify your program to arrange the piles of beepers into descending order?)

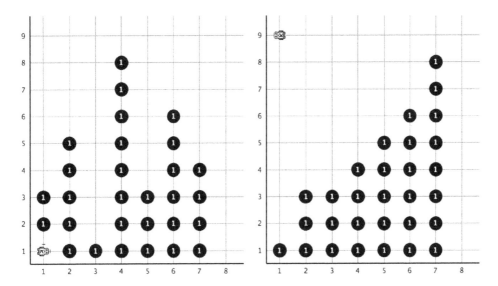

Figure 6-31 A Sorting Task

26. Build a new robot Sweeper class, derived from the Robot class of Chapter 5. The defining property of robots in this class is that they sweep up all beepers on any corner to which they move. Why is this not quite the same thing as saying that they sweep up all beepers on all corners that they occupy?

27. Program the three robots, karel, carol, and karl, to run a relay super steeplechase. karel will start the race at the origin with one beeper in its beeper-bag. Somewhere along 1st street carol will be waiting. When karel gets to carol, karel should pass the beeper to carol and carol should continue the race and karel should stop. When carol gets to karl, karl should likewise continue, with the beeper, and only stop when it comes to a corner with a beeper marking the end of the course. It should put down the beeper it is carrying at this final corner. You may want to put karel and carol in a different class than karl, who can be a Steeplechaser robot. Here you will get a chance to use the predicate **next_to_a_robot**?.

28. Tony the robot is standing at the origin with some beepers in its beeper bag. Write an instruction that will deposit half of the beepers on the corner. The others should be retained in the beeper-bag. If there are an odd number of beepers then the extra one should be left on the corner.

29. Write a Spy Walk program (See Chapter 4) that continues until the Spy arrives on a corner with no Accomplice robot. This is the treasure corner and it should be marked with three beepers. The Spy should end by picking up these three beepers. Test your program using at least 4 Accomplices and at least three strategies. You may assume there are no other robots in the world besides the single Spy and the Accomplices.

30. After doing (or at least thinking about) Problem 29, go back and answer Problem 4.12-10.

31. Suppose a robot arrives on a corner with a lot of other robots of different classes, some of which have overridden the move method in various ways. What happens if we use the list provided by the neighbors method of this new arrival to send a move message to each of the other robots on this corner?

32. Use the idea of Problem 31 to write a program to build a house using a Contractor and a work crew, where the contractor doesn't even need to know how many robots are in the crew or their types. Be as creative as you like. The contractor will just tell each member of the team where the house is to be built by passing a strategy to each.

33. Solve the problem of Exercise 4 in this section without the "hint" pile.

34. Look at go_to_beeper in Section 6.3.2. Does the name truly describe the action? Discuss this and make any improvements you think justified.

35. A robot arrives on a corner with some number of beepers. Leave 1 beeper on the corner if there are originally an odd number, and 0 if there are originally an even number.

36. A robot named karel is at the origin. Somewhere on the main diagonal is a beeper. That is, the street and avenue numbers of the beeper are the same, such as 7th street and 7th avenue. Program karel to find the beeper. Assume there are no walls in the world other than the boundary walls.

37. Solve the problem of exercise 36 again, but this time the world has an arbitrary set of wall segments with the following properties. Each segment is one block long and may be oriented either east-west or north south. None of the segments is connected to any of the others or to the boundary walls.

38. A robot named karel is at the origin facing East with an infinite number of beepers in its beeper-bag. Somewhere in front of karel is a wall. Program karel to compute the distance to the wall by leaving a number of beepers at the Origin equal to the distance between the Origin and the wall.

39. A robot named dersu is in a completely enclosed rectangular room with no beepers in the room. Dersu has an infinite number of beepers in its beeper-bag. Program dersu to compute the area of the room by placing a number of beepers in the south-west corner equal to the area of the room.

7 Advanced Techniques for Robots

This chapter presents a number of quite challenging topics. First we will introduce the concept of recursion. Recursion, like loops, allows robots to execute a sequence of statements more than once. We will also look at the formal relationship between recursion and loops. Next, we study two interesting new instructions that give robots the ability to solve some novel beeper-manipulation problems, including numerical computations. Then we will look again at dynamic object-oriented programming and see some implications of what we have learned here.

7.1 Introduction to Recursion

Having thoroughly looked at loops in the last chapter, we are now going to examine a different way to get a robot to repeat an action. The technique is called *recursion*. The word means, simply, to recur or repeat. When a programming language allows *recursive definitions* or *recursion*, it means that within a new method we can send the same message (the one with the name of the executing method) to the executing robot. This may seem odd at first, but after a few examples, we hope that it will appear as natural as using a WHILE loop to control a robot's execution. We note that recursion is just another control structure and, while it may appear magical at first, it can be understood as readily as loops. It is another programming tool to add to your collection.

In all of the examples prior to Chapter 6, when we asked a robot to move from one point to another, we knew exactly how far it would move. There are many situations, however, in which this is not true. Suppose, for example, that a robot named kristin is standing at the origin facing East, and suppose that there is a beeper somewhere along 1st Street. We want kristin to go to the beeper and pick it up and return to the origin.

```
    kristin.retrieve_beeper()
```

If we knew that the beeper was on 1st and 23rd, we would be able to write a program without loops to do this. If we knew that it was no more than, say, 15 blocks away, then we could find a solution. (How?) But what if we don't know how far it is. To get started, let's build a new class: BeeperFinder.

```
    class BeeperFinder < Robot
       include Turner
       def retrieve_beeper()
          find_beeper()
          pick_beeper()
          turn_around()
          return_to_west_wall()
       end

       def find_beeper()
          # TODO
       end
```

```
def return_to_west_wall()
      # TODO
   end
end
```

Well, that will certainly do the job, if we can write the other two new methods. Let's now attack find_beeper. We know that there is a beeper somewhere on 1st Street. We also know that kristin is on 1st Street facing East. It may be that kristin is already on the beeper corner, in which case there is nothing to do. Therefore, we may get started by writing:

```
def find_beeper()
   if not next_to_a_beeper?()
      ...
   end
end
```

This will correctly terminate having done nothing if kristin is already at the beeper corner. Suppose next that the beeper is on some other corner. Then kristin needs to move, of course, and check other corners.

```
def find_beeper()
   if not next_to_a_beeper?()
      move()
      ???
   end
end
```

Well, what does kristin need to do after a move? Notice that kristin is on a different corner than the one on which it started and that the original corner was checked and found to lack a beeper. Therefore, we may conclude that the beeper is now (after the move) either at kristin's current location or farther East of it. But this is exactly the same situation (relatively) that kristin was in when it started this task. Therefore, we can conclude that what kristin needs to do now is exactly find_beeper and nothing more.

```
def find_beeper()
   if not next_to_a_beeper?()
      move()
      find_beeper()
   end
end
```

Notice that find_beeper has been completely defined, but it has been defined by using find_beeper itself. How can this be done? Well, suppose we needed to empty an ocean with a bucket. To perform empty_the_ocean, we first ask if the ocean is empty. If so, we are done. Otherwise, we just remove one bucket of water from the ocean and then empty_the_ocean.

The important thing in such a definition, called a *recursive definition*, is that we don't define a thing in terms of *precisely* itself. We define a thing in terms of a simpler or smaller version of itself, and also define the smallest or simplest version separately. Here we define find_beeper as either "nothing", if kristin is already on the beeper corner, or "move (); find_beeper()", if kristin is anywhere else. It is also necessary to know before we start executing such an instruction that there is, indeed, a beeper somewhere in kristin's path. Otherwise, after every move, the re-execution of find_beeper will find that the test is true, generating yet another re-execution of find_beeper without end.

The other method, return_to_west_wall is similar, except for the test. Here, however we know that there is a wall to the west. If we can guarantee that the robot is also facing west, then the following method will serve.

```
def return_to_west_wall()
    if front_is_clear?()
        move()
        return_to_west_wall()
    end
end
```

Programming with recursion is a very powerful and sometimes error-prone activity.

7.2 More on Recursion

Given the problem--a robot must clean all beepers from its current corner--we could easily write a loop that looks like the following.

```
def sweep_corner()
    while next_to_a_beeper?()
        pick_beeper()
    end
end
```

This correctly solves the problem and is known as an iterative solution ("iterative" means that a loop of some sort, WHILE or FOR- LOOP, was used). Contrast this solution with a recursive one.

```
def sweep_corner()
    if next_to_a_beeper?()
        pick_beeper()
        sweep_corner()
    end
end
```

The difference between these two methods is very subtle. The first method, which uses the WHILE loop, is invoked once and the robot's focus never leaves the loop until it is finished, executing zero or more pick_beepers (depending on the initial number on the corner). What happens in the second, recursive, sweep_corner? Let's look at it very carefully.

If the robot is initially on an empty corner when the message is sent, nothing happens (similar to the WHILE loop). If it is on a corner with one beeper when the message is sent, the IF test is true, so the robot executes one pick_beeper instruction (thus emptying the corner). The robot then sends a second sweep_corner message (to itself), remembering where it was in the first execution. When sweep_corner is executed the second time, the IF test is false, so nothing happens and the robot returns to the first invocation.

[initial instantiation of]

```
def sweep_corner()
    if next_to_a_beeper?()
        pick_beeper()
        sweep_corner()  # <--This is the second invocation
    end                 # of sweep_corner. The robot
end                     # will return to this point
                        # when that execution finishes
```

[second instantiation of]

```
def sweep_corner()
    if next_to_a_beeper?()  # <--This is now false
        pick_beeper()
        sweep_corner()
    end
end
```

Each execution results in a separate instantiation of the instruction sweep_corner. The robot must completely execute each instantiation, always remembering where it was in the previous instance so it can return there when it finishes.

The process for writing recursive robot instructions is very similar to that for writing loops:

Step 1: Consider the stopping condition (also called the base case)--what is the simplest case of the problem that can be solved? In the sweep_corner problem, the simplest, or base, case is when the robot is already on an empty corner.

Step 2: What does the robot have to do in the base case? In this example there's nothing to do.

Step 3: Find a way to solve a small piece of the larger problem if not in the base case. This is called "reducing the problem in the general case." In the sweep_corner problem, the general case is when the robot is on a corner with one or more beepers and the reduction is to pick up a beeper.

Step 4: Make sure the reduction leads to the base case. Again, in the above example of sweep_corner, by picking up one beeper at a time, the robot must eventually clear the corner of beepers, regardless of the original number present.

Let's compare and contrast iteration and recursion:

* An iterative loop must complete each iteration before beginning the next one.

* A recursive method typically begins a new instantiation before completing the current one. When that happens, the current instance is temporarily suspended, pending the completion of the new instance. Of course, this new instantiation might not complete before generating another one. Each successive instantiation must be completed in turn, last to first.

* Since EACH recursive instantiation is supposed to make some (often minimal) progress toward the base case, we should not use loops to control recursive calls. Thus, we will usually see an IF or an IF/ELSE in the body of a recursive new method, but not a WHILE.

Suppose we wanted to use recursion to move a robot named karel to a beeper. How would we do it? Following the steps presented earlier:

* What is the base case? Karel is on the beeper.

* What does the robot have to do in the base case? Nothing.

* What is the general case? The robot is not on the beeper.

* What is the reduction? Move toward the beeper and make the recursive call.

* Does the reduction lead to termination? Yes, assuming the beeper is directly in front of the robot, the distance will get shorter by one block for each recursive call.

The final implementation follows.

```
def find_beeper()
    if not next_to_a_beeper?()
        move()
        find_beeper()
    end
end
```

Note that this problem could also have been easily solved with a WHILE loop. Let's look at a problem that is not easily solved with a WHILE loop. Remember the Lost Beeper Mine, the corner with a large number of beepers? Imagine we must write the following method in our search for the mine. A robot named karel must walk east from its current location until it finds a beeper. The Lost Beeper Mine is due north of that intersection a distance equal to the number of moves karel made to get from its current position to the beeper. Write the new method, find_mine.

It is not easy to see how to solve this problem with a WHILE loop as we do not have any convenient way of remembering how many intersections have been traversed. Oh, we could probably come up with a very convoluted beeper-tracking scheme, but let's look at a recursive solution that's pretty straightforward. Again, we'll answer our questions:

* What is the base case? Karel is on the beeper.

* What does karel have to do in the base case? turn_left (this will face karel north).

* What is the general case? Karel is not on the beeper.

* What is the reduction? Move one block forward, make the recursive call and have karel execute a second move after the recursive call. This second move will be executed in all instances but the base case, causing karel to make as many moves north after the base case as it did in getting to the base case.

* Does the reduction lead to termination? Yes, assuming the beeper is directly in front of karel.

Let's look at the complete method:

```
def find_mine()
    if  next_to_a_beeper?()
        turn_left()
    else
        move()
        find_mine()
        move()
    end
end
```

How many turn_lefts are executed? How many moves? How many calls to find_mine?

A good way to think about recursion and the recursive call is in terms of the specification of the method itself. In the above case, the specification is that when a robot executes this instruction it will walk a certain number of steps, say k, to a beeper, turn left, and then walk k steps farther. Suppose we start the robot N steps away from the beeper (k = N). When we examine the method above, the ELSE clause has a **move** message first. That means that the robot is now N-1 steps from the beeper. Therefore, by the specification, the recursive (k = N-1) call will walk N-1 steps forward, turn left, and then walk N-1 steps beyond. We therefore need to supply one additional **move** message after the recursion to complete the required N steps.

It will take solving a number of problems and a good deal of staring before recursion becomes as comfortable to use as iteration. A large part of this is because recursion requires some intuition to see the correct reduction, especially in difficult problems. This intuition will come with practice, which is just what the sample problems are designed to provide.

7.3 Tail Recursion and Looping

Suppose we have a method with a WHILE loop and we would like to rewrite it so that it doesn't use a loop, but still carries out the same task. To consider the simplest case, suppose that the outermost control mechanism in a method is a loop. Take, for example, the method

```
def find_beeper()
    while not next_to_a_beeper?()
        move()
    end
end
```

By the definition of the WHILE given in Section 6.3, this is the same as

```
def find_beeper()
   if not next_to_a_beeper?()
      move()
      while not next_to_a_beeper?()  # <--This is just
         move()                       # <--find_beeper
      end
   end
end
```

However, the nested WHILE instruction in this latter form is exactly the body of find_beeper using the definition of find_beeper given first, so we can rewrite this second form as:

```
def find_beeper()
   if not next_to_a_beeper?()
      move()
      find_beeper()
   end
end
```

Thus, the first form, a while, is equivalent to the last form, a recursive program. Also notice that we could just as easily transform the second form into the first, since they are execution equivalent.

Notice, finally, that this is a special form of recursion, since after the recursive step (the nested find_beeper) there is nothing more to do in this method. It is, after all, the last instruction within an IF instruction, so when it is done, the IF is done, and therefore the method of which this is the body is done. This form of recursion is called *tail recursion* because the recursive step comes at the very tail of the computation.

It is possible to prove formally that tail recursion is equivalent to WHILE looping. Therefore, we can see that a WHILE loop is just a special form of recursion. So anything that you can do with a loop, you can also do with a recursive program. There are some deep and beautiful theories in computer science (and in mathematics) that have been developed from this observation.

By way of contrast, the find_mine method discussed in Section 7.2, was certainly recursive, but it is not tail-recursive, because the final move message follows the recursive message. That method is also equivalent to one using only WHILE loops, but, as suggested in Section 7.2, it is very convoluted.

7.4 Going Formal

At the beginning of this chapter we saw that it is possible to get a robot to perform an operation repeatedly without using FOR-LOOP or WHILE instructions. Perhaps you are wondering if there is a relationship between recursive programming and iterative programming. The answer, of course, is yes and we would like to go a bit deeper into the relationship.

In Chapter 6, we learned about the WHILE instruction and how to use it. However, the description we gave of it was somewhat informal, relying on examples and intuition. That is fine at the beginning, but it is also useful to look at a formal definition of a WHILE statement, so that it can be analyzed logically.

Suppose we permit instructions themselves to be named. We don't permit this in the robot language itself, only in talking about the robot language. This is the so-called *meta level*; the level at which we don't use a thing (the programming language), but discuss and analyze it. In any case, suppose that we let the simple WHILE statement form "while <test> : (<instruction-list>)" be known as statement W. We parenthesize the instruction list here to emphasize grouping, but it is NOT valid Ruby syntax. Let us also denote the <test> of the WHILE as T and the (<instruction-list>) as L. Then W can be written as:

W == while T : L

The formal definition of W is

W == if T : (L; W)

This says that to perform the while instruction W we must first test T (if T...) and if T is false, do nothing at all, but if T is true, then we must perform L followed by W, the while instruction itself: i.e. (L ; W). By the definition this means that we must test T again and if it is false do nothing else, but if it is true, we must perform L again followed by W again, etc.

The looping should be clear from this description, but if you look at the definition we have written, you see the recursive nature of the WHILE. This means that the WHILE statement W is defined in terms of itself, since W appears on the right side of the definition as well as the left. We hope that the W on the right is not exactly the same as the one on the left, but a simpler, smaller version of the W that appears on the left. What that means is that for a while loop to make sense, or be defined, the execution of the instruction list L, must partially solve the problem that the entire WHILE set out to solve, and take us closer to termination of the loop. If that is not the case, and the execution of L leaves the robot in the same state, relative to termination, that it was in at the start, then the loop is guaranteed to run forever. This is because in this case the definition is purely circular and so doesn't define anything.

7.5 Searching

This section introduces two new methods named zig_left_up and zag_down_right, that move a robot diagonally northwest and southeast respectively. Both of these methods are defined by using only UrRobot's methods such as turn_left, but we derive immense conceptual power from being able to think in terms of moving diagonally. For reasons that will become clear in the exercises, the class into which we put these methods is Mathematician. It will have the class Robot as the parent class.

The following definitions introduce the stars of this section: zig_left_up and zag_down_right. These direction pairs are not arbitrary; if a robot moves to the left and upward long enough, it eventually reaches the western boundary wall. The same argument holds for traveling down and toward the right, except that in this case the robot eventually reaches the southern boundary wall.

The other two possible direction pairs lack these useful properties: a robot will never find a boundary wall by traveling up and toward the right, and we cannot be sure which of the two boundary walls it will come upon first when traveling downward and to the left.

The following methods define zig_left_up and zag_down_right.

```
class Mathematician < Robot
   include Turner

   def zig_left_up()
      #Precondition: facing_west? and front_is_clear?
      #Postcondition facing_west?
      move()
      turn_right()
      move()
      turn_left()
   end

   def zag_down_right()
      #Precondition facing_south? and front_is_clear?
      #Postcondition facing_south?
      move()
      turn_left()
      move()
      turn_right()
   end
   ...
```

Assume that we have a Mathematician named karel. Observe that no part of these methods forces karel to move in the intended directions. To execute zig_left_up correctly, karel must be facing west; to execute zag_down_right correctly, karel must be facing south. These requirements are called the pre-conditions of the methods. Recall that a pre-condition of a method is a condition that must be made true before a robot can correctly execute the method. We have seen many other examples of pre-conditions in this book.

For this example, the directional pre-condition of zig_left_up is that karel is facing west; likewise, the directional pre-condition of zag_down_right is that karel is facing south. Karel's execution of these methods, when their pre-conditions are satisfied, is shown in Figure 7-1.

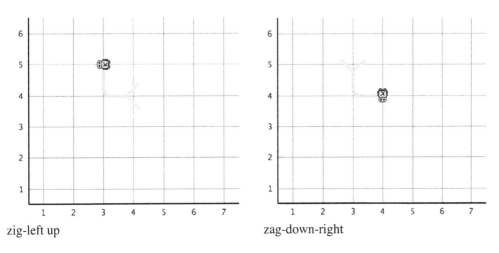

zig-left up   zag-down-right

Figure 7-1: Execution of the Zig-Zag Methods

Here is a statement that is loaded with terminology: the directional pre-conditions of zig_left_up and zag_down_right are invariant over each instruction's execution. This just means that if karel is facing west and it executes zig_left_up, the robot is still facing west after the instruction has finished executing. This property allows karel to execute a sequence of zig_left_up's without having to reestablish their directional pre-condition. A similar statement holds about karel's facing south and zag_down_right. Also observe that each instruction must be executed only when karel's front is clear. This pre-condition is not invariant over the instructions, because karel may be one block away from a corner where its front is blocked (e.g., karel may execute zig_left_up while facing west on the corner of 4th Street and 2nd Avenue).

The first major method that we will write solves the problem of finding a beeper that can be located anywhere in the world. Our task is to write a method named find_beeper that positions karel on the same corner as the beeper. We have seen a version of this problem in Chapter 6 where both karel and the beeper are in an enclosed room. This new formulation has less stringent restrictions: the beeper is placed on some arbitrary street corner in karel's world, and there are no wall sections in the world. Of course, the boundary walls are always present.

One simple solution may spring to mind. In this attempt, karel first goes to the origin and faces east. The robot then moves eastward on 1st Street looking for a beeper. If karel finds a beeper on 1st Street, it has accomplished its task; if the beeper is not found on 1st Street, karel moves back to the western wall, switches over to 2nd Street, and continues searching from there. Karel repeats this strategy until it finds the beeper. Unfortunately, a mistaken assumption is implicit in this search instruction: there is no way for karel to know that the beeper is not on 1st Street. No matter how much of 1st Street karel explores, the robot can never be sure that the beeper is not one block farther East.

It looks as if we and karel are caught in an impossible trap, but there is an ingenious solution to our problem. As we might expect, it involves zig-zag moves. We need to program karel to perform a radically different type of search pattern; Figure 7-2 shows such a pattern, and we use it below to define the find_beeper method.

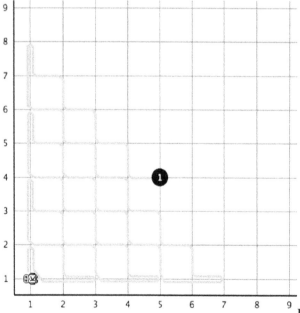

Figure 7-2: A Method for Searching Every Corner

This search method expands the search frontier similar to the way water would expand over karel's world from an overflowing sink at the origin. Roughly, we can view karel as traveling back and forth diagonally on the fringe of this water wave. Convince yourself that this search pattern is guaranteed to find the beeper eventually, regardless of the beeper's location--in our analogy, we need to convince ourselves that the beeper will eventually get wet. We can use stepwise refinement to write the find_beeper method using this search strategy with the zig_left_up and zag_down_right methods.

```
def find_beeper()
    go_to_origin()
    face_west()
    while not next_to_a_beeper?()
        if facing_west?()
            zig_move()
        else
            zag_move()
        end
    end
end
```

The find_beeper method starts by moving karel to the origin and then facing west. (We saw how to write the face_west instruction in Chapter 5.) These messages establish the directional pre-condition for zig_left_up. The WHILE loop's purpose is to keep karel moving until it finds a beeper, and is correct if the loop eventually terminates. The IF condition, which is nested within the body of the loop, determines which direction karel has been traveling and continues moving the robot along the diagonal in this same direction. We continue the stepwise refinement by writing zig_move and zag_move.

```
def zig_move()
    #Precondition facing_west?
    if front_is_clear?()
        zig_left_up()
    else
        advance_to_next_diagonal()
    end
end
```

and

```
def zag_move()
    #Precondition facing_south?
    if front_is_clear?()
        zag_down_right()
    else
        advance_to_next_diagonal()
    end
end
```

The moving methods, zig_move and zag_move operate similarly; therefore we discuss only zig_move. When karel is able to keep zigging, the zig_move method moves it diagonally upward towards the left to the next corner; Otherwise, the robot is blocked by the western boundary wall and must advance northward to the next diagonal. We now write the method that advances karel to the next diagonal.

```
def advance_to_next_diagonal()
    if facing_west?()
        face_north()
    else
        face_east()
    end
    move()
    turn_around()
end
```

The advance_to_next_diagonal method starts by facing karel away from the origin; it turns a different direction depending on whether the robot has been zigging or zagging. In either case, karel then moves one corner farther away from the origin and turns around. If karel has been zigging on the current diagonal, after executing advance_to_next_diagonal, the robot is positioned to continue by zagging on the next diagonal, and vice versa.

Observe that when karel executes a zig_left_up or a zag_down_right method, it must visit two corners; the first is visited temporarily, and the second is catty-corner from karel's starting corner. When thinking about these methods, we should ignore the intermediate corner and just remember that these instructions move karel diagonally. Also notice that the temporarily visited corner is guaranteed not to have a beeper on it, because it is part of the wave front that karel visited while it was on the previous diagonal sweep.

Trace karel's execution of find_beeper in the sample situation presented in Figure 7-2 to acquaint yourself with its operation. Try to get a feel for how all these instructions fit together to accomplish the task. Pay particularly close attention to the advance_to_next_diagonal method. Test find_beeper in the situation where the beeper is on the origin and in situations where the beeper is next to either boundary wall.

Notice something very important about zig_left_up and zag_down_right. When their preconditions are met, they have an interesting invariant. Note that the sum of the street number and the avenue number does not change when they execute if their precondition is first true. For example, zig_left_up decreases its avenue number by one, while increasing its street number. Hence the sum does not change. We will exploit this in the exercises.

7.6 Doing Arithmetic

One of the things that computers do well is manipulating numbers. Robots can be taught to do arithmetic as we shall see. One way to represent numbers in the robot world is to use beepers. We could represent the number 32 by putting 32 beepers on a corner, but we can be more sophisticated. Suppose that we represent the different digits of a multi-digit number separately. Therefore to represent the number 5732 we could, using 2nd street as an example of a place to put the number, put 5 beepers at 2nd Street and 1st Avenue, 7 beepers at 2nd and 2nd, 3 beepers at 2nd and 3rd, and 2 beepers at 2nd and 4th. We could write a whole column of numbers as shown in Figure 7. 3.

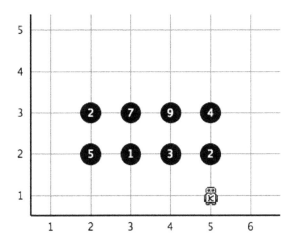

Figure 7.3 A Column of Numbers to be Added.

Let's start with a simpler case, however and just add up a column of single digit numbers. See Figure 7.4 for an example. Suppose we start with an Adder robot on 1st Street with a column of numbers represented by beepers north of it. On each such corner there will be between 1 and 9 beepers. We want to "write" on 1st Street the decimal number representing the sum of the column. Since we must "carry" if the total number of beepers is more than 9 we assume that we are not starting at 1st Avenue.

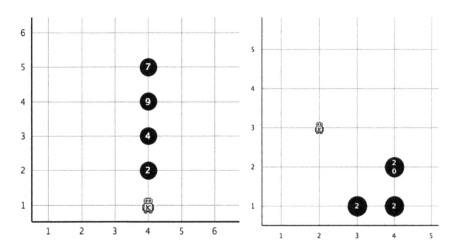

Figure 7.4 Adding Single Digit Numbers Before and After

Our adder robot will utilize two helper robots. The first of these will check to see if a carry is necessary and the second will actually do the carry if it is necessary. Since these robots will need to be created and find the adder robot that created them, we will start with a super (parent) class that provides this *finding* method. All of our other classes for this problem will be derived as subclasses of this base class; Finder. We won't actually create any Finder robots, however. This class is just a convenient place to place methods that must be common to other classes. We will add to it as we go. It could also have been a mixin.

```
class Finder < Robot
    include Turner

    def move_to_robot() # at least one block
        move()
        while not next_to_a_robot?()
            move()
        end
    end
end

class Carrier < Finder

    # Arithmetic carry to next column
    def carry_one()
        # TODO
    end
end

class Checker < Finder

    # Are there enough beepers to require a carry?
    def enough_to_carry?()
        # TODO
    end
end
```

Below is part of the Adder class. We note two things here. First is that we provide a constructor that names only the avenue on which the Adder will begin. It doesn't make sense to start anywhere but on first street facing North. And we won't need any beepers. So we use *default* values for the other required parameters. Note that since we are writing a constructor we must invoke the superclass constructor and it (inherited from UrRobot) requires four arguments. Secondly, the gather_helpers methods introduces the two helper robots whereas this is usually done in the constructor. Since this is the first mention of @carry, for example, and it is on the left of an assignment, the variable will be created here. This is fine as long as no other mention is made of this variable until a gather_helpers message is sent to the Adder robot. In any case, the Adder is responsible for creating its own helpers and bringing them to itself.

```
class Adder < Finder
    def initialize(avenue)
        super(1, avenue, NORTH, 0)
    end

    def gather_helpers()
        @carry = Carrier.new(1, 1, EAST, INFINITY)
        @check = Checker.new(1, 1, EAST, 0)
        @carry.move_to_robot()
        @carry.turn_left()
        @check.move_to_robot()
        @check.turn_left()
```

```
      end

      def add_column()
          # TODO
      end
  end
```

Once the Adder robot has created its helpers, it can execute add_column. To do this it merely picks up all of the beepers north of it until it finds an empty corner, returns to 1st Street, deposits all of the beepers there and then has the helpers finish the task.

```
      def add_column()
          move()
          while next_to_a_beeper?()
              pick_beeper()
              if not next_to_a_beeper?()
                  move()
              end
          end
          turn_around()
          while front_is_clear?()
              move()
          end
          turn_around()
          empty_bag()
          while @check.enough_to_carry?()
              @carry.carry_one()
          end
      end
```

Note that the last while loop computes the quotient and remainder. Carrying is quite simple. Recall that we gave the Carrier an infinite number of beepers in its beeper-bag, so it can't possibly run out. The empty_bag method can also be added easily.

```
      # Arithmetic carry to next column
      def carry_one() # Facing north on 1st Street. -- Carrier class
          turn_left()
          move()         # Note:  Error shutoff here if we try to carry
                         # from 1st Street.
          put_beeper()
          turn_around()
          move()
          turn_left()
      end
```

The Checker robot does all of the interesting work. It must determine if there are ten or more beepers on the current corner. If there are it must return true, otherwise false. It can try to pick up ten beepers to check this. However, it has more to do since it is going to be called repeatedly to see how many multiples of ten there really are. Therefore it must find a way to dispose of each group of ten beepers before it attempts to check for the next group of ten. It has another important task also. If it finds less than ten beepers in a group it must leave them on the current corner. This is to account for the first digit of the answer; the one that isn't carried.

```
# Are there enough beepers to require a carry
def enough_to_carry?() # Facing north on 1st Street. Checker class
    10.times do
        if next_to_a_beeper?()
            pick_beeper()
        else
            empty_bag()
            return false
        end
    end
    # Found ten beepers. Put them on 2nd street.
    move()
    empty_bag()
    back_up()
    return true
end
```

To finish we need only add empty_bag to the Checker class. But note that we also wanted it in the Adder class. It will be worthwhile, therefore to *factor* it up to the Finder class where it will be available by inheritance to both Adder and Checker.

```
def empty_bag() # in Finder
    while any_beepers_in_beeper_bag?()
        put_beeper()
    end
end
```

Now we are ready to tackle the problem of a multi-column sum. Notice that if we start at the right end of the row of values and just slide the adder and its helpers to the left after adding a column, the three robots will be positioned for the next column. Then, working from right to left, we will compute the correct sum since we carry into a column before that column is added.

We need two additional methods in the Adder class: slide_left and add_all. Method slide_left is easy. We need to slide the helpers as well. Therefore we will put a simple version into the Finder class:

```
def slide_left() # in Finder
    turn_left()
    move()
    turn_right()
end
```

We can then override this in Adder and send slide_left messages to the helpers. They have inherited the version above. Note that this is not, strictly speaking, recursion, since the messages go to different robots.

```
def slide_left() # in Adder
    super()
    @check.slide_left()
    @carry.slide_left()
end
```

How will add_all know when it is done adding columns? One way is to have the left most number start on Second Avenue so that there is room to carry any value from the left most column. The Adder will then need to check to see if it is on Second Avenue before adding. This requires a new predicate.

```
def on_second_avenue?()
    turn_left()
    move()
    if front_is_clear?()
        turn_around()
        move()
        turn_left()
        return false
    end
    turn_around()
    move()
    turn_left()
    return true
end
```

We are now ready to write the add_all method in the Adder class.

```
def add_all()
    while not on_second_avenue?()
        add_column()
        slide_left()
    end
    add_column() # don't forget the last column
end
```

As a final check, be sure that this works if there are no beepers at all to "add."

7.7 Polymorphism--Why Write Many Programs When One Will Do?

Polymorphism means literally "many forms." In object-oriented programming it refers to the fact that messages sent to objects (robots) may be interpreted differently, depending on the class of the object (robot) receiving the message. Perhaps the best way to think of this is to remember that a robot is autonomous in its world. We send it messages and it responds. It doesn't come with a remote control unit by which the user directs its actions. Rather, it *hears* the messages sent to it and responds according to its internal dictionary. Recall that each robot consults its own internal dictionary of instructions to select the method that it uses to respond to any message. When we override a method in a new class, the new version of the method, then changes the meaning of the message for robots of the new class but not of the original class.

To illustrate the consequences of this, let's take a somewhat dramatic, though not very useful example. Suppose we have the following two classes

```
class Putter < Robot
   def move()
      super()
      if any_beepers_in_beeper_bag?()
         put_beeper()
      end
   end
end

class Getter < Robot
   def move()
      super()
      while next_to_a_beeper?()
         pick_beeper()
      end
   end
end
```

Both classes override the move method, and nothing more. Thus, a Putter robot puts beepers on corners that it moves to and Getter robots sweep corners to which they move. Suppose now that we use these two classes in the following task.

```
def task()
   lisa =  Putter.new(1, 1, EAST, INFINITY)
   tony =  Getter.new(2, 1, EAST, 0)
   10.times do
      lisa.move()
   end
   10.times do
      tony.move()
   end
end
```

If the world contains a beeper on each of the first ten corners of 1st Street and also each of the first ten corners of 2nd Street, then, when the task is done, there will be two beepers on each of the first ten blocks of 1st Street, and none on the corresponding blocks of 2nd Street. There is nothing surprising about this, but note that both lisa and tony responded to the same messages in identical (relative) situations.

The meaning of polymorphism is even deeper than this, however. In fact, the names that we use to refer to robots are not "burned in" to the robots themselves, but only a convenience for the user. A given robot can be referred to by different names, called aliases.

First, we declare that a name will be used as an alias. We will use the name karel.

Secondly, we need to assign a value to the reference karel. In other words we need to specify which robot the name "karel" will refer to. We do this with an assignment instruction. This assumes that the name tony already refers to a robot as it would if it were part of the above main task block.

```
karel = tony
```

This establishes karel as an alternate name (alias) for the robot also known as tony. We could just as easily make the name "karel" refer to the robot lisa. It is very important to note, however, that an alias doesn't refer to any robot until we assign a value to the name.

Then sending a turn_left message using the name karel will send the message to the same robot that the name tony refers to, since they are the same robot.

```
karel.turn_left()
```

Suppose now that we consider the slightly revised task that follows. We use the same setup and assume the world is as before. The only difference is that we refer to the robots using the name karel in each case. Note that while we have three names here, we only have two robots.

```
def task()
   lisa =  Putter.new(1, 1, EAST, INFINITY)
   tony =  Getter.new(2, 1, EAST, 0)
   karel = lisa
   10.times do
      karel.move()
   end
   karel = tony
   10.times do
      karel.move()
   end
end
```

So note that not only can we have identical messages (move) referring to different actions; even if the message statements as a whole are identical (karel.move()) we can have different actions. Notice though, that we are still sending messages to two different robots, and that these robots are from different classes. It is even possible to arrange it so that different things happen on two different executions of the same statement. Consider the following.

```
def task()
   lisa =  Putter.new(1, 1, EAST, INFINITY)
   tony =  Getter.new(2, 1, EAST, 0)
   10.times do
      karel = lisa        # "karel" refers to lisa;
      2.times do
         karel.move()     # ??
         karel = tony     # "karel" refers to tony
      end
   end
```

```
end
```

Note that the move message is sent 20 times, but 10 times it is sent to lisa, and 10 times to tony, alternately. Again, 1st Street gets extra beepers and 2nd Street gets swept.

7.8 Dynamic Ruby

We have shown a few hints about the dynamic nature of Ruby. Mixins can provide functionality mentioning things they don't provide, but that come from the class mixed in to. Abstract classes leave holes to be filled by subclasses, etc. Here we shall say a few more things about Ruby as a dynamic language, but will only touch the surface. There is much more to be learned than what we can do in this short space.

Back in Chapter 4 we mentioned that methods are actually a kind of object. We have also seen objects used as parameters. Let's put this together.

Suppose that an object named rich wants to open a new store called Rent A Job in which it packages up the solutions to pesky problems of clients. It wants to give the client a solution so that the client can carry it out, rather than rich doing the job itself. The object rich will be a RentAJobber and its main client-facing method will be named rent, with no parameters. We assume that some prior negotiation has gone on with the client before the rent message is sent to rich. The rent message will then return the "solution" to the client.

Now suppose that we have a robot named worker of class UrRobot. Normally we would send worker messages like **worker.move()**. But that is technically called an *application of a bound method*. This just means that the method is executed (applied) by the object to which it is bound (worker). The bound method *itself* can be packaged up into an object of type Method.

We save such a thing in a variable named job, with:

```
job = worker.method(:move)
```

Literally, this means save the method named move (:move) known to the worker object, but don't execute the message.

It is an object that can be saved by assigning it to a reference, like job, or saving it in a list. The method is called bound, since we have named a specific robot that will execute it: move is bound to worker.

Then we can, perhaps at some future time, execute this with just

```
job.call()
```

and the robot originally referred to by the name worker will move at that time. If the name worker has been used in the program for other purposes since we captured the bound method, it will still be the original robot that will move. So, job refers to a bound method and the *call* represents the application of the method. With all of this we can begin to understand RentAJobber:

```
# supplies lists of no argument functions to be
# executed by a client
class RentAJobber

    def initialize()
       @actions = []
    end

    def add_action(action)
       @actions << action
    end

    def rent()
        return @actions.clone()     #Don't let the client modify @actions.
    end
end
```

The initialize method just creates an empty array to save the actions and the add_action method adds
something to this list. What we shall add will be functions of no arguments, including bound methods.

Next we will show the negotiation part of the client's interaction with rich, in which the job is defined. Note
that we have chosen only a simple task, but you can supply anything, harvesting or spying, for example.

```
def task()
    rich = RentAJobber.new()
    worker = UrRobot.new(1, 1, NORTH, 1)
    task = worker.method(:move)
    rich.add_action(task)     # add a method bound to worker
    task = worker.method(:turn_left)
    rich.add_action(task)

    worker = UrRobot.new(1, 2, NORTH, 0)
    task = worker.method(:move)
    rich.add_action(task)     # add methods bound to a different
    rich.add_action(task)     # worker
 ...
```

At this point the job is defined, so the client can rent it from rich.

```
    task_list = rich.rent()
```

This list contains a list of functions of no arguments, so the client can then execute them all at once with

```
    task_list.each do |what|
       what.call()
    end
end # task
```

The two robots will then actually execute their actions. Swell.

As one final illustration, suppose we also have a simple top level method. Top level means that it isn't defined in a class or module (implicitly part of Object):

```
def advert()
    print("Rich's Rent a Job")
end
```

We haven't used print statements before, but they just display strings on your computer screen in a console window. If we invoke the method with just advert() then we will see

Rich's Rent a Job

on the screen. But since this can also be put into the actions list in a RentAJobber. So here is our final version of the RentAJobber's constructor, which guarantees that whenever the client executes the list, it will also see the advertisement.

```
def initialize()
    @actions = [:advert]
end
```

This has been a mere introduction to a very powerful idea. We can capture information known at one part of a program to be used in another.

7.9 Conclusion

Finally, we want to ask the question: When is it appropriate to design a new class, and when should we modify or add to an existing robot class?

The full answer to this question is beyond the scope of this book, because there are many things to be considered in this decision, but we can set some general guidelines here. If, in your judgment, a robot class contains errors or omissions, by all means, modify it. Here omissions mean that there is some method (action or predicate) that is needed to complete the basic functionality of the class or to make robots in the class do what the class was designed to do.

On the other hand, if we have a useful class, and we need additional functionality, especially more specialized functionality than that provided by the class we already have, then building a new class as a subclass of the given one is appropriate. This way, when we need a robot with the original capabilities, we can use the original class, and when we need the new functionality we can use the new one. Sometimes the choice is made because we find that most of the methods of some class are just exactly what we want, but one or two methods would serve better in the new problem if they were modified or extended.

A third, and important, option is to build an unrelated class and delegate part of the operation of the new class to an object of the existing one. This is programming by composition.

7.10 Important Ideas From This Chapter

recursion
tail recursion
searching
meta
formal definition /proof
dynamic programming

7.11 Problem Set

The following problems use the recursion, searching, and arithmetic methods discussed in this chapter. Some of the following problems use combinations of the zig_left_up and zag_down_right methods, or simple variants of these. Each problem is difficult to solve, but once a plan is discovered (probably through an "aha experience"), the program that implements the solution will not be too difficult to write. You may also assume that there are no wall sections in the world unless explicitly shown. Finally, you should assume that our robot, karel, starts with no beepers in its beeper-bag, unless you are told otherwise. Do not make any assumptions about karel's starting corner or starting direction, unless they are specified in the problem.

1. Rewrite your program that solves Problem 6.11-21 using a recursive method instead of an iterative one.

2. Karel has graduated to advanced carpet layer. Karel must carpet the completely enclosed room. Only one beeper can be placed on each corner. The room may be any size and any shape. Figure 7-5 shows one possible floor plan. The central, walled off area, is not to be carpeted by karel. Karel may start from any place within the room and may be facing any direction.

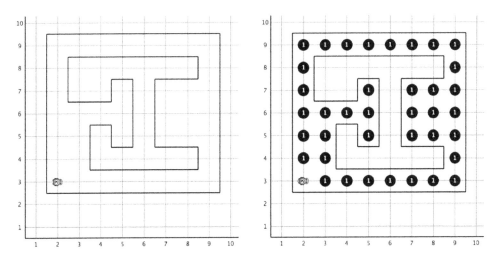

Figure 7-5 A Big Carpeting Job

3. Rewrite both zig_left_up and zag_down_right so that they automatically satisfy their directional pre-conditions.

4. Assume that there is a beeper on 1st Street and N'th Avenue. Program karel to find it and move to Nth Street and 1st Avenue.

5. Assume that there is a beeper on S'th Street and A'th Avenue, and that karel has two beepers in its beeper-bag. Program karel to put the beepers from its beeper-bag on to 1st Street and A'th Avenue and S'th Street and 1st Avenue. The original beeper must remain at the corner on which it starts.

6. Assume that there is a beeper on 1st Street and A'th Avenue. Program karel to double the avenue number; the robot must move this beeper to 1st Street and 2A'th Avenue. (For example, a beeper on 1st Street and 7th Avenue must be moved to 1st Street and 14th Avenue.) Hint: Use the west boundary wall as in Problem 7.10-4.

7. Assume that karel starts its task with an infinite number of beepers in its beeper-bag. Also assume that there is a beeper on 1st Street and N'th Avenue. Program karel to leave N beepers on the origin.

8. Assume that there is a beeper on S'th Street and 1st Avenue and a beeper on 1st Street and A'th Avenue. Program karel to put one of these beepers on S'th Street and A'th Avenue. Karel must put the other beeper in its beeper-bag. Hint: There are many ways to plan this task. Here are two suggestions: (1) move one beeper south while moving the other beeper north; (2) continue moving one beeper until it is directly over (or to the right of) the stationary beeper. If done correctly, both methods will result in one beeper being placed on the answer corner.

9. Assume that there is a beeper on A'th Street and B'th Avenue. Program a Mathematician robot to find the beeper, pick it up and transport it to 1st Street and (A+B)'th Avenue. Hint. When you find the beeper the sum of your street and avenue numbers will be A+B. If you move south one block and also east one block, the sum will still be the same since your Street number will have decreased by one while your Avenue number will have increased by one.

10. Assume that karel has a beeper in its beeper-bag and that there is another beeper on 1st Street and A'th Avenue. Program karel to place one of the beepers on 1st Street and 2 to the Ath power Avenue. This expression is 2 raised to the A'th power or 1 doubled A times. For example, when A is 5, 2 to the A'th power is 32. Hint: This problem uses instructions similar to those used to solve Problem 7.10-6. Karel can use the second beeper to count the number of times it must double the number 1.

11. Repeat Problem 7.10-10, but this time the answer corner is 1st Street and 3 to the A'th power Avenue. Try to reuse as much of the previous program as possible.

12. Program karel to place beepers in an outward spiral until its beeper-bag is empty. Assume that karel will run out of beepers before it is stopped by the boundary walls. One example is shown in Figure 7-6.

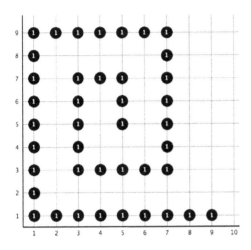

Figure 7-6 A Spiral

13. Assume that karel has two beepers and that there is another beeper on S'th Street and A'th Avenue. Program karel to deposit one of these beepers on the corner of 1st Street and SA'th Avenue. (This expression is S multiplied by A.)

14. Assume that karel has three beepers in its beeper-bag and that there is another beeper on S'th Street and A'th Avenue. Program karel to deposit a beeper on the corner of 1st Street and S to the A'th Power Avenue. (This expression is S raised to power of A.)

15. Assume that karel has three beepers in its beeper-bag and that there is another beeper on S'th Street and Ath Avenue. Program karel to put a beeper on the corner of 1st Street and GCD(S,A)'th Ave. The GCD of two numbers is their Greatest Common Divisor. For example, the GCD of 6 and 15 is 3. Hint: Use Euclid's subtractive algorithm.

16. Assume that karel has N beepers in its beeper-bag. Program the robot to place beepers on 1st Street and all avenues that represent prime numbers between 1st Avenue and (N - SquareRoot of N)'th Avenue.

17. Program a robot named karel to pick up a beeper at the west wall and return to the corner on which it starts. There may be other beepers in the path, but it is known that there is a beeper on 1st Avenue directly west of karel's starting position. Hint: Think recursively.

18. Program a robot named karel to pick up a beeper at the origin and return to the corner on which it starts. Hint: Think recursively.

19. Write a recursive program to solve problem 6.11-25. Hint: If all of the piles of beepers were moved one block north, then 1st Street would be clear. The robot could then use two beepers to mark the beginning and ending avenues that it was supposed to sort. An overall plan could be to move the smallest pile between the two markers to the western marker avenue. That marker could then be moved one block East.

20. Write a recursive predicate to determine if the number of beepers in a robots beeper-bag is exactly the same as the number of beepers on the robot's current corner. You may assume that there is no wall immediately to the north of the robot.

21. Karel the Robot meets carol the UrRobot on a corner. How can karel determine if it has exactly the same number of beepers in its beeper-bag that carol has? Each robot should finish with the same number of beepers that it starts with.

22. Karel and carol again meet on a corner. Have them exchange beepers, so that karel ends with the number of beepers carol has initially and conversely. Assume the corner they both occupy has no beepers.

23. The required instruction creates a robot on each of the first ten avenues of 1st Street. They each have zero or more beepers in their beeper-bag. Their task is to sort themselves in order of number of beepers, with the robot with the smallest number on 1st Avenue, etc. Each robot can visit one of its neighbors and between them decide which of their original corners each should occupy. Repetitions of this will sort the robots. When they are sorted have each robot distribute its beepers along the streets of the avenue it occupies, one beeper per corner. The final picture should be similar to the final figure of Figure 5.31. Assume that there are no beepers in the world except the beepers carried by the robots.

24 What happens if we use an Adder robot to add the numbers 3102 and 4027? Devise a solution that covers this beyond-the-horizon situation.

25. Devise a solution to the problem we left unsolved in Chapter 6. Four robots are supposed to patrol a field of beepers, keeping equally spaced around the perimeter. You might try a solution with one leader and three helpers, as we did in the solution to the simpler problem. The leader will belong to a new class that you must design.

26. Do Problem 29 of Chapter 6 again, but have the Spy find the Accomplices recursively.

27. A Contractor wants to build a house with three helpers, a Mason, a Carpenter, and a Roofer, but the helpers are spread around the robot world. Have the Contractor go on a search for its three helpers and pass each a strategy concerning the location of the house when it finds them. It will also need to tell them to get to work. Then have the helpers build the house.

28. Do Problem 28 of Chapter 6 again, but this time tony must remain at the origin throughout.

29. Use the ideas of Section 7.8 to revisit Problems 13 and 14 of Chapter 4. Build a HomingPigeon class, whose robots keep a list of actions that will undo everything they have done and will take them back to where they began, in the state they were originally in. Assume no other robots are in the world to, for example, pick up beepers that your homing pigeon has put down. When you have learned more Ruby that we teach in this book, you can revisit this and provide an optimized undo list.

30. Write a recursive version of clear_all_beepers_to_the_wall from Section 6.3.4 that also returns a robot to its original location and direction.

31. Write a recursive version of the program to solve problem 38 of Chapter 6.

32. Write a recursive version of the program to solve problem 39 of Chapter 6.

8 Concurrent Robot Programs

In this Chapter we introduce what has been up to now considered a very advanced topic. Real computer systems today run so fast that they can devote small bits of time to many users in quick succession and it seems as if the entire computer is dedicated to each user. Even more interesting, they can let several *processes* operate with seeming simultaneity for each user. This is called *concurrent programming* and we will introduce it here, with some of its pitfalls.

8.1 Simple Concurrent Programs

When a program is to run several pieces at the same time, the individual parts are called threads (threads of control). Each thread in a robot program is just like a task: a sequence of robot instructions executed one after the other until the end. We can make a task run in its own thread quite easily. Suppose we again take up the house building task of Chapter 4.

Only one of our Carpenter robots was needed to make two windows. Suppose we write a task method to do just this. This can be a top-level method.

```
def carpenter_task()
    linda =  Carpenter.new(1, 1, NORTH, INFINITY);
    linda.move_to_first_window()
    linda.make_window()
    linda.move_to_next_window()
    linda.make_window()
end
```

We next need to create a class that can be used to control a thread. Such a class must have a method named run_task. You can do anything you like in this method and it will be run in a thread, concurrently with other threads, if we set it up correctly (shown next).

```
class CarpenterRunner
    def run_task()
        carpenter_task()
    end
end
```

We could have actually avoided writing the carpenter_task method and just put its statements into this run_task method. While the task can be a top-level method, the run_task method needs to actually be a method named *run_task* in some class.

Finally, from our main task block we need to create a new CarpenterRunner and tell the world to run it in a new thread. It is the world that controls the threads, so we tell the world to set up a thread for our runner. Finally, we need to start the threads. We do so here with an initial delay of 1 second (10 tenths of a second).The delay is helpful to let the graphics system display itself before the threads run.

```
def task()
   runner = CarpenterRunner.new()
   world.set_up_thread(runner)
   ...
   world.start_threads(10)
end
```

Now this task will run in its own thread along with other threads that we start in the same way. This same thread could be used to control one or more robots. Each thread behaves like an independent main task block, but, of course, all such threads run in the same world. If we make several such threads for our house building task, it will seem like the workers are working all at once. All the threads start when we send the world the start_threads message. Each thread will execute the run_task method.

8.2 Robot Runs In Its Own Thread

One especially nice way to make concurrent robot programs is to let each robot be controlled by its own thread. Each robot then behaves much more like an independent being than has been possible up to now. This is like the helicopter pilot reading a robot's messages to it all at once and then setting it on its way, rather than reading one message at a time and waiting for it to complete. It also is more faithful to our overall metaphor of robots, which in the real world are usually independent and operate simultaneously. In fact, the helicopter pilot was added to the metaphor to have a way to justify what goes on inside a computer if we don't use threads: everything happens one step at a time in a single thread.

One simple example is to write a class of robots that can race each other to some goal. For example, suppose we start a Racer robot on 1st street and 1st avenue and another on 2nd street and 1st avenue. Both robots face East. Somewhere in front of each is a beeper. We start them up simultaneously, each in its own thread and see who gets there first.

To arrange this, we are going to do two things differently in the Racer class. We are going to tell the World to run this robot in its own thread and we are going to give the class its own run_task method. (Note that UrRobot itself implements the run_task method, so we are really overriding it here.) The constructor itself is used to tell the world to set up a thread for this object's run method. If we have several such objects, all will be started when we send the start_threads message to the world.

```
# Illustrates classic race conditions among threads.
class Racer < Robot

   def initialize(street, avenue, direction)
      super(street, avenue, direction, 0)
      RobotWorld.instance().set_up_thread(self)
   end

   # Race for the beeper
   def race()
      while not next_to_a_beeper?()
         move()
      end
      pick_beeper()
      turn_off()
```

```
      end

   # Runs the race in its own thread
   def run_task()
      race()
   end
end
```

Then, all we need to do in the main task block is to create our robots. We don't actually even need to name them, but we will here.

```
def task()
   world = RobotWorld.instance
   world.place_beepers(1, 10, 1)
   world.place_beepers(2, 10, 1)

   alex = Racer.new(1, 1, EAST)
   jose = Racer.new(2, 1, EAST)
   world.start_threads(10)
end
```

They will automatically start themselves up when we start_threads, since the constructor sent the set_up_thread message when each was created. Even more interesting is to have two such robots race each other to the same beeper. Only one will be able to get it, of course. But it is non-deterministic which one will get there first as the interleaving of operations between threads is not determined. See Section 8.4. The actual behavior also depends on how your computer internally handles threads, so you may not see much non-determinism in a simple program like this.

8.3 Cooperation

Robots have a very rudimentary way to communicate with each other. They can meet on a corner and exchange beepers. This can be the basis of sophisticated programs. Here we show part of a simple relay race in which three robots exchange a beeper (the baton) when the first runs up to the second and the second then runs up to the third.

```
class RelayRacer < Robot
   include  Turner
   def initialize(street, avenue,  direction, beepers)
      super(street, avenue, direction, beepers)
      world = RobotWorld.instance()
      world.set_up_thread(self)
   end

   def run_task()
      while not next_to_a_beeper?()
         spin()
      end
      pick_beeper()
```

```
        run_to_robot()
        put_beeper()
        turn_off()
    end

    def spin()
        turn_around()
        turn_around()
    end

    def run_to_robot()
        move()
        while not next_to_a_robot?()
            move()
        end
    end
end
```

If we start one of these on a corner that contains a beeper, facing down a street that contains another of these then the relay will begin properly. You will need to do some additional things to make it end properly.

8.4 Race Conditions

When threads run concurrently it is usually impossible to predict the order of operations of the individual instructions in different threads. This sometimes leads to undesirable effects in which two things happen in the wrong order. It is generally difficult to reason about the interleaving of concurrent operations because there are so many possibilities. This needs to be carefully controlled. For example, if two computers are connected to the same printer, and the print driver on each isn't careful, it would be possible for two users to print at about the same time and have the individual characters of the two documents interleaved on the output. The usual method of controlling this kind of thing is to have a queue that holds requests to print. A newly arriving print request is put into the back of the queue and the printer takes requests from the front. Eventually each request works its way to the front and gets printed. But, if the print driver isn't careful and two print requests arrive at about the same time, the print queue can get corrupted.

In this section we are going to illustrate one classic problem with concurrency, called race conditions. Since we are using robots we can do this by actually holding races. The term however, applies whenever the interleaving of operations can cause something to happen at an unexpected time.

Suppose we take our Racer robots of Section 8.2 and make them race to pick up the same beeper. We can start one at 10th street and 1st avenue and the other at 1st street and 10th avenue, racing for a single beeper at the origin. We don't know which will reach the beeper first and pick it up. But the other will slam into the end wall, since it won't see any beeper at all. The first robot to get there will pick it up. Since we aren't going to be sending any messages to these robots, we won't even name them. They will be anonymous.

```
def task()
    Racer.new(10, 1, SOUTH, 0)
    Racer.new(1, 10, WEST, 0)
    world.start_threads(10)
end
```

Actually, it is possible for both robots to arrive at about the same time and each check to see if there was a beeper there and each find that there was and only then, each try to pick it up. Thus, one of them would do an error shutoff while trying to pick up a beeper that it just checked for and found, rather than when trying to walk through a wall. Note that we didn't bother to assign the new objects to any variables. We don't need to send them any messages, so this is ok.

8.5 Deadlock

Another classic concurrency problem is deadlock. This occurs when different threads hold some resources (say a beeper) that the other threads need and each waits (forever) for the others to release the resource. One classic illustration of this is called Dining Philosophers.

In the traditional story we have a group of philosophers who alternately think and eat. Each has a place at the table and between each pair of places there is a fork. Each philosopher will think for a while and then decide it wants to eat. To do so, however requires picking up both forks by its place, one at a time. If it doesn't get a fork it waits for the philosopher next to it to put down that fork and then it picks up the fork and continues. When it finishes, it puts down its forks, again, one at a time.

The problem arises when each philosopher has picked up its left fork and reaches for the right one. Each will wait for a fork and none will put one down. This is deadlock. Here is a class that illustrates this example. Note, that it won't deadlock every time. Also note that the run method in the class never ends. You will have to stop the program yourself. We haven't normally shown all of the necessary imports (require) for our programs here, nor the commands we give to the world to set up a situation. Here we show it all. The world will be discussed in some detail in the Appendix and in auxiliary materials that come with Robot simulation programs.

First we show a class, Die, for simulating dice rolls. It is a simple way to achieve some randomness in our programs. It is included with the software for the book.

```
# Creates a die object with any number of faces. If you roll a die you
# get a random integer between 1 and the number
# of faces. You can create a physically impossible die with this, of
# course, with, say, seven faces.
class Die
  # Create a new die with the specified number of faces
  def initialize(faces)
    @bound = faces
  end

  # Roll the die to get a random integer between 1 and the
  # number of faces.
  def roll
    return 1 + rand(@bound) # method rand is built in to Ruby
  end
end
```

Next we show the philosopher class, along with its task and the commands to actually run the simulation.

```
require 'robot'
require 'turner'
require 'die'

# A class of robots that can execute the dining philosophers protocol.
# Demonstrates unchecked concurrency so deadlock can result.
class Philosopher < Robot
  include Turner
  @@die = Die.new(6)

  # create a new Philosopher that will run in its own thread
  def initialize(street, avenue,  direction)
    super(street, avenue, direction, 0)
    world = Robota::World
    world.set_up_thread(self)
  end
  # Waste time in place waiting for a fork
  def spin()
    turn_around()
    turn_around()
  end
  # Think by moving away from the "table"
  def think(time)
    time.times do
      back_up()
      move()
    end
  end

  # eat by moving in to the table
  def eat(time)
    time.times do
      move()
      back_up()
    end
  end

  # get two forks (beepers) to enable eating
  def get_forks
    turn_left()
    move()
    while ! any_beepers_in_beeper_bag?()
      while not next_to_a_beeper?()
        spin()   #nothing
      end
      pick_beeper()
    end
    turn_around()
```

```
    move()
    put_beeper()
    move()
    while ! any_beepers_in_beeper_bag?()
      while not next_to_a_beeper?()
        spin()     #nothing
      end
      pick_beeper()
    end
    turn_around()
    move()
    put_beeper()
    turn_right()
  end

  # return the two forks so as to return to thinking
  def put_forks
    pick_beeper()
    pick_beeper()
    turn_left()
    move()
    put_beeper()
    turn_around()
    move()
    move()
    put_beeper()
    turn_around()
    move()
    turn_right()
  end

  # The task for one philosopher (run in the thread)
  def run_task
    while true
      think(@@die.roll())
      get_forks()
      eat(@@die.roll())
      put_forks()
    end
  end

end

# set up the four philosophers and start them.
def task
  world = Robota::World
  world.read_world("../worlds/beepers.txt")
  p1 = Philosopher.new(2, 3, NORTH)
```

```
    p2 = Philosopher.new(4, 3, SOUTH)
    p3 = Philosopher.new(3, 4, WEST)
    p4 = Philosopher.new(3, 2, EAST)
    world.start_threads(10)
end

if __FILE__ == $0
    window(8, 40).run do
        task
    end
end
```

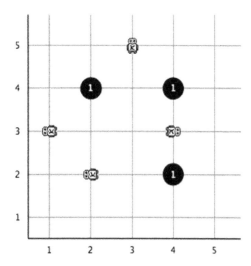

Figure 8-1 Dining Robots

The Die class is shown above. It simulates the rolling of a single die (one of a pair of Dice) to achieve randomization. Thus, the philosophers seem to eat and think for random periods of time. To start up the simulation, you need to use something like the above main task block. The only thing really new here is that the die object has name @@die. Such a name (starting with @@) refers to a single object that is shared by all of the objects of the class. So all philosophers use the same die object. This is why it is not defined within the constructor, which creates single objects.

If you make the Die one or two sided instead of six sided you greatly increase the chance of deadlock. When you run it fast (with a small world delay) it is more likely to deadlock. It might even exhibit another interesting phenomenon of unsynchronized threads. Sometimes a robot will check for a beeper and find that there is one there, but another robot grabs it just before this one picks it up. This robot will then do an error shutoff for trying to pick a beeper that isn't present.

8.6 Important Ideas From This Chapter

concurrent
race condition
deadlock
thread

8.7 Problem Set

1. Run a super duper steeplechase relay race with three robots that run in concurrent threads. See problem 6.11 and problem 6.37.

2. Have two sets of three robots each race against each other in a super duper steeplechase relay tournament.

3. Do Problem 4.12-17 again, where the two Spy robots run in different threads.

4. Do Problem 11 of Chapter 4.12-19 again, where each of the four robots runs in a separate thread.

5. Repeat Problem 4, except that each robot starts at an arbitrary location and each runs in a separate thread. They rendezvous at the origin to exchange strategies.

6. The deadlock problem for Philosophers can be solved if just one of the Philosophers picks up its right fork before the left one. Use polymorphism to implement such a solution. Not all deadlock problems can be solved this way, but asymmetry might be useful in any such situation.

7. One solution to Philosopher deadlock is to have a philosopher put down its first fork if it can't get the second one. It then returns to thinking for a bit. It then tries again later. However, it is possible for a philosopher to never get to eat with this "solution." Because this philosopher example is so important in the history of concurrent programming, this difficulty has come to be called starvation: a thread gets no useful work done. Implement this idea in a subclass of Philosopher.

8. Rebuild the Guard program from Chapter 6 with four guards, each in its own thread. Each guard initially begins guarding a different edge of the field.

9. If you enjoy computer science and eventually take a course in computability theory, fondly recall the days you spent programming Karel R Tuesday and try to solve the following problem: Prove that karel, even without the aid of any beepers is equivalent to a Turing machine. Hint: Use the equivalence between Turing machines and 2-counter automata.

Appendix

1 Ruby Code – run or import

When you put Ruby code into a file you might intend to use it in one of two ways (or both). The file's contents can be imported (with require) or it can be executed. Importing a class or module gives us access to its features. So when we say require "ur_robot, our new code file has access to the name UrRobot and all of the features of that class. You can do the same. Just put a class or module into a file to be imported. And require will load the file's contents. However, any code that is not part of a definition (of a class, module, or top-level method) will be executed when the file is loaded. Sometimes you want this to happen, but often you don't.

On the other hand, we might want to execute a module, rather than import it. You may have classes and modules also, but you will want at least some code that is not in a definition of any kind.

But often you want it both ways. You want to be able to require the things in your file, but you also want to run it as a main program.

This is possible if the module has the code to be executed when run, but not when merely loaded, protected in an if statement of the form:

```
if __FILE__ == $0
    ...
end
```

The IF statement is discussed in Chapter 5. The equality comparison operator in Ruby is ==. The literal meaning of this is to execute the code in the if statement only if the name of the current file (the one just loaded) __FILE__ is the same as the name of the file currently executing ($0). These are both built-in Ruby variables. When a file is loaded with require (or the similar load), the one doing the loading will be the one executing so they will be different and the code will not be executed. When you run the file by invoking the Ruby interpreter, they will be the same, so this becomes the code to be run.

For example, if we have a command/console window open you run ruby code with a command similar to the following (depending on your system).

```
ruby stair_sweeper.rb
```

or more likely

```
ruby -I ".:../karel" beeper_layer.rb
```

and the top-level code in that module will be executed. Other run options are discussed in Section 2. The –I option of the ruby command points the system to the places in which it can find the code. I assume here that your current directory (containing your ruby files) is the default directory of the distribution, or one at the same level of your directory hierarchy. Likewise the simulator code should be another sibling directory named karel. This is how it was distributed. It is also possible to set a directory path on most systems.

2 Executing Robot Code in Ruby

In order to use the simulator that is available for this book you will need to have both Ruby and Tk graphics properly installed on your computer. The installation may be easy or hard depending on your system. Many computers come with Ruby, but many fewer with Tk. You can search on the internet for it along with installation instructions. One easy way to get it running is to install the free Eclipse development environment and then obtain plugins for it for ruby and Tk. The Aptana Studio is the standard Eclipse plugin. The software for the book is distributed as a zip file that can be imported directly into Eclipse without unzipping it. If you don't use Eclipse, you will need to unzip the file and install it manually so your system can find it. Instructions for installing Eclipse, and Tk can be found on this book's web pages.

Most of the sample code discussed in the book is distributed with this software in a directory named default. It is easiest if you work from this directory. The simulator base code can then be found at ../karel, the world files can be found at ../worlds. You will need to add both the current directory "." and the path to the base code "../karel" to the interpreter arguments or the run path for your system to make it work. Numerous examples of run configurations will be available if you use Eclipse.

You can ease the running of robot programs outside any development environment if you include a "she-bang" at the beginning of your executable code files. This has the form (on my computer):

```
#!/opt/local/bin/ruby
```

though it will need to be modified to point to the actual installation of ruby on your system. If you then make the file executable (on unix or macintosh with chmod a+x filename), the code will be directly executable. This is not needed if you intend to use the run commands from within Eclipse or another environment.

3 Typical Imports

There are a number of things that the robot environment provides that you might want to import into your programs. You are unlikely to need all of these.

```
require "ur_robot"
require "robot"
require "turner"
require "sensor_pack"
```

If you require any of the robot classes, the world will also be loaded automatically as there is a cascade of requires in the libraries themselves.

You can also give local names to some things known in the world. Here is a list of them.

```
North = NORTH
East = EAST
South = SOUTH
West = WEST
```

```
INFINITY = Robota::INFINITY
```

4 Constructors in Ruby

In the robot programming language, a delivery specification for a UrRobot looks like this:

```
karel = UrRobot.new(1, 2, NORTH, 0)
```

These specifications need to be defined in the classes that we write. Ruby calls them constructors, since they are used to construct objects. The UrRobot class defines a constructor that requires that we give a positive integer for the street and another for the avenue as well as a direction in which to face the robot initially, and another integer for the number of beepers in its beeper-bag. These values given in the new construct are called *parameters* or *arguments*. Even the word INFINITY that is used to indicate infinitely many beepers is just a name for a special integer. In Ruby, an integer value is just a, possibly signed, number without a decimal point. A constructor looks similar to a method, with some important differences. The constructor for a class is always named *initialize*. It is automatically invoked when you send a *new* message to a class.

You may need to define a new constructor in robot classes that you write. It isn't always necessary, for they are inherited like any other method. For example, the MileWalker class of Section 3.3 needs no constructor. It is only when you need to do something extra, such as define a new instance variable that you need to write a constructor.

Note that the name of a Ruby constructor is always the same: initialize. These are not normally invoked, but if you do need to write a constructor of your own, then its first statement should invoke the constructor of any superclass with super(...), filling in appropriate arguments. This is true even if the superclass doesn't explicitly have a constructor, but inherits one from some ancestor.

For example, a Choreographer does need a constructor, since it needs to initialize its @dancers list. It is a robot (its parent is Harvester) so it needs to implement the following:

```
def initialize(street, avenue, direction, beepers):
    super(street, avenue, direction, beepers)
    @dancers = []
end
```

The meaning of this, in reality, is that in order to construct a Choreographer, we must first construct a super class object (Harvester) and then specialize it if necessary. We could also add additional parameters if we need them.

In general, in Ruby, you may not need to write a constructor for a class. You will need a constructor if both of the following situations occur.

(a) The superclass has a constructor (including ancestor classes).

(b) You need to do something when you create the object to make it immediately sensible and usable.

In the Choreographer case, both (a) and (b) hold. It wouldn't make much sense to create a robot and not deliver it to the world to a specific place, for example. Therefore UrRobot has constructors that require the four parameters above and then sub classes like Choreographer must include a compatible constructor as well.

There is one situation in which you can modify this a bit, actually. Suppose you want to create a class of robots in which it only makes sense to deliver them in one specific configuration. You can then write a constructor without parameters, but in the super construct specify the configuration you need. A somewhat abstract example might be in the class OriginSitter:

```
def initialize()
    super(1, 1, EAST, 0)
        ...
    end
```

The delivery specification would be just:

```
karel = OriginSitter.new()
```

We still need to write a constructor, but we can be more free in its own parameter structure. The important thing is that we do in fact construct a UrRobot that is then specialized to an OriginSitter. You can provide some (rather than all or none) of the parameters and use your fixed values for the rest. The order in super (…) is important, however. You can even add additional parameters of your own to a constructor. This is shown in Section 4.5.

The method super is special, as should be obvious. You don't write it, of course. But it is special in another way as well. We have been careful to always use parentheses when we send messages, including the super message. But if you invoke super with no parentheses it doesn't mean the same thing as if you use them. If you invoke super with super() it sends no arguments as you would expect. If you invoke it with a full set of arguments (in a robot sub class, for example) such as super(street, avenue, direction, beepers) then it will pass those. But if you invoke it with no parentheses and no parameters, it will actually use the parameters of the initialize method in which it appears - another shortcut. So, in class Choreographer we could have written initialize as just:

```
def initialize(street, avenue, direction, beepers)
    super
    @dancers = []
end
```

But we prefer to list the arguments as we do in the text. It is always best to be explicit.

5 Ruby Visibility

There are three visibility levels in Ruby. They determine what other code can "see" the features of a class. Private features can only be seen in the class itself. Fields (and class fields) are always private. A field names begins with @ and is private to an individual object and each object has its own field. A class field name begins with @@ and it is private to the class and its value is shared by objects in the class. But methods can also be private. If you don't give any visibility indications, then methods are public and can be seen by any code that loads the given class (with require, say). The third level is protected. Protected features are available within a class and also in subclasses.

You can mark out sections of a class definition with the tokens public, protected, and private and subsequent defs in the class will have that visibility until the next indicator.

Normally only public and private are very useful. Save protected for experts. But private methods are private to an instance. Thus the only legal receiver of a private message (using a private method name) is self. This is very limiting. Protected allows sending the message to other objects of the same class. You can use this to set a field of a different member of the same class, for example, while still preventing objects from other classes from doing so.

Sometimes you want to have a field in a class, but also want to have a way for client code to access the value. The normal way to do this is to provide a public method that just returns the value. It is very common to name the method with the same name as the field (omitting the @, of course). For example, suppose you were building UrRobot yourself, and decided you want to have an @street field containing the current street of the robot. You could make the value available (but not changeable), with

```
def street()
    return @street
end
```

Note that we have not included such a method with our robot classes as it isn't really necessary and not having it also makes many of the exercises more interesting. But having a method returning the value of a field is commonly done. Such a method is called an accessor, since it accesses information.

Remember we have always said that objects do things and objects remember things. Earlier we said methods like move were how we make robots do things and fields were for remembering. However, an even better way to think of remembering is that it isn't the fields that represent remembering but accessor methods like the one above or next_to_a_beeper? from the Robot class. Methods that don't return anything are called mutators since they must mutate, or change, the state of the computation. Mutators = do things. Accessors = remember things. In actuality you don't know if an accessor is really returning a field to you or if it is doing some behind the scenes computation to get a value to return. To user code (clients) it looks the same. You invoke a method and you get information as if the object had been remembering it – and maybe it was.

Simple accessor methods like the above are very common. So Ruby provides a shortcut. You don't actually have to write a method like that to use it. All you need to write instead is

```
attr_reader :street
```

and the method can be used just as if you wrote it. It will provide an accessor for @street. But the accessor is usually used without parentheses as

```
aRobot.street
```

rather than

```
aRobot.street()
```

And this is a point at which to discuss common Ruby style. We have tried to be very faithful to always use parentheses when invoking methods (sending messages). We have also done this when defining methods. But

Ruby actually requires very little of this and many Ruby programmers would rather avoid them. And it isn't just to do less typing. The following are equivalent.

```ruby
def turn_right()
    self.turn_left()
    self.turn_left()
    self.turn_left()
end
```

and

```ruby
def turn_right
    self.turn_left
    self.turn_left
    self.turn_left
end
```

In fact, these are also equivalent:

```ruby
albert = NeighborTalker.new(1, 5, WEST, 1)
```

and

```ruby
albert = NeighborTalker.new 1, 5, WEST, 1
```

Ruby only requires these parentheses when not having them would be ambiguous, usually because something else follows the construct. We have been consistent in using parentheses as they keep you out of trouble in the difficult cases and so are worth the minimal effort that it takes to get used to using them. Other languages are not so forgiving, and as you learn others it will be a useful habit.

We haven't used *global variables* in the text, but the simulator contains a few. A global variable has a name that begins with a $. One of the important ones in the simulator is $graphical. When true (the default) your programs will run in a graphical window and you will see robots move. If you set it to be false (before you "require" anything) the world will be purely text based. If you tell the (text based) world to trace the robots by setting the global variable $tracing to be true, then a robot will print out information about its state whenever it executes any action. Global variables can be seen and set anywhere in a program.

Another feature of Ruby that is loosely related to the current discussion is class methods. Just as instance variables can be associated with an object and class variables associated with a class, it is also possible to create methods that belong to a class, rather than to the objects created from the class. A class is an object, after all. A class method has a name that is prefixed by the name of the class. RobotWorld.instance() is one that we have used. It is created inside the RobotWorld class and given this name. It is executed by the class itself, which means two things: first, you don't need to create an object before you invoke it, and second, it doesn't have access to instance fields (but it does to class fields). We have not used them in the text, but they do appear (infrequently) in the simulator. By the way, we use RobotWorld.instance() rather than RobotWorld.new(), since the simulator guarantees that there is only one world object. We don't want the robot programmer to be able to create two worlds in the same program. This is an example of a Singleton: a class that guarantees it can only be instantiated once. The new method is actually private in this class.

6 Ruby Cloning

Cloning in Ruby is a bit more complicated than we have suggested in the main text (Section 5.10). Method clone will faithfully create and return a copy of any object that executes the clone method. The important thing is that the type of the returned object will be the same as the receiver of the message. Clone copies the object, but if the object itself has fields, the fields of the new object (the clone) are references to the same things as the original. For example, when we clone an array, we get another, independent array, so that we can append to them independently, but the two arrays at that moment have the same contents, not copies of the contents. If the array cloned contains robots and we copy them as well we will have different lists of different robots, rather than different lists of the same robots. Sometimes you need to do that, in which case you would need to override clone to do it, normally by recursively copying the contents.

We used clone in a couple of places here. We copied *self* in the NeighborTalker's create_neighbor method and we copied the list of actions in RentAJobber. Clone was originally implemented in UrRobot, but here it had to do more work to make our simulator work properly since a clone robot of a needs to be able to talk to the world in the same way.

For this reason, if you want to override a method like clone, and you don't often need to, it is imperative that at the beginning of it you invoke the superclass clone method within it. You can then clone those fields that must themselves be cloned. This is similar to what we do with constructors, and for exactly the same reason. It permits the creation or cloning of an object to occur from the top (class Object) down (to your class). It is top-down because when we execute clone it first invokes the super clone, so that happens first. If every override method in the chain back to UrRobot does the same, then it is actually the clone of UrRobot that completes before any of the others do anything else.

Since Choreographer has a field defined, we would need to take special account of it if we need a clone method there. The inherited clone method will create a choreographer that uses exactly the same array as the original. So if you add a dancer to one, you effectively add it to both. This is unlikely to be useful. We would first need to decide if a "faithful" copy of a choreographer would use the same dancer objects as those used by the original at the point of cloning or a new set. We will show it both ways. Suppose that we want the new object to be independent, but to initially start with the same dancers. Then clone would look like this:

```
protected
def set_dancers(array)
    @dancers = array
end

public
def clone()
    result = super() # get the simple clone
    result.set_dancers(@dancers.clone()) # same dancers
    return result
end
```

The returned object will be independent in the sense that if we add a dancer to it, the dancer will NOT be added to the original, and conversely. But any dancers that are already in the array will now be in both Choreographers.

On the other hand, suppose that we wanted the new object to start with different dancers, cloning them as well. Now we would say instead:

```
def clone()
   result = super()
   result.set_dancers([])
   @dancers.each do |robot|
      result.add_dancer(robot.clone()) # copies of the dancers
   end
   return result
end
```

Here we can just give the result a new empty list and then append clones of the dancers to it. Note that clone is perfectly polymorphic, so that if any of the dancers have special needs in cloning, they will automatically be handled by this message. Remember that in a clone method you are creating a new object. Don't neglect to return it at the end.

7 Open Closed Principle

One of the principles of object-oriented programming is the open-closed principle. A class should be open to extension (subclasses), but closed to modification. Once you see the end of a class it should not be possible to modify it (other than by changing its code in an editor and rebuilding it, of course. Ruby obeys the first of these, but not the second. Ruby objects are always open to change. This is a point of philosophy with the language developer. It can be a dangerous practice, but is also very flexible. In a dynamic language it is fine, as long as you don't over do it. Here we will see two examples. First, it is possible to give an individual object new methods, independent of other objects of its class. We can even give an existing method a different body for just one object, if you like.

Here is how you modify an existing object. It can be of any class. Here we will give an individual UrRobot a different move method.

```
albert = UrRobot.new(1, 5, WEST, 1)
albert.move()
class << albert # note two less-than characters
   def move()
      super()
      turn_left()
   end
end
albert.move()
```

Now, when albert executes a move method it also turns left. Other objects in UrRobot will be unaffected. So albert was not closed to modification. The first move, above, will just be a move. After we modify albert, it will also turn_left when it moves. Note that the class is not given a name and that the "superclass" referenced is just the object that we wish to extend.

But classes are also open to modification in a certain sense. Suppose you would like to add a new method to UrRobot. Say you disagree with the decision to omit turn_right. You can extend a class just by seeming to define a class with the same name (after loading/requiring) the original. The following will work:

```
require "ur_robot"
class UrRobot # an existing class
   def turn_right()
      turn_left()
      turn_left()
      turn_left()
   end
end
```

Now, when you create a UrRobot object it will also know about turn_right, assuming you load this definition instead of the original. There aren't many languages this flexible. But it is a dangerous ability. Remember that public methods, such as we create here have to maintain invariants of the objects in the class. When you modify in this way, you take on that responsibility. But note that the original definition is not changed. Remember that what you require is a file. The class that is loaded is whatever is defined in that file. This doesn't really violate the open-closed principle, however. We really have two classes with the same name. Since they are in different files, which you get will depend on which one you load.

8 Karel's World (RobotWorld) and Testing

The world has a lot of functionality. Actually there are two different worlds distributed with the software. One is graphical and the other is text based. The default version is graphical, but if you set the global variable **$graphical** = false, you will get a purely text based world. The two worlds have the same interface, however. Here is a list of the items that help you set up the world. The first returns a world to your program, and the rest form the interface of that world: the messages the world can respond to.

```
RobotWorld.instance()
set_speed(value) # 1 to 100
read_world(filename)
save_world(filename)
place_beepers(street, avenue, how_many)
place_wall_north_of(street, avenue)
place_wall_east_of(street, avenue)
remove_wall_east_of(street, avenue)
remove_wall_north_of(street, avenue)
remove_all_beepers()
reset() # remove everything
set_up_thread(robot &action) # can be given a block
start_threads(delay)
show_world(
      startStreet,
      startAvenue,
      streetsTowardNorth,
      avenuesTowardEast)
show_world_with_robots(
      startStreet,
      startAvenue,
      streetsTowardNorth,
      avenuesTowardEast)
```

Ruby also has a built in testing framework that has been extended to the robot world. In a testing framework you execute some code fragment from a known starting point and then make executable assertions about the result. The system will give you feedback on the result, so you know whether you get what you expect to get. A robot can execute any of these assertions. If you do it in the testing framework you are notified when they fail. If you use them otherwise, the program will halt when they fail and you will get a lengthly and difficult to read report (a stack trace) the tells you, among other things, the line on which the program failed.

```
assert_street(street)
assert_not_street(street)
assert_avenue(avenue)
assert_not_avenue(avenue)
assert_at(street, avenue)
assert_not_at(street, avenue)
assert_facing(direction)
assert_not_facing(direction)
assert_beepers(howMany)
assert_not_beepers(howMany)
assert_some_beepers()
assert_running()
assert_not_running()
assert_front_clear()
assert_front_blocked()
assert_neighbors()
assert_no_neighbors()
```

Below is a sample test program that is part of one used when the system was being built. Note that it only works in a non-graphical world. You need to require "test/unit" for it to work. A test is a subclass of Test::Unit::TestCase. We are testing a robot named @karel, a field of the test class. Note that such a test knows how it should be executed, so there is no task block. What happens is that setup is first executed and then each method named test_..., though setup is actually executed between the executions of the tests as well. This makes each test independent of the others, dependent only on what is in setup.

```
$graphical = false
require "test/unit"
require "ur_robot"

class TestRobots < Test::Unit::TestCase

  def setup
   super
   @world = Robota::World #note, not a new world for each test
   @world.reset
   @karel =  UrRobot.new(3, 3, NORTH, 0)
  end

  def test_turn
   @karel.turn_left
   @karel.assert_facing(WEST)
   @karel.turn_left
```

```
    @karel.assert_facing(SOUTH)
    @karel.turn_left
    @karel.assert_facing(EAST)
    @karel.turn_left
    @karel.assert_facing(NORTH)
  end

  def test_simple_move
    @karel.move
    @karel.assert_street(4)
    @karel.assert_avenue(3)
    @karel.turn_left
    @karel.move
    @karel.assert_street(4)
    @karel.assert_avenue(2)
    @karel.move
    #@karel.move
  end
end
```

9 Common Ruby Errors

The dynamic nature of Ruby gives it a lot of power, but not without pitfalls. The first of these is that the fact that the Ruby interpreter can do little checking for correctness of our programs.

Misspelled names are caught only at run time. So you may think you have a nice program, and may even have run it a few times, but if you have IF-ELSE statements, for example, you may not have actually executed the statement with the error. When you do, you will get a name error.

Remember that the assignment creates variables as well as using existing ones. There is no warning when it does this. It is especially troublesome if you misspell a name on the left side of an assignment. A new variable will be silently created.

A file that doesn't have a main can still be executed. It will just execute any top-level instructions. I.E. those not part of any definition (class, module, method…).

On the other hand, if you use a good tool like Eclipse, some of your errors will be caught by the tool as you type your program. This is very helpful. Missing end statements and the like will be caught immediately.

10 Ruby Tools

The Ruby documentation module will format documentation from the strings you add to classes and methods. It is also very helpful to understand what is available in the Ruby built-ins. It will create html (web) pages for each of your classes and methods. If you put comments just before a class or method it will include these comments in its descriptions. It is very helpful in seeing the structure of a class without examining its code. The tool also provides indexes of your classes and methods. In eclipse you run it from a menu, but it can also be run from the command line.

The Ruby testing unit is discussed above.

The simulator contains a program called WorldMaker (world_maker.rb) that, when executed will permit you to create worlds with walls and beepers and to save them to a file. A complete set of the worlds that appear in the text is provided.

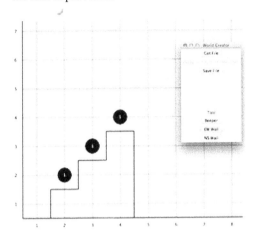

Figure A-1 The World Maker

The simulator contains a class called RemoteControl (remote_control.rb) that consists of a UrRobot but also a dialog window that can be used to manipulate it directly. There are buttons for move, turn_left, etc.

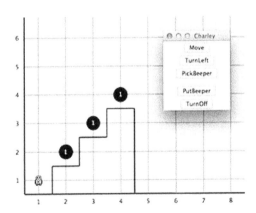

Figure A-2 A Remote Control

There is a Die class (die.rb) that you can use for simple random behavior of things. We used it in the Philosopher class, but it is useful as soon as you understand repetition (Chapter 6.)

Index

www.ingramcontent.com/pod-product-compliance
Lightning Source LLC
Chambersburg PA
CBHW080400060326
40689CB00019B/4087